8.50 ✓
B + 9.

ABREVIATIONS

F.C. — Franche Comté
G — Genoa
M — Monferrat
Ma — Mantua
Mo — Modena
P — Parma
S — Sundgau

Viborg

Vologda

Reval

ESTHONIA

Novgorod

Stockholm

DOMINIONS
OF THE
TEUTONIC
ORDER

DUCHY OF MOSCOW

Riga

Moscow

IC SEA

Vitebsk

Vilna

Kralowiec

POLONO-LITHUANIAN

Gdansk

Vistula R.

Pinsk

Warsaw

FEDERATION

KHANATE
OF
CRIMEA

Lublin

Kiev

ilesia

Cracow

Ukraine

Dnieper R.

Moravia

Kamieniec Podolski

Zaporogian Cossacks

Slovakia

Yedisan

Buda

Moldavia

Kaffa

HUNGARY

Transylvania

Balaklava

Mohács

Croatia

Danube R.

Wallachia

BLACK SEA

Belgrade

Bosnia

Serbia

Nikopol

Varna

Bulgaria

T
H
E

Ragusa

Kossovo Pole

O
T
T
O
M
A
N

Constantinople

Albania

E M P I R E

LES

Otranto

Smyrna

Lepanto

Morea

CRETE

CYPRUS

Damascus

Palestine

Jerusalem

A N E A N   S E A

SPAIN
AND
THE EMPIRE
1519-1643

SPAIN
AND
THE EMPIRE
1519-1643

By

Bohdan Chudoba

1969
OCTAGON BOOKS
New York

Reprinted 1969
by special arrangement with The University of Chicago Press

OCTAGON BOOKS
A DIVISION OF FARRAR, STRAUS & GIROUX, INC.
19 Union Square West
New York, N. Y. 10003

LIBRARY OF CONGRESS CATALOG CARD NUMBER: 71-84177

Printed in U.S.A. by
NOBLE OFFSET PRINTERS, INC.
NEW YORK 3, N. Y.

Castilla visionaria y soñolienta de llanuras, viñedos y molinos, Castilla—hidalgos de semblante enjuto, rudos jaques y orondos bodegueros. . . .

ANTONIO MACHADO

The shadow grows, the lamp burns and I hear about me the sighing of all these peoples trying to settle themselves in the night. It needed night for that lamp to show forth, it needed all this overthrow around me, this world around Prague where there is nothing more to look at.

PAUL CLAUDEL

PREFACE TO THE OCTAGON EDITION

The decision to publish a new edition of this book came shortly before the death of the Nestor of Spanish historians, Ramón Menéndez Pidal—called so not only because of the almost one hundred years he had lived, but also and primarily because of his immense erudition and the dynamic initiative he exercised in Clio's garden. More than thirty years ago he published one of my first studies. But even before that he had already sketched the portrait which he was to finish in his book "La idea imperial de Carlos V." His sketch then became one of the centers of gravitation of this work.

The raw material reached me from elsewhere. A wealth of documents preserved above all in Spanish and Bohemian archives spoke of the fascinating role which the Spaniards, led by their monarchs from the House of Austria, played in Europe's 16th century history. That role appeared to me, from the beginning, under a double aspect. The first of these aspects, Charles V's defense of the continent, I found amply explained by Menéndez Pidal. The second, Philip II's attitudes toward the enmity of the North, seemed to had been intuitively grasped by another man of vast learning, but much more a poet than a historian, Rheinhold Schneider. I did not have to manipulate the testimonies; they agreed with these two visions.

Both visions, true enough, disagreed with some unquestioned tenets—tenets of venerable age—popular mainly among English historians. The first edition of the present work, while it received favorable comments in countries so vastly distant as Austria, United States and Argentine, remained nonexistent to the English. Miss C. W. Wedgewood bypassed in complete silence, in her classical work on the "Thirty

Years War," what this book has to say in a thoroughly documented way about Iñigo de Oñate's decisive participation in the unleashing of the 17th century catastrophe.

Long before, the suspicions against any "olde packe of Spanyshe lyes" which most English historians—with the notable exceptions of Sir Charles Petrie and Miss Bernice Hamilton—have perpetuated, generated also some false trends outside England. In the United States they were readily accepted by Roger B. Merriman. It took some time before one started to set them aside. While writing these lines I have in front of me the last (Oct., 1968) issue of the "American Historical Review" with Andrew C. Hess' study on "The Moriscos; An Ottoman Fifth Column in the Sixteenth Century Spain." What Hess, basing his findings mostly on new Turkish material, has to say must really surprise readers accustomed to sentimental dirges concerning the "victims of Spanish cruelty" and the "tragic expulsion" of 1609. Charles V's defensive European policy—which I was only able to intimate in the present work—comes to full relieve. The military actions of 1535, for instance, which followed Chaireddin's alignment with the Turkish expansionism, are analyzed by Hess in a masterful way. So is the dramatic contrast of Jerba (1560) and Lepanto (1571) or again the sombre, threatening connotation of the word "Lutheran" in the contemporary Ottoman vocabulary.

Hess reaches the following conclusion: "What concerned Philip II was this very attempt at an alliance among the Ottoman Empire, Protestant revolutionaries, and a Muslim fifth column in the center of Spain. If Calvinist destruction of idols prompted Philip II into sending his best general to root out heretical revolutionaries, so much less could he tolerate their infidel counterpart, let alone their allies in the very heart of the centralized Spanish Catholic state that had been created in the war against Muslims who now, again, were approaching the Iberian Peninsula. Even the resources of the mighty Habsburg Empire were not sufficient to confront both Islam and the Reformation . . . Important political reasons, which were deeply rooted in Iberian history, gave free rein to an enthusiasm for a reformed Catholicism that masked many other interests. Whatever may have been Philip II's own motivations, Ottoman evidence provides enough information to indicate that imperial politics, transcending the Mediterranean, made the existence of the Morisco community a definite danger to the state. Self-defense dictated some sort of action. Expulsion was to be the final, tragic solution, and the straits of Gibraltar became the dividing line between two civilizations."

Andrew C. Hess had to come fresh and unprejudiced from his former occupation in a steel-mill. But with the particular issue he discusses we may have reached the heart of some major difficulties. It was not Charles V but his son who finally stood up against Queen Elizabeth and the Cecils. Therefore he was to remain the main object of prejudice, whether original or interpreted. The late Garrett Mattingly was certainly one of the most talented of the interpreters. There is hardly a book which would deserve to be called a masterful narration so much as is his "Armada"—the story of Philip's frustrated onslaught on England. And yet, having read, in Simancas and elsewhere, considerably more of Philip's correspondance than Mattingly, I never noticed that the king's witty marginal annotations were made in a "spidery scrawl." El Escorial, always full of the fresh smell of pines and of swallows swiftly descending to the level of one's head, never impressed me as a "wretched village." Mattingly's "cheerless room" where Philip lived was to me full of the warm afternoon sun and of the distant bluish forests on both sides of the crystal-clear river Alberche. I could not possibly imagine how "the diplomatic corps were shivering in Madrid" (on the last day of March) , wondering "what the king was doing up there on his mountain" (because El Escorial, simply, is not on a mountain) . Nor did I think that "the king's family lodged elsewhere"—because it did not, and because, beside reading the king's gentle family letters published by Gachard, I was allowed by the learned Augustinian friar, Julián Zarco Cuevas—later, in the bloody year of 1936, one of the first victims of the Cheka—to touch the clavichord on which Philip's two daughters used to play, only a few steps away from his own sunny room.

The monarch who used to sign his dispatches "Yo el rey" was, undoubtedly, not a simple man. When Ortega Gasset was writing a preface to the more than frank reminiscences of Alonso de Contreras, he spoke appropriately of the king's secretivness as of an essential feature of the nascent state which impressed itself on the monarch's face. Almost symbolically, Philip's reign seems framed by Lazarillo de Tormes on one side and Guzmán de Alfarache and Quijote's own Sancho Panza on the other—the monarch's own veiled life contrasting mysteriously with all these pictures of the crude reality. During the fifteen years since the first appearance of the present work we have learned more about this personality —from letters carefully edited by C. Riba Garcia, J. Lopez de Toro, V. E. Hernandez Vista or Joseph Lefèvre, from the studies of Luciano Rubio, Oliveros de Castro and Subiza Martin, M. de Foronda Gomez, M. Van Durme or the Count de Atares, but above all from the two volumes of cumulative evaluation written by Luis Fernandez y Fernandez de Retana for Menéndez Pidal's "Historia de España." But still we seem puzzled.

Perhaps we are slightly impeded by our own vocabulary. While—in spite of all the efforts of Ernest Nys and James Brown Scott and now also Bernice Hamilton—it is still the name of Grotius and not that of Francisco de Vitoria which is most often given the epithet of the "founder of the modern international law," we might have also failed to grasp that it just does not pay to confuse a king with a statesman. Even in the field of political theory important new books have appeared, written by J. M. Jover Zamora, J. A. Maravall, A. Truyol Serra and S. Lissarague, M. Fraga Iribarne, J. Beneyto Perez, J. Marín Mendoza, L. Sánchez Agesta, Bernice Hamilton and M. Fernandez Alvarez. But some essential clarification seems still needed. Bernice Hamilton states correctly: "Although Machiavelli's "Prince" was widely read, political thought continued to be expounded within a framework of morality and law." It was the traditional law of the kingdoms —of Castile and Aragon, of Bohemia and Hungary. Bartolomé de las Casas, speaking of the concept of "fatherland" (patria) went as far as to protest against the confusion between the city and any higher body politic. The word "state" ("lo stato degli affari," the recent American "state of the Union") crept only slowly into the Western vocabularies.

Now the birth of the state, one of the subjacent themes of the present book, includes the change from Charles V's rather Dantesque concept of the Empire (as an Instrument of Independence and Peace, not as a Power) to what the Holy Roman Empire became about 1618. It also embraces the personal story of King Philip. When Otis H. Green, author of the recently published comprehensive study of "Spain and the Western Tradition"—whose concept of the Baroque differs in such an interesting way from that of M. Baquero Goyanes and some other Spanish scholars—speaks of the truly Jesuitic "El Discreto" of Gracián Morales, he describes it as "dealing with the problem of self-realization in a world which offers few chances for a man to become a hero." Philip was precisely such a man. He became the victim of the century's main political ambition: the quest for the Power of the State as opposed to the Freedom of the Hero.

As even Mattingly rightfully points out, there was hardly room in El Escorial for the swarms of courtiers. But the "hildalgos" and the "grandes" were increasingly present in the dispatches. Transforming them into bureaucrats, Philip came perhaps closer to Peter of Russia than to the "Roi Soleil" (who let the nobleman rot in the broad corridors of Versailles). Moreover, the fatal word "state" was applied by the XVIth century Spanish writers both to the new form of the body politic and to the Church. They spoke of "temporal and spiritual states." Therein, perhaps, lies hidden the clue to Philip's religious attitudes. The English, of course, have doubted his Christianity ever since the pamphlets of Antonio Perez were published. He was, admittedly, no "Christian statesman"—the concept of the "Christian state" was, in fact, to appear only in the 19th century, to be replaced, after a few decades, by that of the "pluralistic state." But while being far from a "Christian statesman," what kind of a Christian was Philip?

Personally, I could have hardly agreed with Mattingly's opinion that "the church of San Lorenzo had none of St. Peter's gaiety." San Lorenzo is a real church where even the tomb-statues are discreetly hidden and the simple, almost Cistercian architecture of Juan Herrera as well as the warm colors of the canvasses help the mind to concentrate on God —not a pretentious Renaissance arena where the monuments glorifying the bishops of Rome are ostentatiously exposed and adorned with golden inscriptions predicating their "monarchical," truly anti-Christian ambitions. But the question here is not of churches and not of the Church as a Power. Judging from the documents which passed through my hands while I was preparing this book, I am certain that King Philip would have heartily subscribed Francisco de Vitoria's despairing complaint: "The pope, in dispensing from the laws and decrees of councils and of other popes, can err and gravely sin. If only it might be lawful to doubt this conclusion. . . . But we see such extensive, indeed lax, dispensations granted daily by the Roman curia, that the mind revolts . . . It has become a scandal to the strong as well as to the weak." Neither is the question here of that Spanish "conservatism," which another American, William T. Walsh, also free from R. B. Merriman's influence, had set out to defend, starting with Columbus and Isabel of Castile, until he reached not only Philip II, but also St. Theresa of Avila. His efforts would have nowadays probably elicited a commentary similar to that with which a Jesuit weekly commented on the death of Evelyn Waugh: "It is true that he was also a religious conservative, but this fact need not be regarded as tantamount to total damnation."

I am persuaded that Philip had built the small window leading from his bed-chamber toward the main altar of the basilica of San Lorenzo because he really wanted to see that altar even while sick. (A Nordic scholar, once working with me in El Escorial, believed that the king wanted to count the heads of the monks to suppress insomnia.) Philip's tragedy was evidently in the fact that, no matter how much he might have wanted it, he could no longer be a true king— not even distantly resembling those tribal kings of the Hebrews, whose statues he had placed above the main portal of the basilica.

Through the window at the side of his writing desk he could have almost followed, step by step, the descent of that poor boy whose name was Lazarillo de Tormes from the slopes of the Gredos to the gently singing poplars below Escalona and farther to Maqueda and the now deserted "imperial city" of Toledo. Had he been a medieval king, however, he would have met the boy somewhere between Torrijos and Toledo, on one of those desolate roads along which "el ingenioso hidalgo de la Mancha" later liked to wander. He would have heard his complaints concerning the cruel blind beggar and the avaricious priest. And he would have administered justice in the old royal way. As things were, he could only lift, for a moment, his tired eyes from the heap of documents on the desk. He was no longer allowed to be a hero-king.

Thus he dragged his feet through half a century, the living symbol of a kingdom which, in his person, hesitated to become a State and a Power—but eventually became one and having done so in such a belated, grudging way, it lost whatever there was to lose, the Moriscos included. In the medieval Toledo, as Gregorio Marañon used to stress, Christians, Jews, and also Moslems—the ancestors of the Moriscos—lived in perfect peace and mutual understanding. When the Moslems became the fifth column of a foreign militaristic Power, it was not a king who expelled them. It was the State.

BOHDAN CHUDOBA

Iona College
New Rochelle, N.Y.
December, 1968

PREFACE

ABOUT 1931, when I was finishing my graduate studies, my attention was attracted to the extended and profound influence which the Spaniards had exerted on the developments in Central Europe during the "golden century" of their own history. The more research work I was able to do in various archives, the more evident it was to me that not only an interesting and hitherto rather neglected chapter in the story of some European countries—Bohemia, in particular—but also a new aspect of Spanish history itself can be revealed through the study of Spanish imperialism on the European mainland in the sixteenth and seventeenth centuries. The beginnings of Spanish participation in the Thirty Years' War—an event which proved fatal to Spanish might in general —and even the role played by Spain in such important events of religious history as the concluding stage of the Council of Trent appeared to me in a new light.

In the following years, while still continuing my research work, I have published several shorter studies concerned with various minor results of my investigations. They appeared in the *Boletín* of the Spanish Academy of History in Madrid, in the *Mitteilungen für oesterreichische Geschichtsforschung* in Vienna, in the *Český časopis historický* in Prague, and in some other periodicals. A book, *Španělé na Bílé hoře* ("The Spaniards on the White Mountain"), dealing with Spanish interference in the sixteenth- and seventeenth-century history of the Kingdom of Bohemia, was published for the first time in 1939 and, after having been seized by the Nazis, for the second time in 1945, in Prague. Constant broadening of the subject and comparing of the various particular results of research with the general story of Spanish imperialism in Europe brought about, after almost twenty years, the present book.

The story which it contains is perhaps not altogether new. Nor can its conclusions be called definitive, even if they are largely based on hitherto unused documentary material. Nevertheless, I hope that the material I had at my disposal makes it a useful contribution to the knowledge of a dramatic chapter in the story of our civilization.

It is not the aim of this book to revaluate the entire story of Spain during its "golden epoch." Nor does it present completely new portraits of prominent men, such as Charles V, Philip II, or the Count Duke of Olivares. Its purpose is rather restricted—that of analyzing the Spanish will to lead and to control the defense of Europe and of Christian civilization. The most puzzling aspect of the story of Spanish preponderance is the change of the battle fronts on which the Spaniards were successively engaged: the change from the defense against the Turks, which had culminated in the victory of Lepanto, into the conflict with the Protestants, which resulted in the defeat of Rocroi. If this book can help the reader to understand this change better, its mission will be fulfilled.

BOHDAN CHUDOBA

IONA COLLEGE
NEW ROCHELLE, N.Y.
May 16, 1951

CONTENTS

THE ENIGMA OF AN AGE

1

IF THERE was a province of medieval Europe which was commonly considered a borderland, it was the Pyrenean peninsula. Behind it, the mysterious horizons of the Atlantic Ocean guarded in their unfathomable depths cities and civilizations which, according to primeval legends, had disappeared long ago. Another old tradition informed the medieval mind that even St. James, whose missionary endeavors were unparalleled in the annals of Christianity, had to satisfy his apostolic zeal upon reaching that green valley close by the Atlantic shores known to pilgrims as Compostella, where he found his ultimate rest. There, in the Kingdom of the Asturias, was the End of the Earth, "Finis Terrae," beyond which only storms and darkness were known to reign.

Moreover, the Pyrenean peninsula, containing the Roman provinces of Hispania Tarraconensis, Lusitania, and Hispania Baetica, which in the age of the great migrations became the Kingdom of the Visigoths, did not remain permanently in the orbit of Christian civilization. In 711, the Visigothic forces were defeated at Jerez de la Frontera, in Andalusia, by Moslem Arabs, who then overran almost all the peninsula. The following eight centuries were filled with unremitting struggle between the conquerors and the Christians, anxious to recapture the lost territories. This struggle, as well as the internal strife in the newly created Christian states—the kingdoms of Leon, Castile, Navarre, Aragon, and the counties of Barcelona and Portugal—of which the most notable characteristic was the intense competition between Castile and Aragon, exhausted the forces of the inhabitants of the peninsula to a great extent.

Only the kings of Aragon, who gradually had become lords of the rich county of Barcelona—the Catalonia of today—ven-

1

tured beyond the natural confines of their land, adding to it, in the thirteenth century, the island of Sicily. Later, in 1435, after the family of Anjou, which ruled in Naples, had died out, the kings of Aragon annexed also that territory to their dominions, thus becoming rulers of the wealthiest state on the western Mediterranean.

But then, in one swift, unexpected move, the countries behind the Pyrenees became a dynamic force in the history of Christian civilization. The bare facts of this change are known to everybody. It was not the diligent and wealthy Catalans but the Spaniards, the inhabitants of the interior tableland, who gained the upper hand when, in 1469, Ferdinand, king of Aragon, married Isabella, the queen of Castile, thus founding a mighty political unit, the internal cohesion of which had not been, at first, very firm but which was to develop into the unified Kingdom of Spain. The royal pair—the "Catholic Sovereigns" was the honorary title bestowed upon them by the Pope —achieved the reconquest of the peninsula by taking Granada, the last stronghold of the Moslems in its south. They succeeded, at least temporarily, in putting their country's economy in order. They also revived, in 1480, the Holy Inquisition, an institution which, in the High Middle Ages, supported by the state as well as by the Church, had tried to safeguard society against intellectual trends which were regarded as subversive because of their opposition to such essential institutions of Christian civilization as the family, private property, and obedience to lawful authorities.

Thus reunited, Spain stepped forward, took her place at the head of the other European states, and produced two noteworthy achievements: the discovery or perhaps rediscovery of the New World, with its subsequent colonization, and the establishment of a temporary political domination of a large part of the European Continent.

The first of these two achievements—the foundation of the Spanish empire overseas—was accomplished in less than half a century, between 1492, the year of Columbus' first voyage,

and 1541, the year in which Pedro de Valdivia, one of Almagro's captains, founded the city of Santiago del Nuevo Estremo,
the present Santiago de Chile. This proved a relatively lasting
accomplishment. The other achievement, much more problem-
atical from its very outset, started in 1519, when Charles,
grandson and heir of Ferdinand and Isabella, became Holy
Roman Emperor, and to all purposes ended in 1643 with the
disastrous defeat of the Spanish army at Rocroi in northeastern France. Both these stories are connected with each other
through many ideological and personal ties. It is, however,
only the second of the two, the story of the growth and decline
of Spanish might in Europe, to which the present book is
devoted.

Compared with the epic of Spanish conquests in Mexico,
in Peru, in Chile, and in California, ours is perhaps a less adventurous narrative. The romantic haze of the high seas and
of distant unknown countries is certainly absent from it. Nevertheless, it has other qualities that make it none the less interesting. What it lacks in risky undertakings of sailors and explorers it possesses in ambitious designs of kings and ministers.
And the daring of the conquistadors is more than equaled by
the intrepid faith of the protagonists on the European stage.
The discovery and colonization of America had certainly immense importance for the subsequent expansion of Christian
civilization. But the contemporaneous happenings in Europe
were shaping and determining that civilization.

2

The one hundred and twenty-five years covered by our story
comprise an epoch which to many an observer may seem a
time of transition. Old institutions were abolished, and new
were created. Everything was on the move. The age which saw
the great religious reformations and the Thirty Years' War was
an age in which hardly anything appeared permanent. Speaking with Comenius, the great Czech educator who died in
Amsterdam after having looked for an abode, for more than

four decades, in half-a-dozen European countries, we may say that for his contemporaries it was necessary "in time of plenty to think of hunger, in time of abundance to think of need, in time of peace to think of trouble, in time of security to think of escapes, in time of common enjoyment with friends to think of taking leave and of loneliness which may and frequently does overtake us."

The preceding centuries of religious unity, in spite of the elements of tragedy contained in them—elements which are found in every epoch of human history—were times of a much more solid character. The eighteenth-century age of high absolutism—the era of Louis XV, of Frederick II, and of Catherine II—brought its own disasters on mankind, but it also simplified life again. The epoch of Spanish preponderance, however, has remained outstanding precisely because of its agitated course, of which the pandemonium of the Thirty Years' War was the culminating point.

Nevertheless, it was an epoch with its own character. Even if its political trends were "fantastically idealistic"—as Benedetto Croce once called them—even if through such fantasies much was destroyed and little constructed, many ideas which were then conceived had a piercingly dynamic power. In fact, even if in practical life they have proved illusions, they still enrich anyone who contemplates them.

It was a complicated epoch, too. "Two things strike me very forcibly in the 16th century Europe," says Herbert Butterfield. "One of them is the tremendous faith and devotion of which there is such unmistakable evidence in the correspondence and papers of both Catholics and Protestants. But the second thing which always somewhat dazes me is not only the magnitude of the vested interests involved in what are called the wars of religion, but the fact that in one country after another—Germany, France, the Low Countries, the Scandinavian lands, Poland etc.—it seems to me impossible that anybody could begin to understand the wars of religion without studying the class-structure of the region concerned, and the tensions or conflicts between classes." It is perhaps even less imaginable that anybody should understand the sixteenth- and seventeenth-century wars of religion without studying the literature and the pictorial and musical arts of the epoch. Like all the dynamic periods of the story of Christian civilization, the age which produced Philip II, El Greco, St. Theresa of Avila, and Cervantes can certainly not be studied by a positivist method which makes sharp distinctions between the various branches of human cultural activity. All is intimately mingled together. One interest pervades another. Feverish activity and "melancholy," sainthood and ruffianism, replace one another in quick tempo. Don Francisco de Borja, duke of Gandia, one of the foremost Spanish nobles, becomes a general of the Society of Jesus. Albrecht Wallenstein, commander-in-chief of a crusade against Protestantism, is murdered as a traitor. The entire age is stuck in the mire of materialist interests and low ambitions. At the same time, however, in various theoretical concepts, as well as in personal efforts, it reaches the heavens.

Even a student who restricts his research to the political field is surprised by the dynamism of conflicting tendencies which he usually finds difficult to understand. Not only, for example, in various theoretical works but also in official documents of the various councils (*consejos*) of the Spanish court does he encounter a very exalted concept of the moral obligations and purposes of the Spanish monarchy. According to it, the kings of Spain had to transform the political life of the world and to put into effect what no other monarch—with the exception, perhaps, of the ancient Roman emperors—had ever had the possibility of doing. But, at the same time, one of the most frequently used expressions of the Spanish political vocabulary was the verb *dissimular,* which means "to keep hidden," "to conceal." From its persistent presence in all kinds of political documents it is evident how much distrust prevailed in the practical policies of those days. What, then, can be our conclusion? Could a model state be achieved by those who distrusted individuals so much that they hardly ever discussed their problems and interests in an open way? Or, in other words, were people who distrusted even their closest collaborators serious in their ideology?

The judgment of any historian in these matters can scarcely be conclusive. Certainly, no general judgment is possible. If the atmosphere was full of contradictions, it does not mean that the important people of those days were insincere in their political thinking. Theirs was, by all means, an age torn by all the elements by which human genius can be riven. There is much dramatic beauty in such a show. Let us rather contemplate it than judge it.

3

The decades of Spanish preponderance experienced the creation of a new style in the field of plastic arts: the so-called "Baroque" style. It was not a style generally accepted in all Christian countries, as the Romanesque and the Gothic styles have been. England and the Scandinavian countries, for instance, did not accept it. Even in countries in which it enjoyed popularity, such as France, it was never considered a separate style but rather a perpetuation of the fifteenth-century Renaissance. Nevertheless, in Spain itself and in its overseas colonies, in Italy, Germany, the Netherlands, Austria, Bohemia, Hungary, and Poland the Baroque period meant a very real and important epoch in the history of art. Let us not dispute which nationality did most for its development; it was a style which bore its first blossom in the "golden" epoch of Spanish history and which took root in lands which then were in the orbit of Spanish political influence.

Let us, temporarily, accept its name as a symbol of the whole epoch. After the wave of religious skepticism which is known to us under the name of the "Renaissance," the "Baroque age" once again stressed religious values. In philosophy and theology it started early, with Tommaso de Vio, called "Cajetan," the rejuvenator of Scholastic philosophy, who flourished at the very beginning of the sixteenth century. It continued in the life and works of such philosophers as Francisco Suarez and Wilhelm Leibnitz; such theologians as Alfonso de Castro and Melchor Cano; of such mystics as Juan de la Cruz. It also comprised the reformatory activities of Gaetano da Thiene and even of all those reformers who left the community of the Church. It greatly influenced the development of education, especially through the work of Ignatius of Loyola, Joseph Calasanz, and Jan Amos Comenius.

As far as art is concerned, the basic feature in the character of the "Baroque epoch" was its predilection for the theater. Without much help from the ancient dramatists—Greek tragedy was not yet well known—the medieval "mystery plays" and "moralities" were developed by Shakespeare, Lope de Vega, Calderón, Racine, and Molière into vast, but very vivid, visions of the "condition and destiny" of man. Theatrical conceptions prevailed even in some of the other fields of art. The feigned movements of the walls in architecture, for example; the inauguration of landscape painting in the works of El Greco, Claude Lorraine, and Vermeer van Delft; the musical oratorios and the beginnings of opera, all these have a distinct "Baroque" stamp. Another, although less distinctive, feature of "Baroque" art can be seen in its dissatisfaction with the usual ways of expression, as illustrated not only by the stylistic contortions of a Góngora or Bridel but also by the integral predominance of the study of harmony in music, culminating in the works of Bach. Góngorism, it has to be noted, may seem artificial enough to us, but in reality it was the fruit of a quite natural effort to pronounce the unpronounceable.

The historiography of the "Baroque" centuries also had its specific features. They could be summed up as a "search for tradition." Whereas the medieval historians used to take the basic Christian tradition for granted and simply proceeded to relate the "deeds of God through the Franks" and whereas most of the humanists had left out God and concerned themselves merely with the Franks, the sixteenth- and seventeenth-century historiographers turned back again to God's intervention in history. Only this time they did not take it for granted; on the contrary, they tried to explain it in many different ways. This time it was much more an object of controversy than a common property for them. Of course, the humanist imitation of Plutarch still flourished among them. But the typical products of "Baroque" historiography were books such as those written by the Protestant historian Vlasić—Flaccius Illyricus —or his Catholic counterpart, Baronius.

At the same time, the sixteenth and seventeenth centuries were developing other tendencies inherited from the preceding epochs without transforming or changing them. Interest in the material regularities of nature was one of them. The gradual deification of the monarch was another. We shall have ample opportunity to study the latter in the following chapters.

Of such a composite and often contradictory nature was the "Baroque" epoch. And yet it was an age distinct from, and capable of comparison with, all the other famous epochs in the history of our civilization.

4

The sudden and unexpected growth of the political importance of Spain and its subsequent decline coincided with the formative and adult years of the "Baroque" period. Was it just chance, or had this coincidence a meaning of its own? Were the achievements of the "age of the hidalgos" in Europe, with its special creative abilities, facilitated by Spanish political preponderance? Or, perhaps, can the "Baroque" epoch be called a "Spanish" epoch because of the great number of Spanish names among its men and women of genius?

It is natural that the answers of historians to these and similar questions would differ according to their own individual attitudes. Comparing, for example, their judgments concerning the career of Charles V, we find that even those among them—Edward Armstrong, for instance—who have rather severely criticized the achievements of Charles and qualified his character as a "combination of obstinacy and irresolution" have been, at the same time, very careful to stress the opposition he had met in Spain itself. It seems as if they tried to prove that even the little in his doings of which they approve was not Spanish. The Spaniards themselves, on the other hand, do not hesitate, nowadays, to call Charles a "very Spanish figure" and to assume, so to speak, a national responsibility for what he thought and did. The enthusiastic work of Ramón Menéndez Pidal on Charles's imperial policy may be quoted as an illustration of this trend.

Perhaps it would be almost preposterous to try to discover any sort of causal relations between the political ascendancy of the Spanish nation in the hundred years after 1519 and contemporary achievements in theology, philosophy, art, history, and education. The creative spirit knows no barriers and needs no rails—not even political rails—to reach its ends. Rather it should be said that the Spanish policy was just one of the many expressions of an age which was frantically seeking to re-establish the lost equilibrium of man. That alone is sufficient reason for a modern student of history to devote to it some of his time and inquisitive energy.

There were times, especially in the nineteenth century, which did not in the least appreciate the political efforts of the "hidalgos." The unjust infamy concerning the death of Philip II's eldest son, Don Carlos, which Friedrich Schiller used for his popular drama, was typical of the historical estimate which our fathers and grandfathers preferred to any other evaluation. Our own generation has found itself, certainly by no merits of its own, in a situation which makes more accessible at least the various elements of the thinking of the Spanish statesmen, if not the conclusions which they had reached.

Among those elements there is one perhaps which may be regarded as basic. It is the idea of the "traditional policy." If Spanish political ascendancy meant a revolt against the principles of the political trends of the Renaissance, it was because of Spanish opposition to what, in the opinion of Machiavelli, was the natural course of political efforts of any kind.

If the structure built up by the Spaniards collapsed, it was because it had been undermined by the same "natural" conception of human society and of its aims. This "natural policy" then took deeper and deeper root in the European countries. It was used to support the "natural right" of the absolutist monarchs—a veritable travesty of the Christian conception of the natural right. It was exploited to an even greater extent by the apostles of the "natural goodness of man" and of the various nineteenth-century systems of the "natural arrangement of society." For so long a time were modern political prophets and leaders searching after a natural, scientific order, until at least a large part of mankind discovered that such a new order might mean slavery and a beehive-like society in which there is no creative freedom. Thus, after almost three centuries, we are perhaps again better predisposed to understand that a "traditional policy," a policy originating from a set of moral principles which cannot be simply deduced from the evident regularities of the natural order, may be as useful for the preservation of the spiritual freedom of man as any "natural policy."

Of course—and here we may come back to what we have said about the various conflicting tendencies of the age of Spanish preponderance—the story of the years 1519–1643 is not a theoretical but a living example of an effort to put a "traditional policy" into practice. And, in addition, it is the story of an effort which failed almost completely.

Not isolated but set within the broad stream of unpredictable historical developments, the rulers of Spain in the sixteenth and seventeenth centuries tried to formulate their policy and to face opposing trends. Frequently they had to compromise with them—and every compromise means a partial defeat. Fighting Machiavelli in theory, they were not able to avoid completely his influence in practice. Attempting to re-establish the duty of obeying the laws of God as the supreme principle of the monarchy, they not only gradually pushed aside another traditional duty of a Christian monarch—that of consulting his subjects regularly in sessions of parliament—but became as absolutist in their administration as any other ruler of their own and subsequent times. Their situation was even more disadvantageous, as far as new fields of social life were concerned in which the Christian tradition had little or no experience. Colonial policy and relations with the natives of the newly discovered countries was one of such fields. The quickly growing role of capitalist enterprises in contemporary society was another one and perhaps the most important of all. It is always difficult for anyone occupying a high administrative post to face with firmness the challenge of factors which evade the hitherto quite satisfactory formulas of traditional teaching. Before the theoreticians accommodate themselves to the new problems it may be too late for the practical statesman.

Such are the reasons why the general policies of the Spaniards in the "golden age" of their country's history frequently have the aspect of rearguard fighting—or perhaps of "stubbornness and indecisiveness," if one chooses to put it that way. On the whole, it was a dramatic experience. But drama is the essence of history—and here we have one of its most fascinating instances.

AN IMPERIAL PROGRAM

1

IT FREQUENTLY happens to historians, when dealing not only with nations but also with personalities, that by shifting the scenery they change the very character of their heroes without intending to do so. It is quite probable that Charles V, the founder of the Spanish preponderance in Europe and the "last Holy Roman Emperor," has been the victim of such a fortuitous misunderstanding.

Numerous are the books and studies devoted to his life and works. His correspondence, written, curiously enough, mostly in French, has been studied in detail, in spite of its slight legibility. The itineraries of his relentless voyaging from one of his European domains to another have been carefully followed by admirers. We know so much about him that Titian's famous portrait and the smaller picture by Amberger seem to us incomparably more real than many other contemporary pictures. We know him certainly better than that good-natured citizen of Calatayud, who, looking at the seemingly slow, indecisive boy, only recently invested with the dignity of King of Castile and Aragon, and observing his half-opened mouth —a distinctive feature of most Hapsburg faces—told him without hesitation: "Majesty, shut your mouth; the flies of this region are rather insolent."

To us, Charles is the Emperor, wearing his ample cloak adorned with an imperial eagle, as his son Philip had him represented in the kneeling statue at the side of the main altar in S. Lorenzo del Escorial. He is the man who, after having under his rule immense territories, had resigned and died, thinking more of eternity than of the world he was leaving; the man who tried in vain to heal the grievous wound inflicted on the heart of Europe and who despaired of such a gigantic task. And there, perhaps, is the rub of our concept.

12

The initial moral clash between Leo, the Pope who was anxious to build in Rome the greatest cathedral of the world, and Martin, the Augustinian monk who despaired of his inability to control his own sinful thoughts and, to an even greater extent, the theological and philosophical clash between the adherents of the traditional faith and the followers of Luther were undoubtedly important for all the subsequent story of our civilization. Our own age, having become conscious of the fact that in the sixteenth century something decisive happened to the structure of Christian society, sees in those conflicts the central development of the time. And, remembering the deeds of Charles, we look at them in the light of our own predilections, making the lifework of the Emperor and the spiritual achievements of his epoch as closely interwoven with each other as possible. But does such perspective really respond to reality?

Have not the touching scene of Charles's abdication, on October 25, 1555, staged in the Great Hall of the Dukes of Brabant in Brussels, and the signing of the documents of resignation on January 16 of the following year, in the small house by the Louvain Gate of the same city, been repeatedly pictured by narrators of fiction as well as by meticulous researchers precisely because these events seemed to symbolize the end of a chapter in the struggle between the different religious conceptions? It has been accepted as an evident truth that Charles was tired and resigned at the age of fifty-five years mainly because of his failure in suppressing the Protestant Reformation. Charles almost became a secondary personality in the religious drama of his time. He was the last of the Holy Roman Emperors, the last effective successor of Charlemagne, who had been given his title by the Pope seven hundred years before Charles's birth. He was the symbol of the medieval spirit in politics. He had to resign because the Middle Ages were dead.

And yet, are we so sure of all these interpretations? There are certainly some facts which tend to corroborate them. But there are others which should not be neglected.

It is true that the vast power which descended upon the shoulders of Charles was a heritage of the past in the full sense of the word. One of his grandfathers, Maximilian I, who became Holy Roman Emperor in 1493, married Mary of Burgundy, the heiress of the rich Netherlands. Their son Philip, Charles's father, married Juana, daughter of Ferdinand and Isabella, who had united all the Pyrenean peninsula with the exception of Portugal. When Philip died in 1506, Charles inherited his first country, the Netherlands, the land of his birth, when he was only six years old. Ten years later, after the death of Ferdinand, he became King of Castile and Aragon, the ruler of Naples and Sicily, and the lord of all the recently discovered Spanish territories overseas. In 1519, after the death of Maximilian I, he inherited the Duchy of Austria, together with its dependencies, Carinthia, Styria, and Tyrol. And almost immediately afterward he was elected Holy Roman Emperor, becoming thus at least a nominal lord of Germany.

Geographically, his territories were three times as large as the ancient Roman Empire under Trajan, larger than the empire of the Arabian khalifs in the eighth century, and perhaps larger than the Mongolian Empire in Asia of the thirteenth century. Charles, however, never seemed to make much of the vastness of his possessions. Reports concerning the conquests of Cortés, Pizarro, and others were received by him with evident skepticism. If the story, according to which he did not remember what Cortés had done for him, is not wholly true, there certainly is a grain of truth in it. Charles's main interest was not his distant territories—no matter how rich. The Holy Roman Empire, the heart of Europe, was what interested him most. But why?

2

The institution of the empire, a Roman idea which lived much longer than the Romans, had always been an institution dear to medieval Christians. Another idea which they cherished was closely connected with it: the idea of peace. The ancient "imperium" had been the source of law, and law was always the source of peace. Many among those who, in the turbulent Dark Ages, used to sigh for peace also demanded a renovation of the empire. Several such renovations were then attempted; that of Charlemagne at the beginning of the ninth century and that of Otto III at the end of the tenth century were the most famous.

But even later on, during the High Middle Ages, when the various national cultures of the European peoples began to differentiate, the Holy Roman Empire remained in the center of contemporary political thought. In spite of the too ambitious Hohenstaufens, who misused the imperial power, and in spite of the rather phlegmatic Luxemburgs, who did not add much authority to the imperial office, to be a Holy Roman Emperor still meant much. Among those who knew the bitterness of petty medieval conflicts from their own experience and who put their hopes for a lasting peace in Europe in the imperial idea was Dante, the master of Christian poets. He was quite aware that the foundations of the imperial power rested in Germany, not in his own Italy; he was also aware, being one of the most profound Catholic thinkers, that there had frequently been a high tension between the interests of the Church and those of the Empire. Nevertheless, he was sure that the imperial coat of arms was God's own symbol which he would never replace by any minor political emblem:

> ... e non si creda,
> che Dio trasmuti l'armi per suoi gigli.

Charles's three last predecessors on the imperial throne—Albert II, Frederick III, and Maximilian I—were all of his own family, that of the Hapsburgs. The Hapsburgs, originally a Swiss house, had once, at the end of the thirteenth century, already been in possession of the imperial dignity. Now, since 1438, they were invested with it again. But none of them had made himself famous as emperor. Charles IV, the best of their Luxemburg predecessors, endowed with a rare sense of realism, had already restricted the Empire by the terms of the Golden Bull of 1356, which put the election of the emperors

into the hands of three dignitaries of the Church—the possessors of the seas of Mayence, Trèves, and Cologne—three German princes and the King of Bohemia, making it thus practically a German-Czech federation. The Hapsburgs, however,
proved unable to safeguard even this restricted orbit from disintegration.

Frederick III (1440-93) was almost powerless in facing the
thriving forces of territorial patriotism, released by the spirit of
humanism. Matthias Corvinus, King of Hungary, took away
from him even a part of Austria, an old partrimony of the
Hapsburgs. His authority in Germany diminished to such an
extent that he had to ask George of Podiebrad, King of Bohemia, to mediate between him and the German princes.

Maximilian I, Frederick's son, was certainly lucky in his
marriage and possessed no mean fantasy. It was he who arranged two and a half hundred German autonomous states
into ten circles, trying to make the ties between Bohemia, the
Netherlands, and the rest of the Empire strong once again.
But this scheme remained more or less on paper. And Maximilian's attempts to renew imperial supremacy in the Swiss
cantons and in Italy met with complete failure. Was it not
symbolical that this emperor—who at one time, perhaps not
quite seriously, had contemplated the possibility of ascending
the papal throne also—had in vain prepared for himself a magnificent tomb in the chapel of his residence at Innsbruck? Today the bronze statues of this monument still guard an empty
sarcophagus.

Such was the state of the "imperial inheritance" which
Charles, "a youngster of sixteen, but serious as an old man,"
as one of his contemporaries characterized him, hastened to
get hold of. There was a certain avidity for power in his tem-
perament during those years. In 1516 he did not lose a day
but hurried from his native Netherlands to Spain to accept
the Spanish crown with which Providence had adorned him.
Now, in 1519, he did not leave a stone unturned—or a bribe
unpaid—in order to get elected to succeed his paternal grand-

father. His younger brother Ferdinand, although educated in Spain, had been left aside by 1516 and even now, in 1519, he was still almost neglected by his elder. But no matter how much Charles's actions were tempered by personal ambitions, he had a political program, a definite conception of his duties as Holy Roman Emperor.

3

In spite of all his eagerness to rule, it cannot be said that the young Spanish king, who on July 6, 1519, received the news of his election to the imperial throne, had been a great success during his first three years in office. Born in Ghent, in Flanders, and educated there, he had the handicap of being a stranger to the Spaniards. And for some time after his arrival in Spain he continued making things worse for himself. He did not even care to pay a visit to the dying Archbishop of Toledo, the great Cardinal Cisneros, in whose person and works all the glorious tradition of Spain was embodied. His Flemish advisers—Guillaume de Croix, Seigneur de Chièvres, was the most prominent among them—did not help him to understand the peculiar problems of the peninsula. On the contrary, they tried to isolate him from his subjects. Moreover, Charles had to be repeatedly admonished by the Spaniards to learn their language, "in order to understand his subjects better and be better understood by them." No wonder that under such circumstances the Spanish nobles and burghers showed little enthusiasm for the new dignity of their king.

It was not a Spaniard but Seigneur de Chièvres who negotiated Charles's election to the imperial throne. As to his Spanish subjects, they followed the proverb "Rex est imperator in regno suo," by which the political skepticism of the Late Middle Ages gave expression to their doubts about the usefulness of the traditional concept of the "Imperium Romanum." They regarded the Empire as just another kingdom. And what, they asked each other, was the use of having to share their king with another country? Would it not mean just an increase of for-

eign influence upon internal problems? Had not a King of
Castile, Alfonso el Sabio, been elected Holy Roman Emperor
in 1257, and had it not all ended in disaster? And was it not
sufficient that in many Spanish cities dissatisfaction had already
been apparent concerning the King's foreign advisers?

The opposition of the Spanish towns to Charles started with
a letter sent by the Municipal Council (Ayuntamiento) of
Toledo—enraged especially by the appointment of Chièvres's
nephew as new Archbishop of Toledo—to other Castilian
towns on November 7, 1519. In that letter it was suggested
that a petition be sent to Charles, asking him not to absent
himself from Spain, not to give offices to foreigners, and not
to take money out of the kingdom. And yet Charles, anxious
to break the resistance and also because he did not want to
come to Germany with empty pockets, convoked, in the spring
of 1520, the Parliament (Cortes) of Castile at Santiago de
Compostella and astonished it by firmly sticking to his decision to accept the imperial crown. The Cortes, of course,
was reluctant to give its approval and to grant Charles the
appropriations which he needed. After some arguing, Charles
had the Cortes transferred to La Coruña. And there, through
the Bishop of Badajoz—Mota, a Spaniard, who had lived in
Charles's proximity for twelve years in Flanders as well as in
Spain—the noblemen and burgesses of Spain learned about
their king's imperial program.

Two points of this declaration are important.

First, that to have their king elected emperor is a great honor
for Spain. King Charles will, henceforward, be the king of
kings. The Empire itself had to come to Spain to find an able
ruler. The Kingdom of Spain is the foundation, the defense,
and the strength of all other kingdoms. Charles has decided
to live and to die in this kingdom. Spain will always remain
the garden of his delectation, the fortress of his defense, the
strength of his attacks, his treasury, and his sword.

Second, that Charles accepted the imperial dignity only because of his wish to accomplish the defeat of the enemies of

the Holy Catholic Faith, to which cause he was anxious to devote all his energy.

For a full appreciation of this message, it is necessary to take into consideration more than the events which accompanied it. To an observer who would restrict his study to what has immediately preceded and followed it, the declaration may appear as a mere tactical step, aiming at the persuasion of the Cortes to grant the subsidies necessary for the voyage to Germany. Seen from such a point, it was not much of a success. Only after having gained the good will of some of the delegates by special favors and by much persuasion did Charles succeed in obtaining the necessary sum by the bare majority of one vote. And after his departure for Germany—on May 20, 1520—the opposition to his rule spread rapidly. A league of cities, the "Santa Junta," was agreed upon in July, 1520, in Avila. Its program was an openly revolutionary one—against the personal power of the King and in favor of the ancient autonomous governments of the cities. Its declaration was soon accompanied by outbreaks of violence. An open split between the King and the cities was reached in October, 1520. The *comuneros*—as the supporters of the declaration of Avila were called—started recruiting an army but were defeated with decision by the King's regular army at Villalar, in April, 1521. Their leaders were then tried and executed.

Of course, there was much of class hatred to be observed among the *comuneros*. The same was true of the contemporary uprisings of the poor population—organized into "brotherhoods" (*germanías*)—against the nobility and the rich merchants in the region of Valencia and also on the island of Majorca. But the sentiment against the institution of the Empire was to remain a lasting factor in Spanish public opinion. Contrary to Charles's own persuasions, the Spanish nation did not consider it necessary to build its political leadership on a foreign establishment, no matter how traditional. Not only burghers but also the foremost noblemen, such as Pedro Fernández Velasco, and prominent scholars, such as Francisco

Vitoria, were the mouthpieces of this trend. Later on, in 1623, when a political theorist, Jerónimo Zeballos, published in Toledo his *Arte real para el buen gobierno,* he could go so far in application of the principle "Rex est imperator in regno suo" that he dedicated his book to Philip IV as "Emperor of all the Spains." That was one and three-quarters of a century before Napoleon crowned himself Emperor of the French and before Francis I exchanged his title of Holy Roman Emperor for that of Emperor of Austria.

But Charles's declaration of La Coruña not only was not a successful attempt to flatter the Cortes into generosity. It was never meant as such an attempt. It was the real program of a statesman. The proof of that rests in the fact that the complimentary promises which Charles had given when speaking of Spain were later fulfilled by him almost literally. His last voyage to Yuste—when he could freely have chosen to die in Flanders, the country of his birth—became the last seal attached by the resigning Emperor to the fulfilment of what he had promised at La Coruña.

Taking into consideration Charles's whole life and perhaps also that of his son and successor, we have to admit that the declaration of La Coruña had a much deeper significance than that of an *ad hoc* message of an impatient ruler. Indeed, the essence of Spanish policy in the next hundred years was contained in it. If the Empire had been characterized in it as merely an instrument of the very Spanish ideal of the defense of the faith, it was then really considered such an instrument. If Spain and not some other country—any one of the countries of the Empire—had been declared "the fortress, the strength, the treasury, and the sword" of the policy destined to revive the basic European tradition, was it not the first manifestation of a political hope which was then to fill the souls of Spaniards for many years to come?

There is a distinct echo of nationalist sentiment in Charles's message, too. Nationalism, although never altogether absent from the previous history of Christian civilization, had been much in favor with the poets and scholars of the Renaissance. It was now beginning the ascendancy which was to culminate in our own times. The age of absolutism was to make out of it a tool of its ambitions. And in that respect sixteenth- and seventeenth-century Spain, mixing its national pride with its faith in a messianic mission, already acted as one of the great powers of that rapidly approaching age. Charles, praising his country of adoption, plucked the string of the future. And he never ceased playing on it. More and more he accepted the hidalgos, the members of the lesser Spanish nobility, into his service. His diplomatic envoys, his courtiers, and his generals brought the Spanish language—and, with it, the Spanish glory —into all the corners of Europe. To speak the soft Castilian idiom and to observe Castilian customs soon became a fashion —a fashion of a century, not just of a year.

On the other hand, the declaration read to the Cortes at La Coruña by Bishop Mota stuck to the very old concept of the "Christian Empire," which was directly opposed to the Machiavellian and, consequently, also to the absolutist theory of state. Of the "renovations of the Empire," which we have already mentioned, perhaps that undertaken, at the end of the tenth century, by Otto III had been nearest to the ideal of the "Christian Empire." According to this ideal, the Holy Roman Emperor was not a supreme ruler—and even less the only ruler—of the different Christian countries but rather a co-ordinator, a judge who had no ambition to conquer but rather a mission to unite for common action.

This conception remained firmly rooted in Charles's mind. It does not matter so much who of his teachers had implanted it there. Perhaps it was Adrian of Utrecht, a priest and scholar of holy life, whom Charles—at his departure from La Coruña —made temporary viceroy in Spain and who later, in 1522–23, for eighteen months ruled the Church as Pope Adrian VI, the first Pope of blameless character for quite a long period. There was a certain resemblance between his relation toward the young Hapsburg prince and that of Gerbert d'Aurillac, later

Pope Sylvester II, toward Otto III. It is quite probable that it
was Adrian who taught Charles what to think about the Holy
Roman Empire. In any case Charles stuck to his persuasion
in spite of the presence of other persuasions among his counselors. The spirit of the age—which in a few years was to find
a prophet in Machiavelli—was certainly represented among
them; and the spirit of the age was in favor of using power
to acquire even more power.

There were other tendencies represented at the court of the
young Emperor. Mercurino Gattinara, a learned Italian who,
until his death in 1530, had formulated many an aspect of
Charles's policy, was a fervent admirer of Dante. He loved the
treatise *On Monarchy,* in which the prince of poets concentrated his political hopes on the Holy Roman Empire as on an
institution predestined to govern all Christians. Consequently,
he certainly was likely to have advised Charles to use every
possible opportunity to enlarge his dominions. After Charles's
victory at Pavia, in 1525, he admonished his ruler to jump at
the opportunity to extend his domains at the expense of the
King of France. But Charles would not listen to such advice.
Nor would his Spanish counselors, the Marquis of Pescara,
Hugo Moncada, or Bishop Antonio Guevara, author of a famous treatise on the duties of a Christian and humanist ruler,
El reloj de príncipes.

4

When Charles assured his Spaniards that he had accepted
the imperial dignity only because of his wish to accomplish the
defeat of the enemies of the Holy Catholic Faith, whom did
he mean by "enemies"? Let us make it clear that he did not
mean Martin Luther and his followers. In the spring of 1520
the Augustinian monk who had changed the course of his
career as well as that of Europe's history on October 31, 1517,
by proclaiming, at Wittenberg, his ninety-five propositions
was still in the midst of debating his views with prominent
theologians of the Church. It is true that in November, 1518,

he had already appealed from the Pope to a General Council. But that was a step which, as we shall presently see, was not quite strange to Charles himself. At the end of June, 1519, a public discussion had been arranged in Leipzig between Luther and John Eck, a learned theologian of the University of Ingolstadt, during which Luther, after some hesitation, rejected even the authority of a General Council and appealed to the Holy Scripture. But he considered himself still a member of the Church at the time of Charles's convocation of the Cortes at La Coruña. Only on July 10, 1520, after having assured himself of the support of Ulrich Hutten, Franz Sickingen, and other representatives of the "young," humanist Germany, did he write: "I despise the fury and the favor of Rome; I will have no reconciliation or communion with her for ever." And only then, in August, 1520, did he publish his *Appeal to the Christian Nobility of the German Nation concerning the Reformation of the Christian Commonwealth*—note well, not the reformation of the Church—which, for him, did away, once and for all, with the hierarchical concept of the Church and its tradition. Consequently, the Emperor could not mean Luther. He meant a very different enemy, one that had already for more than eight centuries been called by that name—the Moslems.

Let us remember this because it is a fact of basic importance. It is necessary to bear it in mind if we wish to understand Charles's imperial policy and also the almost fanatical religious enthusiasm which quickly permeated the whole structure of the new Spanish empire and which dissipated only under the pressure of the disasters of the Thirty Years' War. The enthusiasm of Philip II, the builder of El Escorial, and of his collaborators and successors was, it is true, mainly a Catholic and anti-Protestant enthusiasm; in that, it differed from the leading idea of Charles V's policy, which was the defense of Europe's faith and civilization against the increasing Moslem danger. But, in its basic character, even the ardent zeal of the Spaniards who lived and worked during the years immediately preceding the Thirty Years' War and during that war was a spirit inherited from the epoch of Charles. And Charles's own ideas, of course, were not of his own invention. They resulted from a combination of the general European tradition, as interpreted probably by Charles's teacher, Adrian of Utrecht, and of the old Spanish experiences in fighting the Moslems on the very soil of the Pyrenean peninsula.

Religious enthusiasm is the noblest of all zeals. But, as Coleridge said, discussing intolerance, "if we clearly perceive any one thing to be of vast and infinite importance to ourselves and to all mankind, our first feelings impel us to turn with angry contempt from those who doubt and oppose it." Intolerance is hardly distinguishable from enthusiasm in human thought and still less in human feelings. In fact, they both are frequently just two aspects of the same trend of thought. Nineteenth-century historians preferred to stress the aspect of intolerance and to judge it very severely. Perhaps our own generation, which experienced the Nazi as well as the Communist heresy and had to institute legal proceedings against both, will be in a better position to understand.

In a panegyric on his country, one of the sixteenth-century Spanish writers, Pedro de Medina, said: "There is and always has been in Spain so much fervor for the Holy Catholic Faith that in it is something which is not to be found elsewhere." It would be perhaps an endless task to retrace the growth of this extraordinary enthusiasm in religious matters. It can be explained—as far as such things can be explained at all—as due to the protracted fighting with the Moslem invaders which had been going on beyond the Pyrenees since the beginning of the eighth century. It can also be explained as an inherent quality of the character of the race. And perhaps it is not an altogether vain speculation to see its origin in the age-long infusion of Arabic blood into Spanish veins. But no matter how it had come into existence, there it was—an important factor in almost every branch of political and communal life. It had redoubled its force in the High Middle Ages during the struggle against the Catharists, who had spread their teaching throughout southern France. At that time, the Church, facing the perverted Catharist doctrine of the sinfulness of procreation and also other sects such as the "flagellants," which tended to undermine the very foundations of civilized society, gradually pushed aside its original negative attitude toward any attempts to use coercion in matters of persuasion and sanctioned the institution of the Holy Inquisition. A Spaniard, Domingo Guzmán, later St. Dominic, founded the Order of the Preachers, the "Blackfriars" of the medieval universities, to provide for and maintain the defense of civilization.

In close connection with the experience of the Middle Ages, the rather particular concept of the "purity of blood" (*limpieza de sangre*) permeated all levels of Spanish society. Actually, it meant a religious purity: to be free from contamination by any heretical blood. But with the unification of the Pyrenean peninsula and especially with the last effort to oust the Moslems from Granada, their last stronghold in the south, it also acquired the meaning of national purity.

In 1478, in connection with the repeated attacks and social and economic injustices committed upon Christians by the *conversos*—Jews who, upon the re-establishment of Christian states behind the Pyrenees, had of their own accord, but only formally, embraced Christianity—Isabella, Queen of Castile, obtained the Pope's permission to renew the Inquisition in her territories. She and her consort, Ferdinand, King of Aragón, put this authorization into effect only after the ruthless Moslem attack on the Italian city of Otranto, in August, 1480, when more than half the city's population, about twenty-five thousand men and women, had been killed as a result of treason of the *conversos*.

Then, of course, the Holy Inquisition again started its activities with a fanaticism which did not hesitate to apply all sorts of torture—as was the custom of the age—to the interrogated. But public opinion and the most learned and saintly men, such as Cardinal Jiménez de Cisneros, who later, before Charles's arrival in Spain from Flanders, managed to hold his territories together for him, were staunch supporters of that institution. And, in spite of all the stress laid upon education and spiritual progress by Cardinal Cisneros himself as well as by Juan Luis Vives, St. Ignatius of Loyola, and St. Theresa of Ávila, the century which had then just begun was to witness many actions originating in Spain and inspired by the vision of a Kingdom of God on this earth, ruled by a monarch so strong that he would be able to defeat the works of evil by sheer political power.

5

Bearing in mind the traditional concept of a unified defense of Christendom against the attacking forces of Mohammedanism, Charles embraced the religious enthusiasm of his Spanish subjects. He made his own the leading ideas of the popular Spanish song about Diego de Vera, the tragic hero of the courageous expedition of the Spanish sailors against Algiers in 1516, the year of Charles's ascension to the Spanish throne. He followed them in his internal as well as in his external policies. He stuck to them to the very last weeks of his life at Yuste.

Some of his actions which resulted from that enthusiasm seem to us hard to understand. In 1525, for instance, he ordered that all *mudéjares*—the Moslem citizens of Spain—should be baptized or expelled from Spain. A modern student of Spanish history is inclined to see in such an act the result of an almost irrational and repulsive fanaticism. He forgets not only that in so doing Charles yielded, quite democratically, to the pressure of public opinion but also that there were some very rational and sound material reasons for such a public opinion.

The *mudéjares* and also the *moriscos*—the baptized *mudéjares*—were considered a sort of fifth column by the inhabitants of the littoral districts living under the constant threat of Moslem naval raids. And—what should be particularly noticed by those modern historians according to whom the Spaniards had deprived their country, because of religious fanaticism, of its best farmers—there were also social and economic reasons which Karl Marx would certainly have understood, had he known them. The *mudéjares* lived mostly under the protection of rich nobles, whose estates they cultivated for much higher rents than the Christian farmers were able or willing to pay. The social hatred against them went so far that, in 1521–22, it resulted in an open revolution in the province of Valencia. Similar social reasons were also at the source of the popular hatred of the *conversos*—Jews who had embraced Christianity and who quickly achieved, in various Spanish towns, economic supremacy over the Christian population.

Spanish religious enthusiasm had, however, still another aspect which should be mentioned here, because it became more prominent later on, when the Spaniards started fighting the Protestants. That was its rationalism—in the sense of the word derived from the concept of a logical faith, a faith which does not contradict the principles of logic.

If medieval thinkers repeatedly asserted the dictum "I believe so that I may understand," they meant it. They knew that faith in facts precedes any reasoning, but they held reasoning in great esteem. And nowhere perhaps had this persuasion found a more important outlet than in the scholarly Order of the Preachers, the foundation of which by St. Dominic, a Spaniard, we have already mentioned. The greatest teacher of the Middle Ages, Thomas Aquinas, was a Dominican. He and his colleagues and disciples fought the non-Christian doctrines not only because they differed from the revealed truth but also because they were unreasonable. In many European countries, the rationalism of scholastic philosophy degenerated, with the decline of the Middle Ages, into logical pettishness, which could easily be derided by the semipagan thinkers of the Renaissance. Spain, however, was spared, to a great extent, such decay. The Renaissance in Spain did not lack initiative in rediscovering the forgotten treasures of civilization. The Greek New Testament, for instance, of the Biblia Poliglota,

edited under Cardinal Cisneros' patronage by the university
which he had founded in 1508 in Alcalá de Henares, was
printed two years earlier than the text published by Erasmus
in Basel. It certainly did not lack scholars such as Juan Luis
Vives and Juan Huarte, who combined a profound Christian
tradition with a noble sense of critical inquisitiveness. Erasmus
himself was appreciated, and his works were translated into
Spanish. When the Inquisition, later on, prohibited their reading—in spite of the fact that even Alonso Manrique, the in-
quisitor-general of the time, had a manifest liking for the
recluse of Basel—it was not because of his arguments and
reasonings but because of his irony, an irony which could mis-
treat even that which was most reasonable. Generally speaking,
the tradition of medieval criticism was preserved during the
Spanish golden century, and even in subsequent times Spain
was spared the witch-hunting so popular in the European
north.

What, under such circumstances, could be the Spanish reaction to Luther's principle: "Ratio est omnium maximum im-
pedimentum ad fidem" ("Reason is the greatest obstacle to
faith")? Some historians have been rather astonished by the
fact that even Archbishop Bartolomé Carranza de Miranda, a
Dominican—one of those theologians who, together with another famous Dominican, Melchor Cano, had been sent by
Charles to the Council of Trent, in 1545-48 and again in 1551-
53 and who later went to England to help to re-establish Catholicism there under Mary Tudor—was, in August, 1559,
arrested by the Inquisition. Was it, they have asked, merely
because he had stressed too much the necessity of faith for
salvation and had not concealed it from the Emperor himself
when he visited him at Yuste shortly before his death? No, the
main reason for his arrest and condemnation was his lack of
respect for the approved, critical terminology and utterances
of his such as that which affirmed that "to Christians it is
necessary to give up the pole-star of reason and to navigate by

faith and rule our works by it, especially in matters which concern Christian religion and the sacraments."

6

The idea of an all-European defense against the Moslems, as proclaimed by Charles at La Coruña, was based on the concept of the Holy Roman Empire as the leading and co-ordinating power. It was also based, although not so explicitly, on the unity of the Church. The trend which was to develop into the Protestant Reformation was, at that time, not yet considered important. Therefore, it was not difficult to presume such unity. And yet it was not such a simple idea as one would think. Even if the unity of faith could be and was expected, the unity of the Church as an organized society was not so clear an issue.

Again we have to remind ourselves of the medieval character of the Spanish tradition on which Charles built his imperial program. It was during the Middle Ages that the originally loose organization of the Church, acknowledging the authority of the Pope in matters of faith but maintaining the independence of its individual communities, was transformed into a monarchical society, in which the episcopal sees were no longer in mere communion but were in greater or lesser organizational dependence on the See of Rome. To safeguard its freedom and its mission from the interference of worldly powers, the Church was bound to achieve this transformation. But the whole process meant such a tremendous change that, after almost three centuries, it had not yet taken firm and deep enough root. Nor had the moral decay of the Church of the Renaissance epoch accelerated it. On the contrary, that decay furnished many an argument to those who opposed the transformation. And the rulers of the various European countries were on their guard; their political interests were not quite in accordance with the freedom of the Church. The decay of morals among the Church dignitaries, especially in Rome itself, was a welcome occasion for them.

The Church, of course, had spiritual strength enough to realize the danger. But as to the ways in which the necessary reform could be achieved there was a diversity of opinions. The Late Middle Ages, in fact, produced two reforming trends: one which concentrated on moral and social reforms and did not touch the constitution of the Church—the "Devotio moderna" which flourished in Bohemia and in the Netherlands, was perhaps the most prominent reforming school of this sort; another which, in opposition to the recently achieved centralization of the Church's internal structure, was concerned also with the organization of the Church and with its relations to the worldly powers, especially to the Empire. The *Defensor pacis,* a manifesto composed by a prominent representative of this second trend, affirmed openly that the Pope derived his authority not from Christ but from the General Council and from the Emperor.

Since the schism which had occurred inside the Church in the latter half of the fourteenth century—and which, in truth, may be regarded as the first major sign of the Renaissance—intervention of the Holy Roman Emperors had been repeatedly requested. The Emperor Sigismund of Luxemburg even tried to persuade the Council of Constance in 1415 to deal with the general reform of the Church before the election of a new Pope. Since the middle of the fifteenth century, when the semi-pagan atmosphere of the Renaissance had swallowed up the Roman Curia itself, the emperors were too weak to profit from the occasion, although Maximilian I, for instance, repeatedly contemplated the possibility of an intervention through the convocation of a new General Council. The more profound the moral crisis inside the Church, the greater were the doubts expressed about the validity of the monarchical constitution of the Church and the greater was the avidity of some worldly rulers to deprive the Church again of its liberty. Maximilian I went so far as to remark, in 1518, that Luther should not be judged too severely because he himself would perhaps need Luther some day.

In Spain the opposition against the immoral policies of the Roman Curia was as great as in any other country. Fray Tomás de Torquemada, the Great Inquisitor of the fifteenth century, was himself in favor of certain restrictions of the papal jurisdiction. And the very Catholic and pious Isabella of Castile, in dispute with Pope Sixtus IV over the nomination of a new bishop of Cuenca, threatened the Holy See by asking the Christian rulers to convoke a General Council against it. When, at the beginning of the sixteenth century, the Moslem danger once again became prominent, with the Turkish forces ready for another onslaught, Spanish enthusiasm was much disturbed by the nonchalance with which the situation was regarded in Rome. At a time when Erasmus, that master of irony who did not spare even the oldest of the Christian traditions, heaped flattering expressions on Leo X, the Spaniards looked at that Medici pope with disapproval. And even before Martin Luther decided to protest against the preaching of indulgences, Cardinal Cisneros, acting as primate of his country, had forbidden them to be preached in Spain. He did this not because he and his compatriots had any doubts about the validity of the indulgences but because they thought it very imprudent to rebuild, in an enormously sumptuous way, the Basilica of St. Peter in Rome—to which the pious donations of the receivers of the indulgences were turned—at a time when much more important duties were pressing. Of those duties Charles V was certainly conscious.

The court of the man whom many historians have pictured as initiator of the Catholic "Counter Reformation" was, of course, not immune to the paganism of the age. The less so because it was a court of poets. We would have found there Jan Dantiscus, the Polish humanist, and also two Spanish poets whose verses were rather void of any traces of Christianity: Juan Boscán Almogáver and Garcilaso de la Vega. Erasmus himself, whose wisdom, hidden among quotations from Cicero and Aristotle, was more skeptical than believing, dedicated to Charles his *Institutio principis Christiani*. Valdés, Guevara,

Cobos, Loaysa, Gattinara, Granvelle, and other imperial councilors were all of them enthusiastic readers of Erasmus. Alfonso Valdés, Charles's secretary and author of a witty dialogue entitled *Mercurio y Carón,* was perhaps the most original personality among them. His skeptical distrust of almost everybody and everything had certainly some influence upon Charles.

Curiously enough, it was Juan Valdés, brother of Alfonso, who settled down in Naples as secretary of Pedro de Toledo, the Spanish governor, and published there, in 1542, a book entitled *Del beneficio della morte di Christo,* in which he expounded a doctrine of salvation very close to that of Martin Luther. Another person who conceived at least a certain liking for Lutheranism was Charles's sister Mary, the Queen-widow of Bohemia and Hungary. And, at the very close of the Emperor's reign, probably by way of the constantly traveling court, Lutheran ideas had penetrated the soil of Spain itself. Not only Archbishop Carranza, whose story we have mentioned above, but also Charles's chaplain, Ponce de la Fuente, and the court preacher, Augustino Cazalla, were disclosed as Lutheran fellow-travelers.

Nevertheless, the Spanish tradition which had pushed aside Erasmus' witty paganism soon overpowered even the Lutheran trend. When, in 1607, Francisco de Quevedo, in one of his satirical scenes, depicted Luther as standing before the judges of the lower world, he placed him at Mohammed's side, and he made both of them claim that they were Judas Iscariot. Upon which Judas himself protested indignantly: "O Lord, I am Judas, and it must be known to you that I am much better than these two; when I sold you, the world profited from it, whereas they, selling themselves as well as you, have brought the world to destruction." And, having saved Europe from Mohammed, the Spaniards made it also their mission to save it from Luther. But that was already at a time when the Emperor had ended his long pilgrimage in search of European unity.

EUROPE—THE DYNAMIC
CONTINENT

1

A GLANCE at one of the crude maps of the sixteenth century shows us Europe as a continent, the boundaries of which were—as they are today—clearly drawn in the west, south, and north by the sea but remained rather vague in the east.

Two vast countries, Muscovy and Turkey, both strange and mysterious to every European, loomed on the eastern horizon. In the year in which Charles ascended the throne of the Holy Roman Emperors, Vasili III, the Grand Duke of Muscovy, who was rather an absolutist ruler, by placing a friendly Tatar chieftain on the Kazan throne had just succeeded in ending, temporarily at least, his war with the Tatar Khanate of Kazan on the Volga. Between his southernmost district, the Riazan region, and the Black Sea, there was still the powerful Khanate of Crimea, against which Vasili vainly attempted to ally himself with the Turks. Of those events almost nothing was known to the Europeans living west of the Muscovite dominions. Perhaps even less was known about the extension and internal organization of Turkey or, more accurately, the Ottoman Empire. However, what was of much interest to the Europeans was the constantly growing power of the Turks in the Balkans.

The rivers Save and Danube served, in 1519, as a demarcation line between the Christian and the Moslem spheres in the Balkans. But a large territory to the north of the Danube—so-called "Walachia," the southern Romania of today—was already in Turkish hands, whereas the Christian possessions to the south of the Save were restricted to a small portion of

33

Croatia, which belonged to the Kingdom of Hungary, and to a section of the narrow Dalmatian coast, belonging to Venice or to the city-republic of Ragusa (Dubrovnik). It was a very insecure and restless frontier.

Neighbor to both Muscovy and Turkey was the great Polono-Lithuanian federation, containing not only the ancient Kingdom of Poland and the Duchy of Lithuania but also the territory of White Russia and the greater part of the Ukraine of today. Together with the Kingdoms of Bohemia and Hungary, ruled at that time by the Lithuanian family of the Jagielons, the Polono-Lithuanian federation represented a part of Europe which, if it did not possess all the rich traditions of the European west, certainly was an integral part of the European community.

A similar regional unit—but still more remote from the western centers—was the Scandinavian federation, formed at Kalmar in 1397 and consisting of Denmark, Norway, and Sweden, which, at that time, also included Finland. Although not confronted by any danger such as that of the Turkish attacks, Scandinavia was soon to be lost to the spiritual unity of Europe and to lose its own unity as well. In 1523, the Kingdom of Sweden was again an independent state, and the whole region was gradually weaned away from the tenets of the Catholic faith.

And then, of course, there was the west, the focal point of Christian culture for the last fifteen centuries. Surrounded, on almost all sides, by seas which had made possible the development of its maritime commerce as well as the great overseas discoveries of its explorers, western Europe could be divided, from a bird's-eye perspective, into five major regions, the predominant languages of which were, respectively, Spanish, French, English, German, and Italian.

Yet the political geography of the European west was not so simple as that. Colorful reports by contemporary travelers and diplomats tell us about a diversity not only of climates but also of dialects, national characteristics, institutions, customs, and folklore. Sixteenth-century Europe was a much more intricate arabesque than the Europe of our own day. Even the commercial routes connecting the ports with the great market places of the interior were not able to change its heterogeneity.

The most cohesive perhaps of the five western European regions was France. An early-instituted absolutism had made it a more centralized political unit than any other European country. But even there we find provinces which had not yet been officially incorporated into the Kingdom of France—such as the Duchy of Brittany or the possessions of the royal family of Bourbon-Navarre in the southwest, around Limoges, Bergerac, Rodez, Albret, and in the Béarn. The Pope, although now living in Rome again, was still the independent lord of the city of Avignon and of the Venaissin. In addition, quite a number of provinces which later on, at the height of the absolutist age, were to be claimed by the French crown were still in foreign hands. The county of Roussillon in the south, including Perpignan, belonged to Spain. The district of Charolles and the Franche Comté in the east, both remnants of the early medieval Kingdom of Burgundy, as well as the province of Artois also belonged to Charles V as heir of his grandmother, the Duchess of Burgundy. The Duchy of Savoy, on the slopes and in the valleys of the Alps, was an independent state. And the Duchy of Lorraine as well as Alsatia, both to the north of Franche Comté, were still considered lands of the Holy Roman Empire. Nevertheless, France was a thriving country much addicted to the semipagan spirit of the Renaissance. It was soon to become the chief obstacle on Charles's way to the unification of European defense.

As to the Pyrenean peninsula, its structure was, as we have already seen, still near to the Christian ideal of the Middle Ages, preserving, at the same time, the moral unity of a whole continent and the autonomy of its provinces. In the comparative prosperity and peace which remained the chief characteristic of life in Spain from the revolt of the cities in 1520 to the end of the reign of Charles V, the Spanish provinces still enjoyed many of their ancient privileges. The Cortes of Castile, as well as those of Aragon, preserved their old constitutional powers—as far as their nobility was interested in preserving and using them. We must also not forget that the Kingdom of Portugal, the country which had started the great discoveries, existed up to 1580 as an independent state.

The islands which now form Great Britain and Ireland were then much less English than they are today. Scotland, governed by the Stuarts, was an independent country. Ireland, with its interior in the hands of tribal chieftains and split by endless conflicts, was rather out of the control of the English kings, who claimed it as their possession. Only during the decades to come was Henry VIII, the Tudor "master of strong government," to reorganize the Emerald Isle. England itself was still a very European country. The political thinking of its inhabitants did not differ much from that of the citizens of any state on the mainland. Even the English Channel did not seem much of an obstacle to frequent contacts with other European countries. On one occasion, Wolsey, Henry's counselor in his younger years, was able to leave Richmond near London at midday, arrive at Dover in the morning, cross to Calais, reach the Emperor's quarters in the neighborhood, return to Dover in the small hours of the third day, and reach Richmond the same evening. But his lord, Henry VIII, had already begun building the navy which, in the course of the subsequent centuries, was to make England almost an independent continent.

The German-speaking orbit was almost identical with the loose political structure of the ancient, but now very restricted, Holy Roman Empire. If there ever was a political unit whose shape and boundaries were in perpetual flux, it was the Empire. Maximilian I, Charles V's grandfather, tried to rearrange it into administrative and judicial provinces which he called "circles." In the number of the circles he included the French- and Dutch-speaking Netherlands, the French-speaking Franche Comté and Duchy of Savoy, as well as the Slovene

Duchy of Carniola—the most western part of Yugoslavia of today. On the other hand, he left out not only the various Italian provinces and the Kingdom of Bohemia, which had had long and close relations with the Empire, but also the largely German-speaking Swiss cantons, the original home of the Hapsburgs, his own family. If the Swiss had been, ever since the thirteenth century, in open revolt against the imperial authority, the citizens of the wealthy Netherlands, although still faithful to the Hapsburgs as to heirs of Burgundy, just ignored the Empire. And the numerous German duchies, bishoprics, and cities did not think much of the Empire either. The time was near in which they would act as completely independent states. We can name as among the most important the duchies of Bavaria, Württemberg, Hesse-Cassel, Saxony, Brandenburg, and the Palatinate; the archbishoprics of Salzburg, Trèves, Cologne, and Magdeburg; the bishopric of Münster; the free cities of Frankfort, Nuremberg, and Lübeck. Actually, the only territories which remained under the direct rule of the Hapsburg emperors were the Alpine duchies of Austria, Styria, Carinthia, and Tyrol with Vorarlberg, which form the Austria of today, and—in addition to some smaller territories—the two strategically important districts on the upper Rhine: Breisgau, of which Freiburg was the capital, and Sundgau.

In Italy much was in foreign hands. The Duchy of Milan was occupied by the French. The Kingdom of Naples, together with Sicily and Sardinia, now belonged to Charles V. The Duchy of Savoy had acquired quite a portion of the western valley-plain of the river Po. There were, however, independent states also, such as the wealthy city-republic of Venice, the city-republic of Genoa, and a number of city-territories and principalities, of which Florence (Tuscany) was the most important. And there was also, in the very center of Italy, the Papal State, extending from the Campagna district, south of Rome, well to the northeast and north and including, among others, the cities of Perugia, Urbino, and Bologna.

2

The Europe of Charles V was certainly not a stable area as far as its economy was concerned.

Many of the so-called "utopias," which sixteenth-century people loved to write and read about, concern the relations between public order and the economic life of the citizens. Some of them are full of wishful thinking, demanding a return to purely agricultural forms of economy and a complete abrogation of the freedoms of the merchants, while others clamor for at least some restrictions of those freedoms. Sir Thomas More, for instance, the English chancellor who, later later on, was to die as a martyr for the Catholic faith, seems to be satisfied with such a partial reform in his *Utopia,* published in Louvain in 1516. Another such book, "The Order of the Land Welfaria" (*Ordnung des Landes Wolfaria*), by a German author, Eberlin von Günzburg, goes much further and suggests that all lords, bishops, and abbots should be forbidden to have anything to do with commerce.

Economic development, however, could not be stopped. It was now clear that the towns, the origin—or perhaps revival —of which in the Dark Ages is not well known to us, were well on their way to instituting much more than a complementary economy, a mere addition to the preponderantly agricultural organization of society. The merchants were no longer mere producers and transporters of goods of secondary importance. They had accumulated considerable pecuniary wealth by enormously extending the exchange of goods and by developing the technique of commerce. In short, they had become veritable capitalists.

The medieval moralists had considered money more or less a kind of goods. For them it was a rare and durable material, cut into small pieces so that it might be stored more easily. On that account they had affirmed that money was unable to beget money—just as a coat is unable to beget another coat— and refused to sanction the levying of interest. Interest was considered usury by them, and we have to admit that their views were perfectly consistent and logical.

As soon, however, as some merchants started to accumulate money—because it was easier to store it than to store anything else—it was found more and more difficult to put the traditional moral principles into effect. This was not only because of the attraction exercised by the power of money on human souls but also because it was more and more apparent that money as a means of exchange was essentially different from other goods. Precisely because a field or an orchard can produce new material values, it was argued, whereas money cannot, the person who lends money for which a field might have been bought is entitled to remuneration.

Capitalist transactions were naturally not an exclusive interest of the merchants. Big landowners among the nobility were soon engaged in them with all their resources. But perhaps the most decisive role in the rapid development of capitalism was played by those wealthy families and groups which had specialized in monopolized trading.

Concentration of all trade in one particular sort of goods was attempted in various parts of Europe. Thus the kings of Portugal, for instance, concentrated all the imports of pepper in their hands. But the greatest successes in this field went to a number of German merchant families. Their influence had been great before Charles's ascension to the imperial throne, not only in the territories of the Empire but also in Bohemia, Hungary, and Poland and in Spain and its colonies. The Fugger family, which had already been engaged in trading silk and spices, in 1498, started an international monopoly in copper. They were associated with other wealthy families, such as the Herwarts, who owned an extended trade in textiles, the Gossembrots, and the Baumgartners. The Fuggers exported copper from Central European mines to Venice and sold it there at prices which they themselves were able to dictate. Another family, the Hochstetters, who previously had traded in corn, wine, and wood, concentrated now on quicksilver, which, for some time, was found almost exclusively in the Duchy of Carniola. When, however, new quicksilver mines were discovered in Hungary and in Spain, the Hochstetters went bankrupt. The Welsers, who owned cane plantations in the Canaries, were the first to obtain authorization to trade with the new Spanish colonies overseas.

All these financial magnates and even other German capitalists were now to profit from the union between Spain and the Holy Roman Empire. Of course, they never restricted their activities to mere banking business. On the contrary, in the long run they showed perhaps a more lasting interest in trading goods of various sorts than did the wealthy citizens of any other European nation. But their impact on the moral, social, and economic formation of Charles's empire was immense. In an epoch in which the predominantly agricultural economic structure of European society was rapidly disintegrating, so that even the perfectly natural ties between the nobles and their villagers were turning in most regions into purely financial relations, the great financiers and their dealings were the source of many an important transformation.

Was it not the Fugger banking-house which had lent 300,000 guldens to a Hohenzollern to help him to become Archbishop of Mayence? To be able to pay his debt, the new archbishop was then forced to accept—even to participate in—the advertising of indulgences, which the Spaniards had refused to accept and which then gave Martin Luther the initial occasion for his reforming action. And, again, was it not the Fuggers who furnished Charles himself with the money necessary to bribe the electors of the Holy Roman Empire?

"Pecunia nervus belli" ("Money is the sinew of war") was the ancient truth which the sixteenth century could reaffirm with greater authority than that of any of the preceding centuries. The medieval rulers used to pay their expenses out of the revenues of their own estates, and extraordinary taxation was accepted by the nobility only if there was an evident and inescapable reason for it. But now the hero of the times was the ruthless ruler, the builder of a state, a man like Cesare Borgia, lord of the papal province of Romagna, whose rough "virtues" were soon to be glorified by a secretary of the city-republic of Florence, Niccolò Machiavelli. A prince of the Renaissance needed much more money to realize his plans than his ordinary private revenues could bring him. Hence his association with the bankers.

Charles was not a hero in the image of Machiavelli's portrayal, a man who would be capable of acting "against faithfulness, against pity, against humanity, against religion." But he had to accommodate his plans to the economic tendencies of the time. He was not just a ruler of one country. He was lord of many lands. And that was the decisive factor.

3

To inherit so many countries meant to increase human envy and human fears. Charles's very candidature to the imperial throne, for instance, set the French king, Francis I, to rapid rearmament. It may be said, of course, that the permanent conflict with France was actually inherited by Charles from his grandfather, Ferdinand of Aragon. Ferdinand, aided not only by the military experience of his great general, Gonzalo de Córdoba, but also by an alliance with Louis XII of France, added the Kingdom of Naples to the other Mediterranean possessions of the House of Aragon. Then he quarreled with his ally over the spoils, and the enmity began. But it would hardly have continued so furiously during Charles's reign, had it not been for the fact that he was the heir of too many countries.

Thus it happened that Francis I, the King of France who had defeated the Spanish troops at Marignano in northern Italy a year before Charles's ascension to the Spanish throne, became our hero's main opponent among contemporary European rulers. Their mutual alienation changed rapidly into an open war, which started in the spring of 1521 on two battlefronts simultaneously: on the frontier between France and the Netherlands—a region which, from now on, was to become an almost permanent theatre of war—and in that green country at the western end of the Pyrenees which is inhabited by the Basques and which, from the beginning of the Middle Ages, had borne the name of the Kingdom of Navarre. The Spanish title to Navarre, which was now incorporated, but not without considerable autonomous rights, into the Kingdom of Castile, was of a spurious nature. Charles himself had recognized this in 1516. But later, influenced by his own growing sympathies with Spanish nationalism, he declared Navarre an integral part of his dominions and thus gave Francis a reason for starting the war.

The initial clash between the Spanish and the French lasted almost four years. At first, there were some successes on the side of the French, who profited from the revolt of the *comuneros* and took Pampeluna, the capital of Navarre—defended, among others, by Iñigo of Loyola, a young officer who was to become St. Ignatius. Then the tables were turned, and Prospero Colonna, one of Charles's generals, drove the French out of the Milanese. This was an event of great strategic importance, since the Duchy of Milan in French hands was like a wedge thrust between the Empire and the Netherlands in the north and Spain and Naples with Sicily in the south. In addition, the French were deserted by Charles Montpensier, Duke of Bourbon, one of their best generals, who resented the tyrannical rule of Francis as well as the ambitions of Francis' mother, Louise of Savoy, and went over to the Emperor. The English were also supporting Charles—thanks more to the ambitious Cardinal Wolsey than to King Henry VIII himself. Then, in the autumn of 1524, a French army, commanded by Francis I in person, again crossed the Alps into Italy, and it seemed almost as if the Spaniards would have to surrender in the fortified city of Pavia, to which they had retired. But then, in a surprising battle—the battle at Pavia, on February 25, 1525—the French army was as good as annihilated, and King Francis himself was taken prisoner.

For a few months it seemed as if Charles was now free to turn to the mission which he had made the pivot of his imperial program: the defense of Europe against Turkish aggression. Already Suleiman the Magnificent—as we shall discuss in the next chapter—had captured Belgrade from the King of Hungary and the island of Rhodes from the Knights of St. John and was preparing to strike at Hungary itself.

But the very fact of the overwhelming defeat of the French at Pavia sent the pendulum of fortune swinging away from Charles again. There was already a marked tendency in the air to regard every territorial change as dangerous to the general peace. The weaker the authorities of the Church became and the less the principles of international Christian morality were appreciated, the more need there was for purely mechanical concepts, such as the "balance of power." The terms of the treaty of Madrid concluded between Francis and Charles in January, 1526, may seem moderate to us. Francis, it is true, was now obliged to give up all claims to the former Kingdom of Navarre and to the Duchy of Burgundy. But Navarre had practically been in Spanish hands for some time now. And the traditional dependencies of the Duchy of Burgundy, which were under French rule, were not included in the treaty. The Milanese was to be given again to the Sforzas, a family of "condottieri" which had already been in possession of that duchy before. Nevertheless, the very fact that Charles's army had established its preponderance on the Continent in such a decisive way was sufficient to arouse animosity and to make the Emperor's position in Europe permanently unstable.

In the first place, France remained hostile to Charles and to his plans, and war was soon resumed. In 1528 a French army under Lautrec invaded Italy again, and only a definite alignment between Genoa—whose navy was commanded by the great admiral, Andrea Doria—and the Emperor frustrated its success. Another peace treaty, signed by Charles and Francis at Cambrai in August, 1529, concluded this chapter. But after Francesco Sforza of Milan died in 1535, hostilities broke out again in February, 1536. A truce was concluded in 1538—at the expense of the small Duchy of Savoy, a large part of the territory of which came into French hands—and Charles was then able to meet Francis personally at Aigues Mortes and even to travel across France. But in 1542, a few months after Charles had granted the Duchy of Milan to his son Philip—which, of course, was an aggrandizement and therefore a breach in Charles's program—the struggle was reopened. Another respite came with the peace of Crespy, in September, 1544, at which Charles offered the Milanese to Francis' younger son if he married one of Charles's own relatives. But nothing came of this offer, as nothing had come from a similar offer made in 1536. In 1547 Francis I died, but his son Henry II renewed the hostilities against the Emperor in 1551 and persevered even after Charles's death at Yuste. We shall presently see how all this affected the Emperor's anti-Turkish plans as well as his position in Germany.

Second, after the victory at Pavia in 1525, Charles began to lose the friendly support of England. Anglo-Spanish friendship dated from the times of Charles's grandfather, Ferdinand of Aragon, who, in 1513, had also affianced Charles to Mary, the younger sister of Henry VIII. Henry himself was already, since 1511, the husband of Charles's aunt, Catherine of Aragon. After Pavia, several factors participated in the breakup of this old alliance. The fall of Cardinal Wolsey was one of them, Henry VIII's decision to divorce his wife was another, and Charles's own marriage with Isabella of Portugal was perhaps a third one—although Henry's sister Mary had, in the meantime, been given to Louis XII of France, Francis I's uncle. After May, 1527, when Henry VIII effectively left Charles's side and concluded an alliance with France, the spirit of friendship between the two rulers was never revived again.

There was, it is true, the period between 1541 and 1547, the year of Henry VIII's demise, when the death of Catherine of Aragon made it possible for Henry to return to an alliance with the Emperor. But their subsequent common operations against France did not obtain any decisive result.

4

To lose French and English support was certainly of great moment for Charles and his plans. But through his victory at Pavia he lost even more than that—he lost the support of the Pope. Already in 1519, when ascending the imperial throne, he had had to take into consideration the fact that the contemporary Pope, Leo X, was a Medici, a member of one of those Italian families which regarded even the high offices of the Church as instruments of their semipagan policies. Then, for a few months, in 1522-23, his own esteemed teacher, Adrian of Utrecht, ascended the papal throne as Adrian VI. But after him came another Medici, Clement VII. It was this Pope who organized the resistance against Charles's newly acquired power with such political skill that even today it is rather difficult to judge what his chief reason was for doing this: a fear that the freedom of the Church was again in danger from a mighty emperor or the political traditions of the Medici family? The Pope's ideas were probably close to those of Guicciardini, a contemporary chronicler, whose advice, addressed to Clement himself, runs: "It would be dangerous indeed to allow the Emperor's power to grow, but it would be equally dangerous to resist him without allies; you cannot be friends, being neighbors; only such rulers can be friends as live far away from each other."

What, actually, was Charles's opinion of the Papacy? Even as champion of the Christian cause, he was undoubtedly influenced not only by the moral decadence of the Curia but also by the still lively doubts about the wholesomeness of the reorganization of the Church as effected by the popes of the High Middle Ages.

In 1521, at the Imperial Diet in Worms, where Charles met Luther and had to admonish him because of the rude words he used, he interrupted his doctrinal explications just once. "Is he," he asked, addressing Luther indirectly, "of the opinion that even the General Councils of the Church can be deceived?" This question gives us a double insight into the religious though of the Emperor. He evidently was surprised when he realized the extent of Luther's doctrinal split with the Church. He had probably been persuaded that the whole difficulty with the professor from Wittenberg consisted in some nonessential theological quarrel. And, second, he was not able to conceive any higher authority in the Church than the General Council.

Always regarding the Church as one and indivisible, he was certainly conscious of its catholic character. When, at the end of 1523, the idea' had arisen in southern Germany of solving the religious difficulties by means of a national council, Charles refused to give his approval. His teacher, Adrian of Utrecht, had always seen in the convocation of a General Council the best way to an internal reform of the Church. Faithful to his memory and refusing to accept any regional or partial reform, Charles supported the conciliar idea to the very end of his reign. The Pope should, in his opinion, convoke the council and bring all the contemporary problems of the Church before it—including the political problems.

It so happened that when, after the Spanish victory at Pavia, Clement VII started organizing resistance against Charles, the imperial troops, unpaid and mutinous, forced their commanders to march with them against Rome. In May, 1527, the Eternal City was sacked and devastated in a most horrible way. And Juan Luis Vives, the eminent Spanish philosopher and psychologist, writing to Erasmus, did not conceal his satisfaction that the Pope would now no longer hinder the Emperor in his task of unifying the Christians. Charles himself did not know about what happened. When he was informed by a brief from Pope Clement, full of wrath and indignation, he replied by a declaration composed by his secretary of Latin letters, Alfonso Valdés, reproaching the Pope because of his slight willingness to help with the pacification of Christendom. The Pope, affirmed the declaration, was the cause of what had happened to Rome. And if he was not ready to change his disastrous policy, the Emperor would appeal to a General Council.

5

Charles never appealed to a General Council. In the very next letter to the Pope he restricted his threat to a possible appeal to the College of Cardinals. Later, in 1529, he signed a special treaty of peace with Clement VII. In 1530, at Bologna, he received the imperial crown and the crown of Italy at the Pope's hands. And in 1534 Pope Clement died. His successor, Paul III (1534–49), collaborated with the Emperor not only in the unification of Christendom and its defense against the Turks but also in the convocation of the General Council.

The affairs of the Church were rather strange to Charles. His thoughts and those of his courtiers were probably never concerned with a religious and philosophical revival. After all, what political suggestions could there be in the writings of a Hernando de Talavera, Alejo de Venegas, or Pedro de Alcantara, although all of them and many other religious thinkers were Spanish subjects? Also, Charles was not interested so much in Luther the theologian as in Luther the politician.

As early as in 1520, in his *Appeal to the Christian Nobility of the German Nation,* Luther had come forward with a very narrow, nationalist concept of the Empire. Then, after he had been banned by the Emperor, he published, in 1523, the treatise *On Worldly Power,* which was openly directed against Charles. Thus he started a new school of German political thought, contrary to all traditions, a school which was continued after his death by Sleidanus, author of *Commentarii de statu religionis et reipublicae,* published in 1572, and later by Philip Chemnitz, author of the *Dissertatio de ratione status in imperio nostro Germanico,* published in 1640. The doctrine of the Christian empire was flatly rejected by this new current of political ideas, full of national pride and self-assurance.

The fact that the Emperor did not want or was not able to enforce the ban against Luther was perhaps not a sign of serious weakness. It could hardly be expected that the new and inexperienced ruler of the Empire would impose a better discipline on the realm than his three predecessors had been able to do. Nor was such a step contemplated by Charles. He wanted peace and collaboration, not coercion.

When, however, it became apparent that there were political threats concealed in the Lutheran reform, the danger menacing Charles's plans was obvious to all. It had been a favorite theme of Luther and his friends to depict the poor Christ accompanied by fishermen as suddenly encountering the Pope and his Cardinals in all their splendor. But then Luther's best propagandist, Hans Sachs the poet, wrote a play on Cain and Abel, culminating in the prophecy that Abel's posterity would consist of kings, princes, and dignitaries, whereas the sons of the murderer Cain would have to satisfy themselves as farmers, shepherds, and vagabonds. By such an allegory Sachs only expressed the real tendency of Lutheran thought. In 1522 a revolt of the knights, in 1525 another revolt, this time of the peasants, resulted in anarchy and much bloodshed before they were suppressed by the wealthy German dukes and counts. Although the revolutionaries were, in both cases, faithful Lutherans and had built all their expectations on the Lutheran doctrine, the reformer's sympathies were against them. *Against the Pillaging, Murderous Hordes of the Peasantry* ran the title of the violent tract launched by him against the farmers.

It was under the pressure of these events, portending chaos in the very center of Europe, and also under the pressure of revived French hostility that Charles's delegates accepted, at the Imperial Diet at Spires in August, 1526, a declaration of the states of Germany to the effect that each of them should act individually in the matter of the Lutheran propaganda. Thus all Germany was divided into two groups, a Catholic and a Lutheran—the League of Dessau and the League of Torgau were their first names—and the foundations of the policy were laid which, later on, was expressed by the maxim "Cuius regio eius religio." The only hope for a renewal of spiritual unity remained in the clause of the declaration of Spires which said that it should be valid "until the summoning of a General Council."

If the message to the Cortes of La Coruña in 1520 expressed the theoretical foundations of Charles's policy, the experiences of the years 1525–27 constituted the elements from which the practical aspect of that policy had been formed. The Turkish menace was and remained the most important among those elements. The year 1526 brought the fall of Hungary and the rapid progress of the Turkish army toward the heart of Europe. French hostility, pacified for a short period after the battle of Pavia, underwent a fresh recrudescence. For a couple of years it was necessary to consider even the Papal State as an enemy. The opposition in Germany assumed a religious countenance, and henceforth it could not be regarded as a disciplinary problem only, but also as a matter for a General Council of the Church to decide upon.

Taking all these factors into consideration, the young Emperor made his peace with the Holy See and arranged the General Council to meet in the city of Trent in 1545. He was less successful, as we have seen, in regulating his relations with France. And as for the troubles in Germany, their subsequent story is a sad one.

First, they never could be dealt with as a separate problem. If their solution had been made dependent upon the decisions of a General Council, then the convocation and the proceedings of the Council were dependent upon the Emperor's relation with France. Second, the intense nationalism inherent in the Lutheran doctrine was now combined with the personal ambitions of various German dukes and counts.

At the Diet of Augsburg, in the summer of 1530, at which Charles himself was present, Melanchthon, representing Luther, tried to explain, in a new solemn statement known afterward as the "Confession of Augsburg," the Lutheran doctrine of justification through faith alone as a "consolation for timid consciences"—whereas the rude common men "must have the law and repentence preached to them." When the Diet outlawed the Lutheran teaching, the Protestant princes, under the leadership of Philip of Hesse, transformed the League of Torgau into a military alliance, constituted, in February, 1531, at Schmalkalden, a small town in Thuringia. Charles, again thinking first of the Turkish peril, accepted a truce, at Nuremberg in July, 1532, granting temporary immunity to the states which had not obeyed the decision of the Diet and postponing final settlement until a General Council could be convoked.

This respite contributed greatly to the triumph of Lutheranism in the European north. Greed, debauchery, and nationalism led the German princes into the camp where confiscation of ecclesiastical goods and moral profligacy were encouraged. The Protestant reformers went so far in subservience to the powerful of this world that Melanchthon and Bucer, two of the most learned among them, signed, together with Luther, a document authorizing Landgrave Philip of Hesse to commit bigamy. Everything was possible in Germany as long as people acted in accordance with the maxim "Kein Welsch soll uns regieren, dazu auch kein Spaniol" ("No Italian shall be our ruler, a Spaniard even less so"). New German states, such as Saxony and Brandenburg, joined the League of Schmalkalden. Outside Germany, where Sweden had already become a Lutheran country in the late twenties, Norway, Denmark, and Iceland now passed over to Lutheranism. Other reforming trends gained ground elsewhere in Europe. Zwinglianism, which had originated in Zurich, continued spreading even after the death of Zwingli in 1531. In England, Henry VIII had broken with the Holy See, although he did not introduce any change in doctrine. In Basel, Calvin published, in the spring of 1526, his *Christianae religionis institutio*.

As most reformers who had broken with the Church, and particularly Luther, favored a society in which all authority would rest exclusively with the political sovereign, it was only natural that the princes, anxious to plant their absolutist rule as firmly as possible, saw in the Reformation a welcome opportunity. They also saw to it that public order should be preserved. Nevertheless, the Lutheran doctrine, according to which works did not avail to salvation, asserted itself in the debaucheries and slaughters which accompanied the popular uprisings in Münster and in Lübeck in 1534–35. Luther's own last days—he died in February, 1546—were filled with lamentations and protests against the lawlessness of his followers. "Who amongst us," he wrote, "would have thought of preaching as we have done, if we could have foreseen how much misery, corruption, scandal, blasphemy, and wickedness would result from it?"

In such an atmosphere it could hardly be expected that any Protestants would participate in the long-desired General Council. In 1545, when the Council was at last convoked at the episcopal city of Trent on the upper Adige River, they refused to come.

What else could be done to save the imperial authority in Germany from complete collapse, except to enforce the decisions of the imperial diets by an armed hand? Charles's counselors, especially Garcia de Loaysa, had long been of that opinion. And in the letters of one of them, Juan de la Vega, the imperial ambassador in Rome, we find again the conception of the Empire as a hereditary and absolutist monarchy.

Charles for a long time kept to the policy of appeasement. He did attack the Duke of Cleve—a minor German prince who had not hesitated to come to a military agreement with the French—but, on the other hand, at almost the same time, he tried to win over the immoral Philip of Hesse. At last, at the beginning of 1547, when it was probable that another peace with the Turks would be concluded in a few months, he decided to strike. In Maurice, a younger member of the family of the Duke of Saxony, he had found, as early as the summer of 1546, a man ready to betray the Lutherans. Nobody moved in England or in France when Henry VIII and Francis I died, in February and in March, respectively. A short war started—the "War of Schmalkalden," since it was fought against the league of that name. It ended on April 24, 1547, with the decisive victory of the imperial troops, com-

manded by Charles himself and by the Duke of Alba, at Mühlberg on the Elbe. Both the Duke of Saxony and the Landgrave
of Hesse, the leaders of the Protestant League, were taken
prisoners.

6

The victory at Mühlberg seemed to be another Pavia. To
celebrate it, Hernando de Acuña, one of the poets who lived
at Charles's court, wrote a sonnet announcing the approaching
golden age in which there would be only one ruler on the
earth and one flock of his subjects. But, once again, the simple
ideas of the poet—as well as the equally simple wishes of the
imperial counselors—were rather far removed from complicated reality. Neither a unification of Germany—not to speak
of a unification of the world—nor an extirpation of Lutheranism, but the so-called "Interim of Augsburg" of May, 1548,
resulted from the imperial victory.

The reasons for this step were twofold. First, Charles's own
ideas still adhered to the concept of the office of emperor as
that of a moderator and judge, not that of an absolutist ruler.
Second, to use his victory for a complete suppression of Lutheranism, Charles would have had to be fully conscious of the
social impact of that new trend in religious thinking; and that
was clearly not the case.

Did not Alfonso Valdés affirm that Lutheranism was just a
theological quarrel which had resulted from the old rivalry
between the Augustinians and the Dominicans? Charles, in all
probability, had identical or similar views. The efforts of the
German dukes and counts to assert their independence of imperial authority were for him a problem inherited from the
preceding centuries. In coping with it, he was ready to display
energy equal to that with which he had withstood the opposition of the Spanish cities. Had the princes profited from
Lutheranism for their political aims? In that case the more
quietly Lutheranism could be disposed of, the better for the

Emperor. The political disunity of the Christians simply could not be complicated by petty theological dissensions.

The first period of the Council of Trent, opened finally on December 13, 1545, was observed and judged by Charles from the same point of view. As soon as the question of the sources of revelation had been clarified and the Christian doctrine of original sin defined and the bishops and theologians had started to discuss the problem of justification, the Emperor, through his representatives, did his best to frustrate any dogmatic definition of the matter. He still had some hope that the Lutherans would, on second thought or forced by circumstances, accept the invitation to join the council. And he evidently did not consider the difference between Luther's most cherished idea and the Christian tradition a matter of great importance.

In spite of the Emperor's resistance, the Council did redefine the doctrine of justification—in the sense of the traditional teaching of the Church—in January, 1547. In addition, it also defined, in March of the same year, the general doctrine of the Sacraments. Thus the Emperor approached the battlefield of Mühlberg, in April, 1547, with much bitterness against the Pope and the other bishops. The breach widened even more when, in September of the same year, Ferrante Gonzaga, the Emperor's governor in Milan, organized an uprising in neighboring Piacenza, ruled by the Pope's son, Pierluigi Farnese, and occupied the territory.

As the result of all this, at the time of Charles's second and perhaps greatest military triumph, such a thing as a "Catholic" or "Counter-Reformational" policy simply did not exist. The first period of the Council of Trent—which, because of an epidemic, was transferred to Bologna—ended by adjournment in September, 1549. Its second period, convoked by the new Pope, Julius III (1549–55), in November, 1550, dealt with the special doctrines of the Sacrament of the Altar and of Penance and, for a time, suspended its deliberations until a few Protestants arrived. But then, in April, 1552, seeing the impossibility of a compromise and aware of the new events in Germany, it once more interrupted its labors. The new occurrences in Germany did not themselves result from any "Catholic" policy. On the contrary, through the "Interim of Augsburg," which approved of the confiscation of the Church estates as well as of matrimony for the clergy and communion under both species, and through orders sent to those bishops at Trent who were his subjects, Charles held to the policy of compromise at any price. In spite of all this, Maurice of Saxony, who had helped Charles in 1547, came now to an understanding not only with another *kerndeutsch* prince, Albrecht Alcibiades of Brandenburg, but also with King Henry II of France, to whom he promised the imperial cities of Metz, Toul, and Verdun, and, without warning, struck at the Emperor.

The storm aroused by Maurice and Albrecht came as unexpectedly as heavy clouds, which, driven by a gust of wind, cross the peaks of mountains and descend upon a valley. At the bottom of the deep valley of the river Inn, in Tyrol, in the city of Innsbruck, the Emperor waited unarmed and tired. When he realized the danger—in May, 1552—he first tried to flee directly to the west, but, finding that way closed, he hurriedly crossed the Brenner Pass to the south. Not until he had arrived at the town of Villach, in Carinthia, did he find any rest and security.

It meant an evacuation of Germany, thirty-two years after La Coruña. It almost meant that Charles left Central Europe out of his plan for unification of European defense. A year later, in the summer of 1553, another and the last epoch in Charles's career started—that which was based on the marriage of his son Philip with Mary Tudor, who, unexpectedly, became Queen of England after the death of her young brother, Edward VI. Residing in Brussels until 1556 and then, until his death, in the Spanish monastery of Yuste, the Emperor thought of England much more than he used to think of it in the years of his youthful friendship with Henry VIII. But the Empire was no longer the central piece among his chess figures. It receded definitely to the second row, along with the territories which were in the hands of Ferdinand, the Emperor's younger brother, and which were to remain in the hands of Ferdinand's descendants.

The flight to Villach did not mean, however, any basic change in the ideology of Charles's policy. The continuation of the General Council was now postponed *ad infinitum*. The chances that it would be resumed diminished even more with the ascension to the papal throne, in 1555, of Paul IV, one of the Carafas, who had never hidden their Italian anti-Spanish nationalism. The Interim of Augsburg was completed, in September, 1555, with Charles's consent, by the Peace of Augsburg, which was signed by Ferdinand and confirmed the main clauses of the Interim, sanctioning not only Lutheranism as a religion but also all the gains of the Lutheran dukes and counts in Germany which had resulted from the "secularization" of the property of the Church. The same principle was adhered to in England after Philip's marriage with Mary Tudor. There the Hapsburgs resisted all the attempts of the Pope and of the English Cardinal Reginald Pole to obtain the restitution of the estates which had belonged to the Church—especially to the monasteries—before Henry VIII had authorized their spoliation by the nobles.

A few ordinances against the Protestant propaganda were published, before and after 1550, in the Netherlands. Also, the last days of the Emperor were filled with an unusual interest in the work of the Holy Inquisition in Spain. All this, however, resulted from efforts aiming at the absolutist unity of the countries in question rather than from any enthusiasm for the internal revival of the Christian tradition. There was a world of difference between the Emperor's policy, on the one hand, and the activities of the Theatines, the Jesuits, and the bishops and theologians assembled at Trent, on the other.

ON THE LAND, ON THE SEA

1

FOR a short time, Garcilaso de la Vega, the poet, was confined on a small island in the Danube near the Bavarian city of Regensburg. The confinement had been inflicted upon him by the Emperor because of disobedience. There, looking down the mighty stream toward the east, Garcilaso composed a *canción*.

> Danubio, río divino,
> que por fieras naciones
> vas con tus claras ondas discurriendo ...
> en tierra tan ajena,
> en la desierta arena. ...

It was, perhaps, not for the first time that a Spaniard was able to contemplate the forlorn horizons of the European east and the life hidden behind them. The sixteenth-century liturgical books of the Spanish dioceses of Zaragoza and Tarragona, for instance, contained prayers to be used on the feast of St. Orosia, a Slavonic princess who had become the patroness of the Pyrenean town of Jaca. Old legends dating from the thirteenth century celebrated this daughter of the Czech Duke Bořivoj and his wife Ludmila, who, engaged to Fortunio Garcia, Prince of Navarre, met the glorious death of a martyr when on her way to Pamplona, the capital of Navarre. The bloodthirsty Saracens who, only a hundred years before, had entered the half-mythical world of medieval heroic poetry by killing the valiant Roland in the Pass of Roncesvalles, did away also with Orosia. And their sons and grandsons, slowly retreating toward the south and stubbornly defending the peninsula which they had occupied so rapidly, were probably the main reason why the Slavonic virgin and martyr remained alive in the memory of the citizens of Navarre and Aragon. As late at 1530, Bartolomé Pau, a Catalonian author, composed his tragedy called *Historia de Sancta Orosia.* The Mohammedans were still the enemies. And Garcilaso de la Vega, following in his dreamy thought the garrulous waves of the "divine river Danube," was able to think of the "fierce nations" living on its shores. Those "fierce nations" were not only the Slavs and the Magyars but also the Mohammedan Turks. And the lower valley of the Danube was now the battlefield.

The blue and white waves of the *mar latino*—the "Latin Sea," washing the shores of Valencia, Murcia, Almeria, and Malaga—were now almost identified with the fast-running water of the Danube. There was danger in store for anyone who would intrust his fate to those waters. Beyond the Mediterranean or down along the Danube there were the fierce enemies of Christendom. That is why Garcilaso de la Vega spoke of the "strange land" and of the "sands of the desert" when thinking of the countries on the lower Danube. To his mind, Africa and the Balkans were almost one and the same region.

The fight with the Moslems once again assumed universal importance. A generation before, in the days when Ferdinand and Isabella entered the city of Granada after a long and bitter campaign, some people in Spain could believe that the task which they had tried to bring to a successful end for so many centuries had finally been accomplished. But then, with the growing might of the Moslems on the sea, the problem of the defense of Christian civilization acquired a new meaning and a new urgency. It became, once again, a European problem. Not only Spain but also Italy were in danger from the sea. And the very core of the European mainland was threatened by an attack on the land from the southeast.

2

The source of the revived Mohammedan danger was Turkey. Since the days of the thirteenth-century empire of the Mongols, there had not been such a mighty power in the immediate neighborhood of Europe. Indeed, the first appearance of the Turks was connected with the dramatic events of the epoch in which the culture of the Christian Middle Ages culminated and in which Alfonso el Sabio fought with the Moslems in Castile, and the Polish and Czech knights stopped the Mongolian hordes at Lehnice and Olomouc. It was in the same century, the events of which impressed themselves so vividly upon the memory of Dante Alighieri, that the Turks were separated by the Mongols from their old home in central Asia. Having entered the Arabic world, they accepted Mohammedanism but, at the same time, did not forget how to assert and reassert their military supremacy. In a short time they became the most dynamic and powerful element in the Moslem world.

After the occupation of Asia Minor the Turks crossed into Europe about 1350, subjugating, one after another, the outer provinces of the Byzantine Empire in the Balkan peninsula until, on May 29, 1453, their Sultan, Mohammed III, called "The Conqueror," took Constantinople itself and made it the capital of his realm.

The Turkish move northward toward the center of the Balkan peninsula had already started before the capture of Constantinople. In 1389 in the fields of Kossovo, Lazarus, King of Serbia, was defeated, and the freedom of his land was basically reduced. In 1416, Mircea, Voivode of Romanian Walachia, was forced to pay tribute, and the Turkish units penetrated even Transylvania. Then, however, even the conscience of a decadent Europe was aroused, and the struggle began—at least such a struggle as could be put up by the Kingdom of Hungary, with some very slight help from its neighbors. János Hunyadi, Duke of Transylvania and later governor of Hungary, became the hero of this valiant but vain opposition. In 1442 he drove the Turks out of Transylvania, and two years later, in alliance with Ladislaus I, King of Hungary, and supported by the Pope, he crossed the lower Danube and reached the Bulgarian town Varna. But there the Turks proved to be stronger. Another attempt was made by Hunyadi in 1448, but again without success. The Hungarian army was routed by the Turks, this time on the same fields of Kossovo where the Serbs had been deprived of their liberty more than half a century before.

Hunyadi's son, Matthias Corvinus, King of Hungary, continued in his father's footsteps and in those of St. John Capistran, the great preacher and spiritual leader of the defendants of Hungary. He was able to count on some support coming from the city-republic of Venice, whose commercial interests had been put in danger by the Turkish conquest of the Peloponnese—then called "Morea"—and whose war fleet was now speedily built up. Also the much smaller city-republic of Ragusa (Dubrovnik) on the eastern coast of the Adriatic Sea became a factor in the struggle for the freedom of Christendom. Nevertheless, the results were far from satisfactory. Serbia—with the exception of the city of Belgrade—now became a province of the Turkish Empire, and so did Bosnia and Albania. Walachia was transformed into a tributary protectorate. Even to the north of the Black Sea, the Tatar Khanate of Crimea—which, besides the khanates of Astrakhan and Kazan, both on the Volga, was the only remnant of the medieval Mongolian push against Europe—now became a part of the Turkish sphere of influence. Several fortresses on the Crimean coast, of which Kaffa was perhaps the most important, were garrisoned by the Turks and maintained the Tatars in submission.

Thus it happened that at the end of the fifteenth century the boundaries between the Turkish Empire and Christian Europe ran straight across the Balkans, roughly along the forty-fifth parallel, as we have described it in the preceding chapter. Hungary—since 1490 united with Bohemia—was still the major obstacle to Turkish imperialism on land. Venice played a similar role on the sea and was still in possession of a number of important islands, among which Cyprus—the last remnant of the territories occupied by the Crusaders and acquired by Venice in 1479—was the largest, followed, according to the degree of strategic prominence, by Crete, Zante, Corfu, and the small islands of the northeastern Adriatic.

In the meantime, however, the Turks also contemplated the occupation of other Mediterranean countries. For some time, after a sudden attack from the sea, they had held the city of Otranto in southeastern Italy. After 1512, with the ascension of Selim I to the sultanate, Turkish expansion turned to the east and southeast. The Shah of Persia, head of the Shiites, whose Mohammedanism differed from the Sunnite credo of the Turks and the Arabs, was defeated, and Kurdistan was added to the Turkish Empire. Then, in 1516 and 1517—the first two years of Charles's reign in Spain—Selim conquered the state of the Arabian Mameluks, which had its center in Egypt and to which Syria, Hejaz, and Palestine also belonged.

With the fall of Cairo, the capital of the Mameluk state, the spiritual as well as the political leadership of all the Mohammedans passed from the Abbasids to the Turkish sultans. It was in this role that Suleiman I—Suleiman the Magnificent, Selim's son—embarked upon new imperialist adventures in 1520. A successful assault on fortified Belgrade in 1521, followed, during the next year, by the conquest of Rhodes, marked the first stage of his victorious progress. And then in 1526 came the main attack against Hungary. By-passing the valley of the Save, through which, in the preceding decades, the Turkish raids had reached the Piave and the confines of northern Italy, Suleiman directed his large army along the Danube, into the very heart of Hungary. There, on the marshy fields near Mohács, he met the quickly assembled forces of Louis Jagielon, King of Bohemia and Hungary, and defeated them in a short but decisive battle. A few days afterward, the Turks were in Buda, the capital of Hungary. The heart of Europe now lay open to them.

The news of the battle of Mohács spread terror throughout central and southern Europe. A new and strange power was threatening Christian civilization. Similar, to a certain extent, to the future Soviet Union, with its enormous human resources serving one huge military machine, the Turkish—or Ottoman —Empire was a dictatorship in which all executive and even judicial power was concentrated in the hands of the army. Its production, of course, was left in private hands and was soon to become entangled in the international machinations of the capitalist merchants. But between the producing inhabitants and the military governing body there was an immense gap such as Europe had never witnessed. The spirit of the Turkish laws was the spirit of nomadic primitivism and of the fanatical *sheria* of the Moslem tradition. In the background there was some pessimistic and sensual Persian and Arabic philosophy, the cultivators of which never had the slightest interest in the well-being of human society.

The Turkish army which in the first half of the sixteenth century counted some two hundred and fifty thousand soldiers was a body as cruel and ruthless in fighting as it was disciplined and well equipped. The core of the army was a body of particularly well-trained and indoctrinated professional soldiers called the "janissaries" and recruited from sons of Christian subjects and young prisoners of war. Their enthusiasm was the enthusiasm of a ruling class which knew well that its advantages would grow only with the extension of its power.

3

A distance of only one hundred miles divided Buda from the eastern frontier of Austria, the province of the Holy Roman Empire, which since the thirteenth century had been regarded as the hereditary property of the Hapsburg family. Maximilian I, Charles's grandfather, had lived in Austria, as had his predecessors. Charles himself, however, did not care much for the tranquil seclusion of the Alpine valleys or for Vienna, the small, peaceful town on the Danube. In February, 1522, by an agreement signed in Brussels, he ceded the land of his forefathers to his younger brother Ferdinand, who thus became Archduke of Austria.

Did that happen just because the young Emperor had no

time left to devote to the administration of Austria? Or was it the result of a certain tension between the two brothers? Ferdinand, unlike his elder brother, had been educated in Spain, and many Spaniards used to look on him as their future king. After the death of Ferdinand of Aragon and before Charles's arrival in Spain from Flanders, at the time when the aged Cardinal Jiménez de Cisneros held the regency for the absent heir, the house of Prince Ferdinand became the center of intrigues aiming at the overthrow of the regent. This had been reported by the Cardinal to Charles, and the young king ordered the dismissal of the rebellious courtiers from his brother's household—with the exception of Cristóbal de Castillejo, the poet. Even a guard was posted in front of Ferdinand's house. As soon as circumstances were favorable, the Emperor transferred his brother to Germany, making him, in 1521, his permanent representative in that country. And in 1522, as has been said, he sent him to Austria.

Such a promotion was certainly not to Ferdinand's liking. As early as 1521, Louis Jagielon, King of Bohemia and Hungary—whose sister Anne married Ferdinand a year later, while Louis himself espoused Ferdinand's sister Maria—had to advise Ferdinand to stay and not to try to return to Spain against the Emperor's will. In January, 1526, Ferdinand wrote to Charles asking to be appointed governor of one of his territories in Italy. But then, all of a sudden, only a few weeks after King Louis's death at Mohács, he was elected king of two ancient states in the neighborhood—Bohemia and Hungary.

The election in Prague came first, on September 24, 1526—that is, after the Diet at Spires, which had witnessed Charles's acquiescence to the spread of Lutheranism. The Czech nobles convened, according to ancient usage, in three separate assemblies in the capital cities of Bohemia, Moravia, and Silesia. The first elected Ferdinand by vote. The other two accepted him as their hereditary ruler, as a result of his marriage with Anne, sister of Louis Jagielon.

In Hungary, developments were more complicated. There,

almost immediately after the disastrous battle of Mohács, a certain number of Hungarian noblemen elected János Zápolya, Duke of Transylvania, and had him crowned in the ancient town of Székesfehérvár. Whereupon Maria, the widow of Louis, summoned a regular Diet to Bratislava and there, on December 16, had her brother Ferdinand proclaimed King of Hungary.

Thus the already immense sphere of power of Charles V was extended by the accession of two ancient kingdoms. Circumstances, however, modified this extension essentially. Did it not mean new conflicts for the Emperor? What were the actual plans of Suleiman? It was known that some troubles in Asia Minor had forced him to leave Buda almost hurriedly and to return to Constantinople. But for how long a time? Would Hungary be able to re-establish its defenses?

On the other hand, was not the military fame of the victor at Pavia one of the reasons—or perhaps the main one—why the Czech and Hungarian noblemen chose the Emperor's brother for their king? At the time when the Bohemian Diet was in session at Prague, some Turkish troops were only a few miles from the southern frontier of Moravia. And as to the decision taken by the Diet in Bratislava, was it not evident to the Hungarians that even the valiant Zápolya would not be able to resist Suleiman without foreign help?

4

The fame of the Spanish army was world wide. The struggle with the Moors, which had been going on for centuries on Spanish soil, had made the Spaniards born soldiers and soldiering the fashionable profession not only of the hidalgos but of the whole population. Also, a military career brought to everybody the hope of earning some money and being able to settle down on the land or to choose another more quiet profession later on. Thus the Spanish military units of the sixteenth century were recruited from better and more disciplined people than any other contemporary army. In addition, the hardship of the Spanish climate endowed the sons of the peninsula with special powers of endurance.

But the personal pre-eminence of the Spanish soldier would hardly have been sufficient to achieve such victories as that of Pavia, had it not been integrated into a magnificent military machine, equipped with new tactical methods. The real father of Spanish military fame was Gonzalo de Córdoba, the "great captain" of Ferdinand and Isabella, who, in the Italian wars at the beginning of the sixteenth century, had improved the endurance of the Spaniards by the introduction of a new method of fighting, a method which lasted until Rocroi. The essence of this method consisted in the combination of the use of various arms. Of the three thousand men of a Spanish *coronelia* or *tercio,* fifteen hundred were armed with long pikes, one thousand with short swords and javelins, and five hundred with arquebuses. A *tercio* consisted of twelve or fifteen companies. Each company was commanded by a captain, each *tercio* by a *maestro de campo.* In battle formation—which was now often strengthened by technical field works—the pikemen would form squares, with the javelin men in the center so that these might surprise the enemy when it came to hand-to-hand fighting. The arquebusiers and also the artillery would be placed separately in positions from which they would be able to support the squares by fire.

What could the old-fashioned archers or even the German *Landsknechte* do against such an organization? It is true that the arquebuses or muskets—about five or six feet long and so heavy that in a battle they had to be supported by a forked rest—were still very clumsy and that they had an accurate range of only a hundred yards. Even the pikes, sixteen or eighteen feet long—a unit of pikemen in battle looked like an enormous porcupine—were quite heavy, and the soldiers used to drag them along the ground when marching. Nevertheless, the Spaniards made almost a virtue out of slow, circumspect advances. Their famous commanders who succeeded Gonzalo de Córdoba were all eminent tacticians and very prudent strategists. They were Antonio de Leyva and Fernando Alvarez, Duke of Alba, both of whom made themselves prominent in the times of Charles V; Alessandro of Parma, who served under Philip II; and Ambrosio Spinola, who commanded Spanish troops under both Philip III and Philip IV.

In 1526, however, it was by no means clear whether the Spanish soldiers would be available for the defense of the Danubian valley. The inhabitants of Spain well knew of the Turkish danger, but they wanted to have the defense of their own country assured first of all. In 1527, when Charles asked the Cortes of Castile at Valladolid for a grant of money to pay a military expedition to Hungary, he was refused.

In the meantime, Zápolya, whose supporters had found themselves in the minority and unable to resist even the insignificant forces which Ferdinand had at his disposal, retired to Poland and from there, imitating the French, asked Suleiman for help. The Sultan, who undoubtedly had regarded his expedition to Hungary as unfinished, listened to his request readily and, in the late summer of 1529, invaded that divided kingdom for the second time. By September 3, he was in Buda again and had Zápolya solemnly raised to the throne of St. Stephan as his own vassal. Then, by forced marches, he proceeded toward Vienna. For more than two weeks his troops tried to take the city by assault; during the last four days the fighting was especially fierce. There was some Spanish infantry on the walls of Vienna, commanded by the experienced Antonio de Leyva, whom the Emperor had sent to his brother; several small units of Spanish cavalry participated in the skirmishes in the surrounding country. Failing to take Vienna, however, and deterred by the approaching winter, the Turks fell back again on Buda, where they left a strong garrison in support of Zápolya's claims.

In the course of the following decade, the fighting in Hungary was almost continuous. In 1532 it was particularly violent, and, although about six thousand Spanish troops participated in it, a large part of lower Austria was devastated by Turkish raids. Ferdinand was able to get some help from the Bohemian and Moravian nobles but almost none from Germany. "To fight against the Turks," said Luther, "means to resist God, who, through the Turks, punishes us for our iniquities."

Among the military aspects of the war in Hungary, besides the use of special fighting boats on the Danube, built in the Austrian river port of Gmunden—according to the Ukrainian model of the so-called *tchaikas*—the organization of the defense between the upper parts of the rivers Drave and Save and to the south of Save was of particular importance. That region, inhabited by the Croats and the Slovenes, was given, in 1538, an autonomous military administration which proved efficient not only against the Turkish onslaughts but also against the *uskoks* and the *hajduks,* small but very ruthless military units formed by the indigenous Slavs, who were ready to fight the imperial, as well as the Turkish, troops. A similar problem had to be coped with by the defendants of the Venetian possessions on the Adriatic coast; there also the native partisans, the *zagorci,* caused no little trouble.

In 1542 Suleiman, having in the meantime won a new conflict with Persia, arrived again in Hungary, appealed to by the widow of Zápolya on behalf of her infant son. This time, however, the Sultan was ready to go much further than the mere protection of other people's interest. He was now going to make Hungary an integral part of his empire. His plan was to establish—besides the main part of the realm, consisting of twenty-four provinces *(vilayets)*, each of them governed by a high pasha and divided into regions *(sanjaks)*—a series of self-governing territories, placed directly under the suzerainty of the Sultan. The "Garb-Ojaklari," i.e., the provinces of North Africa (Tripoli, Tunis, and Algiers), the Sherifate of Mecca, which was administered by the descendants of Mohammed, the Sherifate of Hejaz, the Khanate of Crimea, and now the Kingdom of Hungary and perhaps also Transylvania and

the Romanian principalities of Walachia and Moldavia were
to be included among them.

Both the Hapsburg rulers, Charles and Ferdinand, had to
content themselves with the defense of a narrow strip of Hungary, ranging from the Croatian-Slovene military district in
the south toward Slovakia in the north, under the Carpathian
Mountains. With all the troubles in Germany and elsewhere,
they gladly accepted, in 1545, a truce which the Sultan was
willing to agree upon.

5

On the sea the situation was even worse. The Spanish navy,
which in those days—like all other contemporary fleets—util-
ized many former convicts as sailors, was weak indeed in comparison with the combined strength of the small but numerous
fleets of the Mohammedan pirates of North Africa, who now
worked in close alliance with the Turks and had the support
of Suleiman himself. In 1516 the corsairs nearly captured Pope
Leo X, when he was fishing in the proximity of Cività Lavinia.
In 1529 they raided the Spanish coast near Valencia and took
many thousands of captives. Not until the early thirties was
Charles V able to do something against the naval power of the
Mohammedans. He now had the help of Genoa, his ally
against the French. After several smaller attacks against the
strongholds of the pirates in the region of Algiers and Oran,
he sent the Genoese admiral, Andrea Doria, to the southern
shores of Greece and into the Gulf of Corinth. Doria was able
for a short time to occupy Coron, on the shores of southern
Peloponnese, and also to seize Patras.

This expedition, which coincided with Suleiman's drive
along the Danube in 1532, had a decisive effect upon the Sultan
—the attack on Austria was stopped. But in the long run it
only forced the Sultan to take more care of the navy, to make
Kheireddin Barbarossa, a renegade Christian and the most
ruthless of the African pirates, commander-in-chief of the

Turkish fleet, and to start negotiations for a closer alliance with France.

The alliance between Francis I, King of France, and Suleiman, the Mohammedan conqueror, is one of the most significant results of the Renaissance decay of European morals. Paolo Veronese, one of the prominent painters of the epoch, celebrated it in his "Marriage at Cana," a typical Renaissance picture in which a religious scene furnishes the stage for a symbolic feast offered by the King of France to Suleiman the Turk. Francis was the real author of that memorable accomplishment. On the eve of the battle of Pavia, one year before the Turkish attack on Hungary and the heroic death of King Louis at Mohács, Francis had sent his signet ring, accompanied by an offer of military friendship, to Constantinople. The offer was accepted, and Francis was now an ally not only of the Sultan himself but also of Kheireddin, his bloody admiral.

As a heritage of older days, there were still some Christian possessions on the coast of North Africa. Tangier belonged to the Portuguese; Melilla, Oran, Bona, and Bizerta were occupied by the Spaniards. Tunis with its fortress, La Goletta, was governed by a Moorish chieftain, vassal of the Spanish king. Tripoli, taken in 1510 by Ferdinand of Aragon, had been given by Charles V in 1522 to the Knights Hospitalers when this order, a venerable institution of the epoch of the Crusades, had to evacuate Rhodes. The Knights also took over Malta, a small but strategically important island to the south of Sicily. It was against these strongholds of the Christian Mediterranean that Kheireddin, the new commander of the Turkish navy, directed his onslaught. In 1534 he took Tunis, and Charles, aided by the Pope and by Portugal, drove him out in 1535 only after a long siege. Having achieved that, however, the imperial forces were not strong enough to follow Kheireddin to Algiers, where the pirate took refuge. New piratic raids against the Balearic Islands and the Valencian coast in 1536 and another large-scale attack against southern Italy in

1537—in combination with the renewed French offensive mentioned above—were the result.

The Emperor, who in April, 1536, speaking in Spanish before the Pope and diplomatic representatives of many European states, explained his policy of European defense and protested against the French treason—even the guns found in Tunis were of French provenance—concluded, in February, 1538, an anti-Turkish league with the Pope and with Venice. But in spite of an allied naval victory in the Gulf of Prevesa, on the western coast of Greece, in September, 1538, the league disintegrated again when Venice made a separate peace in 1540, ceding to the Turks a number of smaller islands in the Aegean Sea and even some ports in the Adriatic, such as Nadino and Laurana.

Late in the summer of 1541, the Emperor, in the hope that he would be able to bring over to his side one of Kheireddin's lieutenants, Hassan Aga, decided to attack Algiers, of which Hassan Aga was the governor. This time, however, he was even less fortunate than in 1535. Hassan Aga refused to surrender, and heavy gusts of wind and rain helped him to defeat the Emperor, whose fleet, under Andrea Doria, lost about a hundred and fifty ships in the storm.

This unlucky expedition, which had been prepared with so many hopes and in which, besides Charles and Andrea Doria, the Duke of Alba and Hernando Cortés, who had returned from Mexico, also participated, was the last of Charles's major naval actions. Engaged in a new conflict with France—from 1542 to 1544—and later on in a war with the League of Schmalkalden, the Emperor had to witness a constant deterioration of the situation in the Mediterranean. Franco-Turkish friendship went so far that the Turkish fleet even spent the winter of 1543-44 in Toulon with all its cargo of Christian slaves. Kheireddin himself died in 1546, but his place was almost immediately taken by another ruthless sailor, called Dragut, who, himself a renegade of Greek origin, operated often in alliance with the galleons of small groups of independent pirates—the *ponentini,* as they were called in the ports of the eastern Mediterranean. Sea commerce between the Christian countries of the Mediterranean, such as Spain itself or Naples, almost ceased to exist. In spite of the truce agreed between Ferdinand, Charles's bother, and Suleiman, on November 10, 1545, and renewed in June, 1547, Dragut continued to rule over the western Mediterranean according to his piratical custom. A solemn protest addressed by Charles to Suleiman from Augsburg in October, 1550, could not stop him.

On August 14, 1551, the city and fortress of Tripoli had to be evacuated by the Knights Hospitalers, who henceforward were restricted to the exclusive possession of Malta and consequently were called the "Maltese Knights." Other fortified places on the North African coast fell gradually into Mohammedan hands. The fleet commanded by the aged Andrea Doria was defeated off the Italian coast near Terracina in August, 1552. The next year the French, with Turkish help, attacked Corsica, a Genoese possession. And in 1554 Turkish political and military influence was extended, by an expedition of Dragut's lieutenant, Salah Reis, to Morocco, hitherto ruled by independent Moorish chieftains. There were certainly more losses than gains in the story of the naval defense of Europe under Charles V.

6

Taken together, the religious and political disintegration of Germany and the engagement of Ferdinand in Hungary and Bohemia resulted in the formation of an area, embracing Germany, Austria, Bohemia, and Hungary, which Charles V, at the end of his reign, regarded as only a secondary sector of his sphere of political influence. Naturally, it took a long time before the Emperor came to regard things in that way. Only after his son's marriage with Mary Tudor of England was he ready to concentrate his planning on western Europe. And even then, discussing the question of succession with his brother Ferdinand and with his sister Maria, the widow of

Louis of Hungary, he hesitated to give up altogether the idea which he had cherished so long, the combination of Spain's might with the traditional mission of the Holy Roman Empire.

Ferdinand, on the other hand, was pushed forward by developments. A frustrated competitor for the Spanish throne, governor of Germany, ruler of Austria, King of Bohemia and Hungary, and, since 1531, successor presumptive of the Emperor himself, he was gradually ascending toward higher and more important offices. Not that he had, in all probability, a political plan of his own. On the contrary, he was of the type that is controlled by circumstances instead of controlling them according to his own ideas. As King of Bohemia, Ferdinand was, according to the imperial constitution, one of the Electors whose duty it was to select the emperors. That, however, was not deemed sufficient by Charles, who did not wish to let central Europe slip out of sight even when the naval defense against the Turks called him to the Mediterranean. On that account, in 1531, he arranged Ferdinand's election to the office of King of the Romans, a title traditionally given to the future emperors. It is interesting to notice that, at the same time, Maria, the widow of Louis, was appointed governor of the Netherlands.

But then the special circumstances in central Europe themselves began to mold the policy of Ferdinand, whose character, in spite of his youthful opposition to his brother in Spain, was always inclined to compromises.

At the beginning of his political career, Ferdinand was not quite able to get rid of the remnants of his Spanish education. The language was undoubtedly the most enduring among them. Up to 1550, there lived at Ferdinand's court the gallant cleric and poet, Cristóbal de Castillejo, acting as his "secretary of Spanish letters" and composing old-fashioned songs in the traditional Spanish meters. Spanish customs also lingered for some time around Ferdinand's residences in Vienna and in Prague. At Easter, the King used to wash publicly the feet of twelve old men; tournaments were arranged according to Castilian usage by Pedro de Córdoba, one of the King's courtiers. And there were some counselors who had come from Spain, such as Gabriel Salamanca, a poor "hidalgo" from Argos, who was intrusted with Ferdinand's treasury and managed it in such a selfish way that, in 1525, the Austrian nobles obtained from Ferdinand his dismissal from office. Even afterward, in 1527, the Czech nobility protested against the advice he had been giving to the King in financial matters.

Salamanca was probably of the type of financiers, such as Juan Vasquez or Francisco Eraso, who served Charles V by entangling his finances more and more with those of the international capitalists. Ferdinand's own financial administration was necessarily bound to that of his brother and thus to the interests of the big moneylenders. When Ferdinand took over Austria, all the revenues from the mines in Tyrol, for example, were already in the hands of the Fugger family. To help Ferdinand in building up the defense against the Turks, Charles V placed at his disposal some of his own revenues from the Kingdom of Naples. Those revenues, however, were not cashed by Ferdinand directly. They were paid in Naples to a representative of the Fuggers, and Ferdinand received them in Augsburg from the Fugger treasury. Naturally, he obtained much less than had been granted.

Through the joint influence of international commerce and the influx of precious metals from America into Spain, the economic structure of European society—in which the use of money was gradually becoming indispensable even in the relations between noblemen and their farmers—was undergoing a profound change. Year by year, more and more bullion was streaming into Europe by way of Spain, and prices were mounting. The Emperor and his bother needed money to pay their soldiers and sailors as well as to cover the expenses of their constant voyages—expenses unknown to the rulers of small states of the previous centuries. At the same time, fewer and fewer direct revenues remained in the hands of the Hapsburgs. Since 1524, even the revenues from the three orders of knights—those of Santiago, Calatrava, and Alcantara—which hitherto had been paid by the noblemen directly to the King of Spain, were paid to the Fuggers, who had got hold of them as mortgage for their loans.

It is interesting to observe how Ferdinand strove to accommodate the economic life of his dominions to that of his brother's territories. A conflict arose between him and the Diet of Moravia in 1538 when the Diet tried to defend itself against devaluation of money. Four years earlier, the Diet of Bohemia had refused to adopt a special tax on sales which Ferdinand had tried to impose in imitation of the Spanish *alcabala*. On the other hand, Ferdinand succeeded in concentrating the treasuries of all his lands into one Court Treasury, thus taking the first step toward absolutist centralization. At the same time, he attempted to replace the individual Diets of his lands by a single general Diet. But in that he failed.

Only one advantage resulted from this trend of economic affairs. In 1552, after Charles's flight across the Alps to Villach, it was Anton Fugger, the head of the Augsburg capitalist family, who, by advancing a substantial loan to Ferdinand, enabled him to deal firmly with the German rebels. The Emperor was certainly not a "prince without a penny," as Rabelais depicted him—in the person of "King Picrochole"—in his *Gargantua*. Nevertheless, it took some time before money could be obtained from Naples and from Spain, and many an important thing might happen in the meantime in Germany. Thus the same banking-house which had helped Charles to the imperial crown had now also saved Germany—if not for Charles, this time, then at least for his bother and successor.

7

The treaty of Passau, through which Ferdinand in 1552 settled the conflict between his brother, the Emperor, and Maurice of Saxony, the rebel, and the peace of Augsburg, completed in September, 1555, were both concluded under the impression that the decisive battles against the Turks would have to be fought on the Mediterranean. That was the main idea which pushed Charles toward arranging the English marriage for his son Philip. That was also the main reason why it was decided that the Emperor would settle down in Brussels, before retiring to Spain.

But the arrangements of Passau and Augsburg also meant the definitive legalization of the spirit which had been best expressed by the principle "Cuius regio, eius religio." Was Ferdinand, who indorsed that principle much more readily than his brother, guided in his decision by some particular experiences of his own? What was the religious situation in that triangle of countries which he had inherited and which he now had to defend against the Turks?

The Danubian valley had been infiltrated by the spirit of the Renaissance somewhat later than France or Germany. Also the impact which the Renaissance had upon architecture and the other arts of Austria, Bohemia, and Hungary—as well as on those of Poland—did not amount to much; the Gothic style, in new modifications, remained prevalent up to the middle of the sixteenth century. But social life was thoroughly permeated by the new semipagan trends of thought and customs. The moral disintegration of society which followed was to a great extent responsible for the defeat of the Hungarians at Mohács and for the inadequacy of the help they had received from the Czechs and other neighboring nations.

On the other hand, Lutheranism found fertile soil in the regions to the east and southeast of Germany. Lutheran preachers like Paul von Spretten in Austria and Mátyás Devay in Hungary were supported in their efforts by young noblemen who had studied in German universities. It may be said that German nationalism in Austria and Germanization in Hungary—and also in the Kingdom of Bohemia—were the concomitants of the Lutheran propaganda.

The case of the Czech inhabitants of the Kingdom of Bohemia was a peculiar one. Only a hundred years before, they had been engaged in one of the most spiritual adventures that the Middle Ages had witnessed—in the great religious movement, striving to establish God's kingdom in the very heart of Europe. The idea around which that movement finally concentrated— under the leadership of Jan Hus and after its original ideals of social reform through religious revival had been distorted by an influx of irrational Wycliffism from England—was the idea that no exercise of authority, not even the exercise of private owner- ship, was possible without the presence of the sanctifying grace which accompanies only those who lead a moral life. Much blood had been shed in Bohemia between 1420 and 1440 be- cause of this fantastic ideal. "Behold, O men, your duty: to root the sins out of your heart, to punish all the sins which have been revealed, to admonish all whose sins have been dis- closed."

But then, with the second half of the fifteenth century, an epoch of disillusionment started in Bohemia, full of skepticism and pagan ideas. Even the Czech (Moravian) Brethren, a sect which had originated in the religious movement and which believed that it had rediscovered the teaching of "primitive Christians," was now, in 1520, seeking spiritual help from Erasmus of Rotterdam, the man who doubted all traditional teaching, no matter how "primitive." At the same time, a wave of Lutheran propaganda, accompanied by rapid Germaniza- tion of cities and schools, swept through the country. Martin Luther himself, who at the beginning of his career had em- phatically denied having anything in common with the Czech "heretics," became the most influential person in Bohemia.

The Czechs, who in the last years of the movement had put the teaching concerning the public prosecution of sins and the advisability of receiving Communion under both species before the General Council of Basel and had obtained its approval, were now led by men who, accepting the Lutheran doctrine, professed the precise contrary of what their fathers had taught.

Not the necessity of perfect sinlessness but the complete independence of salvation from deeds was now the maxim of the day.

In 1543 Mystopol, regent of the Prague Hussite consistory—the so-called "Lower Consistory"—and an enthusiastic follower of Luther, ordered his priests not only to cease all devotion to the Sacrament of the Altar, for the greater glory of which the Czech religious movement had fought for so many years, but also to cease observing the feast of Jan Hus himself —a feast which had been kept in Bohemia by Catholic priests of the Czech rite ever since the execution of Hus at the General Council of Constance in 1415. A few days afterward Prague had the opportunity to witness one of the most paradoxical scenes of the century. King Ferdinand, grandson of the "Catholic Kings" of Spain, himself educated in the tradition of Juan de Palomar, the Spanish theologian who had opposed the Czechs at the Council of Basel and even at Prague, and of Cardinal Juan de Torquemada, author of the treatise *De corpore Christi adversus Bohemos,* asked Mystopol to come to see him and ordered him to revoke his decree and to observe the feast of Jan Hus with all the usual solemnity.

It seems that Ferdinand had more in mind than just a tactical maneuver against Lutheran influence. In 1538 he had already told Joachim, Duke of Brandenburg, that a General Council would hardly be able to solve the present religious difficulties and that more practical ways for a solution must be found. He named two such "practical" ideas: the introduction of Communion under both species and the authorization of the marriage of clergy.

Psychologically, undoubtedly, this suggestion was clever enough. The revival of Communion under both species—an idea which Ferdinand had obviously taken from the Czechs— would have satisfied, to a certain extent, the Lutheran tendency toward a literal explanation of the Bible. The authorization of the marriage of clergy would have satisfied the sensual fever of some of the reformers. There was, however, a third element in Lutheranism, perhaps the most important of all: an opposition to the authority of the Christian tradition. Frequent quotations from the Bible, it is true, seemed to be an exception to this opposition; but the books of the Bible had been selected and preserved by tradition. Therefore, in the long run, even the authority of the Bible was bound to disappear. And this tendency could hardly be stopped by Ferdinand's plans.

8

As the years passed, the Emperor's brother found it more and more difficult to formulate a general policy for the sphere which Charles had left in his hands. In 1547, when some towns and noblemen in Bohemia, won over by the German Lutheran princes, refused to help the Emperor and prepared, on the contrary, to help the League of Schmalkalden, Ferdinand, returning to Prague after the Emperor's victory at Mühlberg, restored order in Bohemia in such a rigorous way that it can only be compared to that in which Andrés Hurtado de Mendoza, having been nominated, ten years later, Viceroy of Peru, restored order in the South American colonies torn by the civil war between Diego de Almagro and the four Pizarro brothers. Ferdinand had two noblemen and two burghers decapitated, restricted the judicial autonomy of the provinces, concentrated the administration of Bohemia, Moravia, and Silesia into one office—the Royal Bohemian Chancery—and imposed special royal governors on the towns, imitating thus the *corregidores* which had been imposed on the Spanish towns by his grandfather and the *Stadtanwalten* which he himself had already imposed on the towns in Austria. Shortly afterward, in 1550, he introduced the *alcabala* tax into the province of Moravia. And gradually, by establishing a number of central "court offices," he proceeded toward uniting Austria, Bohemia, and also Hungary—as far as he had the territory of this kingdom in his hands—into one administrative whole.

In Germany, however, the general trend of the times pointed to goals of a very different nature. Not the victory of Mühlberg but the peace of Augsburg was to provide a pattern for the future. Thus, at the time when Charles was preparing his abdication and his retirement to Yuste and when Philip, his son, was embarking upon the ambitious task of organizing the European west around the Madrid-London axis, Ferdinand's Central European domain still faced a double danger: that of a Turkish attack on the land and that of internal, ideological disintegration.

> Orbis cuncta meos tenuerunt sceptra triumphos,
> Gallus, Turca potens, Antipodesque feri.
> Terrarum imperium deieci, sceptra, coronas,
> Nam mihi regnandi spes fuit una, Deus.

Such were the words which, later on, were chosen to adorn the library of the University of Salamanca and to glorify Charles, the "last of the Emperors." But even they, although mentioning France, the Turks, and even America, did not mention that part of Europe beyond the Alps which had had such an attraction for the young ruler in 1519. A sad result of a magnificent program—but the end of a life's career is, of course, not always the end of the story.

I, THE KING

1

AT MÜHLBERG in 1547 there was a young man of twenty years standing beside the Emperor and surveying the battle. He was the Emperor's nephew, Maximilian, a rather impulsive youngster, who, only a month before, had left the Emperor's camp at Ulm without permission when news was brought to him about the death of his mother, Queen Anne. His first teacher, Wolfgang Schiefer, had explained the ideas of Martin Luther to him. In 1543 he had met August of Saxony, brother of Maurice, in Prague, and the two young men had become good friends. What was his opinion of the War of Schmalkalden?

After the war had ended, Charles appointed his nephew to preside at the Diet at Augsburg, in the place of Cardinal Otto Walburg, one of the spiritual leaders of the German Catholics. Thus it happened that the Interim of Augsburg was concluded under the auspices and perhaps not without the active participation of the young prince who knew Central Europe very well, having been brought up at Innsbruck in the deep valley of the Tyrol. As to his future career, nothing had been settled as yet, with the exception of the decision to make him the heir to the crown of Bohemia.

In the autumn of 1547, however, Charles conceived the idea of marrying Maximilian to his own daughter Maria. What were his reasons for this rather fatal step which made the already degenerated family of the Hapsburgs even more feeble? Our information concerning these matters is scarce. There had already been differences of opinion between the Emperor and his brother Ferdinand. Their sister Maria, the widow of Louis of Bohemia and Hungary, had had to act as mediator between them. Ferdinand's policy differed more and more, as we have seen, from that of the Emperor. And now it seemed as if the younger generation would inherit more of those differences than of the interests which Charles and Ferdinand had in common. It was obvious, above all, that Maximilian's character was precisely opposite that of Philip, Charles's only legitimate son and heir.

If Maximilian was a difficult young man, Philip proved quite docile and true to most of his father's ideals. Born in the same year as Maximilian—1527—at Valladolid and educated by his mother, Isabella of Portugal, by Juan Martínez Guijeño, a patriotic humanist known under the pen name of "Siliceo," and by Juan Ginés de Sepúlveda, a historian and an emphatic critic of Erasmus, Philip was, above all, a Spaniard. Latin remained his only foreign language. The ochre and white plains sprawling from the shores of the Duero to the distant mountains of old Castile were his only true fatherland.

When he was two years old, his father left Spain and came back only after four years. When he was twelve, his mother died, and his father again had to go away for two long years. Between 1541 and the spring of 1543 there was a short period of respite for Charles, during which he devoted as much attention as possible to the education of his son. But then he had to leave Spain again. In spite of that, the young prince proved to be a devoted admirer of his father.

It would have been probably most satisfying for Charles to be able to make Philip his sole heir. But, with Ferdinand's constantly growing influence in Central Europe, such a solution was hardly conceivable. Some place in the hierarchy of the Hapsburg family had to be found for Maximilian. For some time— as may be seen from the instructions brought to Philip by the Duke of Alba in January, 1548—Charles had been considering the possibility of making Maximilian Duke of the Netherlands. But then he made another decision: Philip and Maximilian were, for a time, to change places and gain new experience in countries hitherto unknown to them.

In June, 1548, Maximilian, accompanied by young men from the foremost Czech and Austrian families, such as Vratislav Pernštýn, Jaroslav Smiřický, and Adam Dietrichstein, set out for Spain. Philip awaited him in his native Valladolid. The meeting of the two cousins took place in the splendor of complicated ceremonies which Charles had known in his youth in the Netherlands and which he had ordered Philip to introduce in Spain. The Spaniards proved particularly inept in grasping the spirit of those ceremonies; they turned them into a somber and rather tedious demonstration. The same ceremonies surrounded Maximilian's marriage to Maria. They even accompanied the sessions of the Spanish Council of State, of which Maximilian, representing his uncle, was now the chairman. The young prince did not care much about Spain. He knew that he would never make it his home. In February, 1549, Volf Krajíř, a Czech nobleman, brought him the news that he had been elected to succeed his father on the Bohemian throne. That, at least, was an assurance that his visit to Spain would not last forever.

Philip, who left Valladolid a month after his cousin's arrival, in October, 1548, had a different task. His father wanted him not only to become familiar with life in foreign countries but to make those foreign countries familiar with his own person. Philip, however, was too much a Spaniard to be willing to give up the manners and customs of his country. In Brussels, where he arrived first, he celebrated Palm Sunday, with a group of other Spaniards, by accompanying an ass through the streets of the city—much to the sarcastic amusement of the Flemings. In Germany, where he went in the summer of 1550, he tried his best to imitate the rough diversions of the German noblemen. But all in vain; he was just not able to drink as much as they did. Thus, as the diplomatic rumors of that time affirmed, he was little liked by the Italians, was disliked by the Flemings, and was hated by the Germans, who kept on repeating that Charles's successor must not be a foreigner or too powerful a person.

In September, 1550, Maximilian obtained permission to return home. A family meeting was arranged in Augsburg, which resulted in a secret agreement, signed in 1551, according to which Ferdinand was to become Charles's successor on the imperial throne, but was, in his turn, to support Philip as his successor. Maximilian was to inherit the imperial title only after the death of Philip. In addition, Italy and the Netherlands were to be inherited directly by Philip. We may see in this agreement a compromise between Charles and Ferdinand, but also a compromise between Charles's ideals and the spirit of the "new Germany."

A few days after the conclusion of the family meeting, both cousins set out for Spain again. Philip was going to take charge of his native country. Maximilian went to fetch his wife, who had stayed at Valladolid. They traveled separately. Philip was anxious to avoid all mention of the family agreement. Maximilian succeeded in doing so only during the journey to Spain. On his way back he met Micheli, the Venetian minister in Genoa, and spoke to him in very frank terms about the Emperor; Charles, he said, hated his brother's family and could hardly be considered a great statesman, since he had always had more luck than talent. Then, continuing his journey home, he stopped at Trent and entered into hot discussions with the Spanish representatives at the General Council. A few months later, at the beginning of 1552, now at home at his father's court, he fell ill and did not hesitate to affirm that the Spaniards at Trent had tried to poison him. In a short time, however, he recovered.

The cohesion of the Hapsburg empire was thus made dependent on the cohesion of the Hapsburg family—a usual condition of large empires, but this time colored by an ideological discrepancy which became evident on the occasion of Maximilian's visit to Trent and to which we shall return in the next chapter. It was in the following months that the utter uncertainty of Charles's hold on Germany was revealed by the sudden revolution organized by Maurice of Saxony. Even after Charles's flight to Villach and after peace had been restored once again by Ferdinand—with the help of the Fuggers—the basic problem remained unsolved.

Charles, after having partially recovered, tried to regain the imperial cities of Metz, Toul, and Verdun, which the rebel, Maurice of Saxony, had sold to the King of France; but the rest of his energy soon left him, and he retired to Brussels. There, as we have already seen, he inaugurated, after July, 1553, when Mary Tudor became Queen of England, his last diplomatic action aiming at the inclusion of England in a western European block. There also he made public his resignation.

The fragmentary accounts of those days give us little evidence of any improvement in Hapsburg family relations. On the contrary, a profound divergence of plans is evident from the fact that, as soon as the death of Edward VI of England had become known, not only Charles on behalf of Philip but also Ferdinand on behalf of his younger son, the Archduke Ferdinand, sent envoys to England asking for Mary Tudor's hand. Curiously enough, Ferdinand's ambassador was a Spaniard, Martin Guzmán. The new Queen of England, nevertheless, preferred Philip.

Nor did Maximilian change his opinion of his uncle's policy. He commented upon the unexpected death of Maurice of Saxony, which followed soon afterward, by saying that this Protestant prince had offered his life for his country. In December, 1553, he wrote to Albrecht of Bavaria: "May God give my father the strength at last firmly to oppose the Emperor and not obey him so sheepishly as he has done until now." Charles undoubtedly knew about it. Juan de Ayala, his envoy to Poland, had instructions to stop in Vienna for a while and to collect as much information concerning Maximilian as possible. And Luis Vanegas de Figueroa, who at that time acted as the Emperor's ambassador at the court of his brother and who had, on a previous occasion, mediated between Maximilian and his wife's Spanish ladies-in-waiting, was instructed to try and change the Augsburg family agreement once more in Philip's favor by having him declared heir of the Duchy of Austria. Had that been realized, Maximilian would have had to be satisfied with the Kingdoms of Bohemia and Hungary. Naturally, Ferdinand and Maximilian refused to listen to such an offer, and Vanegas had to assure Maximilian that Charles had nothing against his becoming his eventual successor.

Mutual suspicion persisted to the very last. According to the Augsburg agreement, Philip was to be appointed Imperial Vicar in Italy by Ferdinand after his ascension to the imperial throne. Charles, however, to assure that dignity for Philip, issued a secret decree appointing him to that office at once. Even Maximilian's journey to Brussels in 1556, to take leave of the Emperor, did not alleviate their reciprocal distrust.

Charles departed for Yuste, and Philip was left in charge of what remained of his father's ideals and alliances. It was now up to him to make the best out of the idea of a West European block. It may be said that, as far as England was concerned, he always remained true to the diplomatic character of Charles's last plan. He never in the least considered the realm of his unhappy wife as anything other than an allied country. After Mary's death, he did not try to impede in any way the succession of her half-sister Elizabeth. But he also had to find a way in which to handle his uncle and his cousin. And—what was most important—he was left with the main task which his father had left unaccomplished, the defense against the Turks.

2

The man who ascended the papal throne in May, 1555, a few months before the conclusion of the peace of Augsburg and before Charles's resignation, was, as has been mentioned, one of the Carafas—a family which strongly opposed Spanish predominance in Italy. A reformer from his youth—it was with his help that Gaetano da Thiene had founded the reforming Theatine order in 1524—he knew Spain, where he had been active as nuncio, and he did not like it. He had been in Rome when the city was sacked by Charles's army in 1527. As Pope he now appointed a new Bishop of Triani—an Italian diocese but in territory which belonged to Spain. Philip protested, because he wanted to have a say in the nomination of bishops to the sees under his sovereignty. As a result, the relations between him and the Pope, Paul IV, deteriorated rapidly, and the French, observing this development, took to arms once more against the Hapsburgs. The Pope sided with the French. Thus the first two years of Philip's rule were taken up with a war against the Pope as well as against Henry III of France. The Spanish army under the Duke of Alba had to occupy Rome once more, this time without any pillaging. Another Spanish army, under the command of Emanuel Philibert of Savoy and personally supervised by Philip, defeated the French at St. Quentin in northeastern France in August, 1557. Peace was re-established only in April, 1559, by the treaty of Cateau-Cambrésis.

In one sense, the peace of Cateau-Cambrésis meant a milestone in the history of Spanish imperialism. It meant the temporary end of a strong, ambitious France; there would no longer be any competition with Spain in Italy. Until 1635, when France, led by Richelieu, would again be ready to fight, the French would be unable to resist Spanish policy with any vigor.

But, on the other side, if we take into consideration the main object of Spanish foreign policy, the defense against the Turks, we have to realize that Philip's position was far from satisfactory even after the peace of Cateau-Cambrésis had been concluded. First of all, the event almost coincided with the death—in November, 1558—of childless Mary Tudor, Queen of England. With her demise the last scheme conceived by Charles—who himself died in Yuste only a few weeks before the English queen—was frustrated. Philip, of course, had some hope that Mary's successor, Elizabeth, daughter of Anne Boleyn, would remain true to her solemn promise and hold to the Catholic faith. But he was to know better. Second, with the break with Rome, the main pillar of the common defense in the Mediterranean area had collapsed. And even when contacts with the Pope were re-established, it was very difficult to build this pillar up again.

Someone, undoubtedly, will question the affirmation that the defense against the Turks was still, in 1558, the main object of Spanish foreign policy. Yet such was, to our best knowledge, the reality. Philip was not altogether young when he replaced his father. He had worked with Charles for a couple of years. He was also that type of man who is ready to accept the advice of his elders. Charles's program was to be, for a long time, his own.

Let us not forget—to make this point even clearer—that, up to 1572, the rebellion in the Low Countries, that protracted affair which was to involve Spain in full conflict with Protestant Europe, was a local matter. Precisely at the moment when Juan de Austria won the decisive naval victory at Lepanto, the Duke of Alba had the best chances to do away, once and for all, with the rebels in the Netherlands. Up to April, 1572, also, Philip, even if he had already lost all illusions about Elizabeth's sincerity, did not wish to break with her. Even after the bull of February 25, 1570, by which Pope Pius V excommunicated Elizabeth, the King of Spain still adhered to the foreign policy which his father had formulated and in which a friendly, or at least neutral, England played a prominent role.

Let us therefore do justice to Philip and regard the first epoch of his reign, up to the spring of 1572, from the viewpoint from which he himself had chosen to regard it.

3

Spain itself, as Philip had inherited it, was not yet internally secure. Nominally, the great majority of the Spanish families with Mohammedan ancestry were now Christians. Inwardly, however, they were full of hatred for Christian principles and institutions, thus constituting a fifth column inside Spain.

It is interesting to observe how this fact and the clash between the heirs of the Mohammedans—the "Moriscos" as they called them in Spain—and Philip's administration were regarded by the historians of the following centuries. To the chroniclers of the sixteenth and seventeenth centuries who had themselves experienced the danger, the measures taken by Philip II and, later on, by Philip III were inevitable and necessary. The eighteenth century regarded them with skepticism and irony. The nineteenth century put Philip in the defendant's box and, after having preached at length of intolerance and bigotry, condemned him. The main difficulty, perhaps, consists in the varying belief in the efficacy of persuasion. Some generations—especially such as accept the dogma of the natural inclination of man toward good—are sure that all evil can be overpowered by argument. From such a point of view, the Spanish Christians of the sixteenth century can be blamed for lack of love and apostolic zeal. But there are also generations whose historical experience testifies to the existence of evil so full of hatred that no force of persuasion and no argument are strong enough to overpower it. In such generations survival is a matter of fighting for life and death.

With the growing danger of a Turkish attack from the sea, of which we shall presently speak, Philip was forced, first of all, in January, 1567, to issue a *pragmática,* ordering the Moriscos to use only the Spanish language and forbidding them all customs and usages of Arabic origin. In spite of this pressure or perhaps accelerated by it, the clandestine resistance of the Moriscos broke out into open revolution in December, 1568, under the leadership of Aben Humeya. The region of Granada and especially the strip of country between Sierra Nevada and the Mediterranean were soon in flames. The Christian population was massacred in hecatombs. Those who escaped death were taken away as slaves by the ships, which came speedily from Africa bringing arms and ammunition. Uluch Ali, the Turkish governor of Algiers, transported troops to Spain, and a regular war started. It was on this occasion that Juan de Austria, half-brother of the King—a bastard of Charles V—distinguished himself for the first time as a soldier. About sixty thousand Spaniards lost their lives in the war. By the end of 1570, however, all was over, and the interior of Spain was safe again. Perhaps it was lucky for Philip that the rebellion broke out at a time when the Turkish fleet was engaged against Venice.

Otherwise the chances would not have been favorable to the Spaniards.

The revolt in Granada influenced Philip's government in matters of education. From 1570 onward, the Spanish state accepted the old Christian principle that the right to education is a natural right of everybody. Attendance at the parish schools was made compulsory—the first step of that kind in the history of our civilization. It soon became apparent, however, that even then the Moriscos were not to be persuaded.

4

The strategic situation on the Mediterranean, as seen from the Spanish point of view, had rapidly deteriorated. Since 1556, when the Turks took Tripoli from the Knights Hospitalers, Mohammedan supremacy on the sea had been indisputable. Of Turkish plans for the future Philip had no doubts whatever. His instructions to Bishop Aguila, whom he sent from Brussels, in May, 1558, to his uncle Ferdinand, made a clear distinction between the circumstances in Hungary, Bohemia, and Austria and those in Spain and southern Italy. Ferdinand is free to conclude peace with the Turks if he wishes to do so, says Philip; for Spain, however, it is better to arm—even if the possibility of a peace in the distant future is not excluded.

A few weeks afterward, in the summer of 1558, an expedition was arranged with the Knights Hospitalers in Malta to regain Tripoli. Commanded by the Duke of Medina Celi, it set out from Messina, in October, 1559, and proved a complete disaster. After having taken the small island of Djerba in the Gulf of Khabes, it was destroyed in the spring of 1560 by the Turkish fleet under the command of Piali Pasha. A few months later, even Djerba was regained by the Turks. Only a very few fortified places on the coast of North Africa were now in Christian hands. On the other hand, Turkish influence was taking firm root in Africa, and the Venetian island of Cyprus was becoming more and more isolated.

Were the forces of the Sultan to dominate Europe? For the

time being, such a possibility was not to be excluded. Nevertheless, Europe had not yet shown its real strength. And there was the European east, too. Poland observed with much apprehension Turkish occupation of the Romanian province of Moldavia; the Zaporogian Cossacks in the Ukraine were engaged in constant warfare with the Turks of Yedisan—the region of Odessa of the present time—and with the Tatars of the Crimea. And there was also some news about the military successes of the rapidly growing Duchy of Moscow, which had recently, between 1552 and 1554, occupied the Tatar Khanates of Kazan and Astrakhan. Nevertheless, the following five years, 1561–65, were marked by anxious waiting. Suleiman the Magnificent had some new difficulties in Persia but would certainly attack the West soon again. Some fighting was going on against the African pirates, and Oran was saved, in 1563, from a Mohammedan attack. In 1564 the situation once again became more dangerous because of the revolution in Corsica, organized against Genoa, the holder of the island, by Sampiero Corso, a pirate supported by the French as well as by the Turks.

The attack, so long awaited, came at last in May, 1565, when a large Turkish fleet appeared before Malta, the island which had been given to the Knights Hospitalers by Charles V. For almost four months the Knights, commanded by the Grand Master of their order, Jean de la Valette Parisot, resisted the fierce onslaughts of the Turks, who had disembarked on the island. García de Toledo, who at that time was in charge of the Spanish fleet in the Mediterranean, was rather tardy in his preparations, but the news of his arrival caused the Turks to give up and depart, in spite of the terrible sacrifices which they had already made. The next year, 1566, the Sultan decided once again to attack Austria.

We know very little about the actual sources of Turkish policy of those days. Certainly not all its component parts were the personal ideas of Suleiman himself. There was a group of religious enthusiasts in Constantinople, led by Mohammed Sokolli, which urged the Sultan to attack Spain itself. The revolutionaries in Granada were in contact with this group. But there were also other influences active in the Turkish capital. International commerce had actually never left the city, and Greek as well as Jewish merchants flourished under Turkish rule. By means of contacts which these merchants had with the court of the Sultan, not a few capitalists of oriental origin but lately living on the Pyrenean peninsula succeeded in gaining influence among the Turks. Naturally, these merchants did not use their new-found power in favor of Spain, which they had left. On the contrary, they were usually full of hatred against Christendom—hatred which perhaps even surpassed that of the Mohammedans themselves. One of the most important among them was a Jewish merchant, called Joseph Miques-Mendes, who had arrived in Constantinople via Venice about 1550. Accepting, at first, the title of *Nasi*—which means "leader of Israel"—he added to it, later on, that of the Duke of Naxos. Evidence of his powerful personality may be found in all the Turkish plans for attack, including that against Cyprus in 1570.

The onslaught along the upper Danube in 1566 was the culminating and also final stage of the career of Suleiman the Magnificent. In Vienna as well as in Prague, such an attack had been expected since the early 1540's, in spite of all the peace negotiations which had resulted in a peace treaty concluded in Prague in 1562. The permanent defensive arrangements on the Save and on the Drave were reorganized. The Diets of Austria, Bohemia, and Moravia enacted special measures against the Turkish spies, who were especially numerous among the Jewish merchants. After the death of Ferdinand in 1564, Maximilian, facing the Turkish demands for tributary payments stipulated in the previous negotiations and, resenting his own dependence on Philip, tried to find the necessary money in Italy. He even told his ambassador in Madrid, Adam Dietrichstein, that he would rather not beg at the Spanish court. At the beginning of 1560, however, he sent Juan Manrique to Madrid with an urgent demand for help.

Philip's interest in the defense of Central Europe was undoubtedly much smaller than the concern which his father had shown. Nevertheless, since the autumn of 1556, he had forwarded—through the Fuggers—the pay of two thousand soldiers, and Manrique now obtained 300,000 florins from him. Philip was even willing to participate in a defensive league of which the German princes could become members; thus, he hoped, would Germany be forced to help the Emperor against the Turks. Maximilian, however, did not like the idea.

The clash in Hungary started with a small-scale Turkish attack, commanded by Arslan, the pasha who was in charge of the Buda garrison. The imperial troops repulsed it, and the Slovak towns and villages of northern Hungary saw that there was hardly any difference in point of behavior between the Turks and the *desperados* of which the imperial units were composed. But then Suleiman's main army, well equiped and accompanied by thousands of camels, transporting all sorts of necessities, was stopped in the southwest of Hungary, where the fortress of Sziget, under the command of the heroic Nicolas Zriny, resisted for quite a time its fierce attacks. Whereupon, suddenly, Suleiman died in his tent. The immediate danger had passed.

It reappeared, however, in the summer of 1570, when the new Sultan, Selim II, who was not much of a warrior, decided to take Cyprus, the last Christian outpost in the eastern Mediterranean. The Venetians, unable to defend their property, were at last ready to join a league, proposed by Pope Pius V. The fleet of the League, consisting of Genoese, Spanish, Papal, and Venetian ships, under Juan de Austria as commander-in-chief, annihilated the Turkish fleet near Lepanto, off the eastern coast of Greece, on October 7, 1571. About three hundred Turkish ships were destroyed, and some ten thousand Christian galley slaves were set free. Thus, half a century after the proclamation of La Coruña, at least a kind of European victory was finally achieved.

The naval victory at Lepanto certainly did not mean the destruction of the Ottoman Empire. Cyprus had already been taken by the Turks and remained in their hands. The Turkish land army was untouched, and the ships of the North African pirates were still able to capture Christian ships and enslave their passengers—as happened, in 1575, to Miguel Cervantes, author of *Don Quijote*. La Goletta, a fortress near Tunis, was captured by the Spaniards, only to be lost again. The city-republic of Venice lacked money as well as manpower—it was looking for oarsmen for its galleys as far as Switzerland and Bohemia—and at last, under the influence of Salomon Aske-nazi, a close friend of Joseph Miques-Mendes, it left the League again and in 1573 concluded a separate peace with Turkey, giving up, in addition to Cyprus, several places on the coast of the Adriatic.

Why was the victory of 1571 not used as the basis for an offensive? There were two main reasons. First, sixteenth-century naval technique was insufficient for such a task. Transportation over long distances was too risky an undertaking. Second, and most important, the year 1566 had seen the beginning of Protestant hostilities in the Low Countries, and in 1572 the tide there turned definitively against the Spanish Empire. A new chapter in the story of Spanish preponderance started. The year 1572 is a veritable milestone—halfway between 1516 and 1643.

Relations between Spain and Turkey during the next twenty years may be characterized as repeated attempts for a stable peace. The powerful Ottoman Empire still constituted a major danger not only to Christian civilization but also to Spain as a state and an empire. The negotiations of Martín de Acuña and Giovanni Margliani in Constantinople, the death of Mohammed Sokolli, the difficulties the Turks had in Persia and even among the Berbers of North Africa—all those factors contributed to the preservation of a relatively peaceful status quo on the Mediterranean. In 1593, when the hostilities were renewed, it was on the land only, and once again in Hungary. Thus the victory at Lepanto indeed marked the end of Turkish ascendancy on the sea.

And the Emperor? He did not participate in the league

organized by Pius V, although Philip invited him to do so. In the winter following the victory at Lepanto, Pedro Fajardo came to Prague as an envoy extraordinary from Madrid. His instructions were to persuade Maximilian to join the League and then to go to Moscow. Philip had been informed about the successes of the Russian push toward the Baltic Sea in 1558–65 as well as about the utter failure of the Turks, in 1569–70, to enlarge their hold upon the Tatars by occupying the Khanate of Astrakhan. He wanted to establish a military alliance with Moscow or perhaps even with Persia. Fajardo, however, did not go farther than Prague. Maximilian's main argument for refusing to participate in the League was the unpopularity of any league with the Pope among the German Protestants. When Fajardo expressed his disbelief in the argument, Maximilian sent to the Princes Electors, demanding their opinion. The Duke of Saxony's answer was evasive, that of the Elector Palatine negative. The discussion was then taken up by the conference of Princes Electors in Mühlhausen in July, 1572; their decision was a negative one. Thereupon, Fajardo returned to Spain. The plan to win over Russia was dropped.

We may add that Ivan IV, the Terrible, in the meantime, was trying to win Turkish friendship through the good offices of Novosiltsov, his ambassador in Constantinople. The Poles, whose own relations with Turkey were neutral at that time, did not like the prospect of a Russian-Turkish friendship. It was probably through their influence that the Spaniards—the Duke of Alba, for instance, as early as 1571—warned the German manufacturers of arms not to export their products into Russia.

5

When Philip, returning from the Netherlands, disembarked at Laredo on September 8, 1559, he did not know that he would never again in his life leave Spain. And he certainly, as we have demonstrated, did not think of giving up the plans which he had inherited from his father. Why did he not attempt to govern his dominions from Brussels, where he would have been able to exert much greater influence on England as well as on Germany? The answer is obvious: because he remained true to the leading idea of his father. The defense against the Turks was his main task, and the Mediterranean area was to be his main field of operation.

Nevertheless, by fixing his residence in Spain and by making first Madrid and, later on, the Escorial the center of his administrative activities, Philip laid the foundations of a new system of government. His father, the Emperor, traveling from one place to another and attempting to realize the ideal of an international, "Roman" ruler, was nearer to his medieval predecessors of the ninth or eleventh centuries than it would seem to an observer taking only the distances in time into consideration. Philip, on the other hand, although fully participating in the religious controversies of his age, was much closer to the late seventeenth- or early eighteenth-century type of absolutist ruler, indifferent to religious matters but governing his domains from his stable residence by means of hitherto unheard-of administrative apparatus.

Hundreds and hundreds of bulky volumes of documents have been preserved until our own days, which bear his annotations or his short signature, *Yo el rey*—"I, the King." He used to delegate foreign campaigns as well as political negotiations to soldiers and diplomats who were in his pay and who were often recruited from among the hidalgos. But he required them to keep closely in touch with him and to report to him every detail of their activities. On the other hand, he furnished them with minute instructions. Little freedom of action was left to them. The fate of the Great Armada in 1588, which might have destroyed Elizabeth's fleet near the English coast, had its commander not been tied by precise instructions, may be noted as just one illustration of how great were the disadvantages of such a system of government. Also, Philip's principle that his servants should each work in his own sphere or at his own task without any knowledge about the work of his colleagues proved to be a great strain on the King himself and a major impediment to those who were anxious to help him. On the other hand, of course, it brought him as much direct information as has ever been placed at the disposal of a single statesman.

Even the most detailed parts of the various problems of administration were reserved for the personal decision of the King. And usually up to the last minute nobody knew what such a decision would be. Listening with utmost patience to what his counselors had to say and reading, word by word, the reports which had been sent to him from his representatives in the various parts of his dominions, Philip remained calm and reserved, hiding his personal opinions behind the mask of his imperturbable majesty.

The idea of the necessity of "dissimulation" in politics was not invented by Philip himself. The Italian and French political theory of that time was saturated with it. Machiavelli had propagated it. Charles V appreciated it and recommended it to his son in his letters. Both with Charles and with Philip it had acquired a meaning which was not quite incompatible with Christian morals. The Spanish verb *dissimular,* which comes forward so frequently in Philip's letters and instructions, means "to conceal one's own will." It means a screen behind which the ruler can, slowly and undisturbed, make up his mind. It also means the consciousness of the bad inclinations of human nature. We would find it adopted later on by the Spanish theoreticians such as Pedro de Ribadaneira or, to a certain extent, even by Juan de Santa Maria.

The main reason, after all, which Philip had for the secrecy of his deliberations—and sometimes also of his actions, such as the confinement of his ailing son, Don Carlos, the main reason for which remained known only to him and two or three of his closest collaborators—was his zeal for justice and an extremely developed sense of duty. If there was ever a ruler who was anxious not to be unfair in the least to anybody, it was Philip. "He has always shown such gentleness and humanity as no prince could surpass," was said of him by Michele Soriano, a Venetian diplomat who certainly had not the least reason to flatter him. Taciturnity and secretiveness were the other side of that humanity. Are we not reminded, studying Philip's thoroughly moral attitude toward politics, of that extremely sober treatise called *Del regimento del governo della città di Firenze* and written by the austere and lonely champion of moral discipline, Girolamo Savonarola? Perhaps we do not even have to go so far away from Philip's own times. In 1556, Sebastián Fox Morcillo—the "great Platonic metaphysician," as Menéndez Pelayo calls him—published his *De regni et regis institutione,* in which he proposed an extremely rationalist theory of government: not outward form or organization, but the efficiency of a system of administration and the personal efficiency of the ruler are what matters. It is a clear picture of the man who, in the same year, became King of Spain.

No matter how diligent and prudent an absolutist ruler may be, his forces are as restricted as those of any other human being. In 1640, at the very time when the political and military preponderance of Spain was rapidly approaching its end, Diego Saavedra Fajardo deemed it necesary to stress, in his *Idea de un principe político christiano*—one of the last treatises on that subject produced by the "Golden Age" of Spanish history—that it is better to govern in accordance with human capacity than according to some perfect but unattainable pattern. To impose, he said, upon the citizens of a state a perfect system is the usual characteristic of tyranny; human nature cannot bear it. Had he in mind, perhaps, when writing those lines, the builder of El Escorial? An atmosphere of disillusion is perceptible even to a modern student of the later years of the reign of Philip II. Too much conscientiousness and anxiety had frequently ended in what Philip's contemporaries used to call "melancholy." Many among Philip's diplomats and officials and even some of his relatives had fallen victims to this illness, which was characterized by prolonged mental depressions as well as by fevers and various physiological disturbances. If the

Renaissance had its "macabre dances," the age of Philip II reflected its failures in the melancholy sufferings of its prominent personalities.

6

The administrative system of Philip II had its roots in the development of the central Spanish government under the Catholic Sovereigns, Ferdinand and Isabella. With the growing centralization, the number of advisory councils of which the central government was composed had to be enlarged. At the end of Philip's reign, there were twelve councils of unequal number of members. The councils of Castile, of Aragon, of Italy, of Flanders, of the Indies, and, after 1580, of Portugal dealt with the administration of territories which had autonomous rights. The Council of State (Consejo de Estado) dealt with foreign affairs and with problems of general policy. The councils of Finance, of the Cruzada, and of the Military Orders dealt with royal revenues and with the distribution of subventions and remunerations. The councils of Justice and of the Inquisition were intrusted with the administration of justice and security.

The Council of State, seen from the point of view of a student of Spain's international relations, was the most prominent of all. Although it dealt with the foreign policy of the Spanish empire as a whole, only Spaniards were generally appointed by the King as members, and, with the exception of Bishop Granvelle, a native of Franche Comté and educated at Louvain, no member of any other nationality ever had a prominent place in it.

One positive result of Philip's reticence was the tradition of relative freedom of speech which soon established itself in the Council of State. Comparing the summaries of its proceedings with what we know, for instance, of similar consultations held at Versailles under Louis XIV, we are surprised by the frequency of divergent views occurring in it. Indeed, such freedom in the consultative body of an absolutist monarch was so

unusual that many historians, especially those whose own ideas
conflicted with the principles of Philip II, expressed the opinion
that Philip had taken deliberate care to have the council always
divided and unable to reach any unanimous conclusion. We
need not remark that there is no ground whatsoever for such
an opinion. If there was rivalry between the intransigent group
headed by the Duke of Alba and the more conciliatory group
led by Ruy Gómez de Silva or, later on, between other divergent groups, it was because Philip did not impose his own
views upon his counselors. And that was certainly a rare thing
with an absolutist monarch.

The various councils, however, had no executive power. The
king was the only person who had the right to decide. And he,
of course, had to sustain the immense financial burden which
had been created by Charles's military activities and which was
constantly growing with every new expenditure on the armed
forces or on the administrative and diplomatic apparatus. The
debt which Philip inherited from his father amounted to some
seventy million ducats. Every year, the high interest rates added
new sums of money to that figure. And the wars against the
Turks and against the Moriscos and, since 1566, the increasing
difficulties in the Netherlands forced the King of Spain into
new loans. *Si no falta el dinero* ("if the money is not lacking")
became a most frequently used conditional phrase. The silver
from overseas, imported in ever increasing quantities, caused a
constant rise of prices but proved insufficient to cover all the
current expenses.

Spain shared this burden with its ruler. It had never been a
very rich country. Castile especially was a much poorer country
than many other regions of Europe, including such as the Low
Countries or the Milanese, which were now politically dependent on it. The citizens of Spain used to support themselves
mainly by various sorts of agriculture. Lately, however, a crisis
arose in agricultural production which was probably due
mainly to the conflicting interests of the grain-producing farmers and the sheep breeders. The production of wool, governed

by a special guild under royal control—the "Honorable Assembly of the Mesta"—had certainly been an important source of revenue for the Spanish kings. The taxes levied on the enormous flocks of sheep as well as upon the wool shipped to France, the Low Countries, and England, yielded large amounts of money. But the influence exerted by the Mesta on the small landowner was pernicious. Its privileges were such that thousands of farmers were forced to abandon their fields. Others, especially the young generation, abandoned them because they thought it of more advantage to seek employment with the army or to look for adventurous careers overseas. Thus Spain, which had once produced more grain than it needed, had now to look for it elsewhere.

In the first years of Philip's reign, the revenue which had hitherto flowed from the Mesta started declining too. A series of intricate economic difficulties arose. The old medieval social order was gone. To establish a new one was anything but easy. A curious mixture of economic liberalism, state controls and restrictions, and traditional feudalism presents itself to the student of the Spanish economy of those days. Philip II had certainly not been educated by teachers who would have induced him to consider interest in economic problems a part of his duties; such an idea was totally strange to the epoch. Nevertheless, we find him continually exacting detailed information on the price of bread, the best thermometer of the economic situation. We also find him attempting to regulate trade with the newly discovered possessions overseas. All imports from America were limited to a single port—that of Seville—and subordinated to a special "House of Trade," which registered and licensed every single shipload. But to find honest officials for this and similar duties was extremely difficult.

From the very beginning of Philip's reign, it may be said, the Spanish economy had been declining—and that in spite of the increasing imports of bullion from America. The financiers were stronger than the King. In 1557, in the second year of his reign, Philip suspended the subletting of his revenues to the bankers and changed the interest on his debts to them to only 5 per cent. But he needed more and more money. In vain did he seize the silver imported by private firms from America and convert it also into forced loans. He had to borrow again and pay higher and higher interest. Thus by the year 1575, when the problem of the defense against the Turks had been at least partially solved but when new troubles were arising in the Netherlands, the King's treasury was rapidly approaching insolvency.

A kingdom on the verge of powerlessness? Certainly not. A kingdom which was going to exchange its traditional mission— that of defending Europe against the Mohammedan invaders— for another one and to plunge, as an ultimate result of this change, into a long and disastrous war.

THE PRINCES AND THE BISHOPS

1

PHILIP II was a person of deep religious feeling. Not only the symbolism of El Escorial, where the church of St. Lawrence forms the center of the palace (how different from the almost hidden palace chapel of Louis XIV at Versailles!) but also the testimony of people who lived near Philip tell us about his piety. It permeated all his activities, it accompanied him in all the important steps of his life. Nor was there any difference between his political principles and his religious ideas. Being probably of a deeper character than his father, he never made a political decision without carefully consulting his conscience and perhaps also his confessor. It was, however, his Catholicism which differed a great deal from the living trends of the contemporary Church.

To describe this difference, we have to stress, first of all, the fact that it was not the humanist indifference to the doctrine of the Church which separated Philip from many other Catholics —as was the case with Charles V, Philip's father. Erasmus, who had died in 1536, had no supporters among Philip's counselors. In matters of faith the King of Spain was always very serious and admitted no skepticism into his thoughts. He did not vacillate in the least as far as dogmas were concerned.

What, however, was rather strange to him—as it had been strange to his father—was the Catholic reformation. Was that perhaps because Philip was a Spaniard? The organizational reform of the Church, achieved during the High Middle Ages, was nowhere less successful than in Spain. The rights of the Papal Curia were restricted behind the Pyrenees not only by a law forbidding the appointment of foreigners to Church offices but also, since 1514, by a royal decree forbidding the publication of any papal bull in Spain without a royal authorization. And yet it must be remembered that the leading personalities among the Catholic reformers were much in favor of all that had been achieved by the medieval Popes in the organizational field. The efforts of the most spiritual and unworldly men and women were concentrated around the Roman Curia. Bridget of Sweden and Catherine of Siena devoted their energy to the task of bringing the Pope from Avignon back to Rome. In a similar way the new generation of reformers, although concerned chiefly with the revival of Christian education, saw a close connection between the intensified monarchical administration of the Church and their own task. Gaetano da Thiene and the Theatines came to Rome to the papal altar of St. Peter's to make their solemn profession. And Ignatius of Loyola, founding his "Company of Jesus" in distant Paris, placed it at the unconditional disposal of the Holy See. In short, the Catholic reforming trends of the sixteenth century had inherited the medieval zeal for the complete autarchy and independence of the Church.

It was not so with King Philip. His conception of the relations between Church and state was that of a ruler of the Early Middle Ages who considered the care of the Church his moral duty but did not recognize any authority which might interpret this moral duty. Philip stuck to the decree of 1514. He also opposed, for a time at least, any uncompromisingly religious line in foreign policy. Regarding his alliance with England as a factor of great value in his general scheme of international policy even after the death of Mary Tudor, he sided with Elizabeth against Mary Stuart and for a number of years tried to dissuade the Pope from excommunicating the new Queen of England.

Nevertheless, the very problem which Philip thus tried to avoid was gradually closing in upon him. Like his father, Philip understood Christianity as a tradition. But, when it came to distinguishing what was a part of that tradition and what was not, he necessarily found himself at a loss. In a similar way his Protestant contemporaries were puzzled when they tried to find out what had been the "original" teaching of the "primitive" Church.

2

The person in Philip's immediate surroundings who brought out most clearly the inherent problems of a religion based exclusively on tradition was his cousin Maximilian. His fame in Spain had declined in the early 1550's, at the time of the Hapsburg family conference at Augsburg, and had not improved since those days. Some people at the Spanish court later suspected him of having instigated the small Spanish Lutheran group led by Augustin Cazalla and discovered at Valladolid about eight years after Maximilian's departure from that city. It is not likely that Maximilian's sympathies for the new religious trend had been so active at the time of his stay in Spain. Nevertheless, they were strong enough.

After the family conference at Augsburg, as we have already mentioned, the young prince made one more short visit to Spain, to fetch his wife Maria, Philip's sister. On the way back, he paid a formal visit to the Council of Trent. Listening to the bishops, who, at that time, were discussing the doctrine of the Holy Communion as expressed in the Gospel of St. John, Maximilian did not conceal his skepticism. What, he remarked, was the value of determining whether the Evangelist had in mind a "spiritual" or a "sacramental" communion, if the important thing was to reach an agreement with the Protestants concerning the Communion under both species? Naturally, his observations were criticized by the assembled theologians, and the princely pair left Trent in no friendly mood.

A hatred against everything Spanish was not slow to develop in Maximilian's mind. The Spanish courtiers and ladies-in-waiting of his wife were to feel it on their own skins. On the other side, very friendly relations started between the prince, who was now also elected King of Bohemia and Hungary, and some of the prominent Protestants among the young German princes, such as Frederick, son of the Duke of Brandenburg. Kaspar Nidbruck, author of the *Magdeburg Centuries,* entered into correspondence with him. Another Lutheran, Christopher Eitzig, was appointed his *mayordomo.* On top of all this, Johann Sebastian Pfauser, a Protestant preacher, became his chaplain in the autumn of 1554. Was it a result of a real change of religious persuasion, or should it be considered only an aspect of Maximilian's aversion to the policy of the Emperor which we have already mentioned? It is difficult to say.

No matter what was the real reason for Maximilian's inclination toward the Protestants, his attitude became a real factor in Hapsburg family policy. As it was more and more probable that not Philip, but Maximilian, would become Holy Roman Emperor after Ferdinand's death, Philip—who in the meantime had become King of Spain—was faced with the possibility that all central Europe, including Bohemia and Hungary as well as Germany and Austria, would turn Protestant. Evaluated according to the principles which had been adopted by Philip's father, such a situation could hardly have been considered tragic. After all, central Europe had been left by Charles V to his brother; the King of Spain was no longer responsible for it. Politically, the only thing which mattered was the revival of imperial authority in Germany.

Philip felt responsible, however, for the religious actions of his relatives. In 1556, almost immediately after his father's resignation, he sent a learned theologian named Gallo, a friend of Archbishop Bartolomé Carranza, to Vienna and to Regensburg to find out the actual religious persuasion of Ferdinand and Maximilian and what attitude could be expected from them toward the growing influence of Protestantism. This almost secret mission of a Spanish priest was the first symptom of Philip's new policy—the policy dictated by the sense of moral responsibility which made Philip's character so different from that of many other rulers.

We do not have any reason to doubt the sincerity of the

Spanish king. His secretiveness, his life in seclusion, his frequent lack of confidence in his collaborators—all that made his character very strange. When he decided to imprison his son Carlos, he did not communicate the reasons for his decision to anybody—not even to the Pope. But that precisely is an argument in favor of his honesty. An impostor would have tried to create legends to disguise his motives. Philip kept quiet. He really believed in responsibility in matters of religion, for his relatives as well as for his subjects. And, believing in such a responsibility, he laid the foundations of that new policy which Spain was to continue even after his death—the policy of leadership in the struggle for the traditional culture, the policy which, in the long run, brought about the inclusion of Spain among the protagonists of the Thirty Years' War. Other factors, certainly, co-operated in that development. But Philip's moral sense in matters of religion remained for years the main driving force.

3

Master Gallo, the theologian, did not find his task easy. It was apparent, in the first place, that Ferdinand still remained much more conservative than his son. But his conservatism was political in character, of the same kind which Charles V himself had adopted in the course of his reign. The former disciple of Cardinal Cisneros became accustomed to act not according to any fixed principles but according to the pressure of his opponents. He also proceeded in different ways in the various territories under his rule. In Bohemia he tried to resist Lutheranism by supporting the old, medieval, reforming trends of the Czechs. In Austria, following the advice of Peter Canisius, a Jesuit priest of great energy and saintly life, he had issued in 1554 a series of decrees, the so-called *Generalia,* prohibiting the spread of Lutheranism. In 1556, however, the Austrian Protestant nobles prevailed upon him and obtained the revocation of the decrees. In Germany, Ferdinand would probably have prefered to follow the example of the Duke of Bavaria, Albrecht, and to pacify the Protestants by authorizing the Communion under both species and the marriage of the clergy.

As for Maximilian, his attitude toward religious problems obviously sprang from something more than mere opportunism. It seemed as if the skepticism of Erasmus had come to life again in his thoughts. Maximilian despised all dogmatic controversy. He let Master Gallo discuss various questions with the Protestant theologian Skalić, but obviously he did not care for the conclusions of such discussions. When, at a conference in Worms, the adherents of Melanchthon quarreled with another Protestant group led by Flaccius, Maximilian refused to take any interest in the wrangle. He contracted, at the time of Gallo's stay in Vienna, a new friendship with John Frederick, Duke of Saxony; their corrpesondence frequently mentioned religious subjects, but never in a profound way. He also found an adviser in his new chaplain Pfauser, a man of very simple, but manifestly Protestant, ideas.

To make things—at least for some time—more complicated, the impetuous Pope Paul IV, who only in September, 1557, had made his peace with Philip, jumped at the opportunity presented at Ferdinand's promotion by the Princes Electors from the dignity of King of the Romans to that of Holy Roman Emperor. The Pope issued a public condemnation of the imperial policy of the Hapsburgs. He denounced, in the first place, the activities of Charles V himself, whose negligences, he affirmed, had enabled Protestantism to spread. He equally deprecated the tactics of Ferdinand and the indifference of Maximilian. The only person who found grace in the eyes of the Pope was Philip II. And, as a sort of conclusion, the Pope refused to recognize Charles's abdication and Ferdinand's election. He asked Ferdinand to accept the imperial crown at his own hands and to forbid Protestantism in his dominions. It all sounded like a voice coming from other times.

Philip himself found it difficult to take a standpoint of his own. He could not sympathize with his uncle or with his cousin. To sympathize with the Pope's demand, however, would have meant to accept his ideas concerning the submission of the imperial throne to the Holy See. To win time, therefore, Philip appointed a commission to investigate the "misunderstanding" between the newly elected Emperor and the Pope. Master Gallo, Bishop Granvelle from the Netherlands, and Philip's confessor Fresneda became its members. It is difficult to imagine what would have been the decision of such a tribunal. As things developed, no decision was necessary because Paul died in August, 1559, and his successor, Pius IV, a Medici, readily gave his approval to Ferdinand's election to the imperial office.

The problem of what should be the Emperor's policy in matters of religion remained open, however. And as to the behavior of Ferdinand's eventual successor, the qualms of Philip's conscience were not to cease. In the late summer of 1558, almost at the last moment before the death of Charles V, Philip sent Archbishop Carranza to Yuste to ask the Emperor's advice. But Charles was sinking fast, and Carranza was hardly able to inform him of his mission. Instead, he could only grant final absolution to the dying monarch. And, paradoxically enough— if we are to believe the testimony which Juan de Regla, the Emperor's confessor, gave later to the Holy Inquisition at Carranza's process—it was on this occasion that the Archbishop's own doubts in matters of dogma became apparent. As if he had not come to ask the Emperor's opinion on Maximilian's inclinations toward Lutheranism, he kissed Charles's hands and said: "Let Your Majesty have great confidence, for if there is any sin or has been any sin, the Passion of Christ alone suffices."

Then there was also Maria, Philip's sister and Maximilian's wife. Would she be able to convert her husband? Her own religious education had not been of the most dependable kind. For a time she had had a confessor, Vicente de Rocamoro, who was of Jewish origin and who, later on, was to flee to the rebellious Netherlands and to join the Jewish community in Amsterdam. In the spring of 1559, rumors spread from Vienna that Maximilian had decided to divorce her. But even when such reports had not been confirmed, Maria had evidently little influence on her husband or, having it, was not inclined to use it.

Gradually, but incessantly, the drama of Maximilian's formative years approached its climax. In 1560, under the combined pressure of Master Gallo and of Peter Canisius, he dismissed his chaplain Pfauser but refused to listen to the learned and witty Polish Cardinal Hosius, who had just arrived in Vienna. Soon afterward he also refused to accept Communion under one species only. Hastily, Ferdinand wrote to Rome, asking the Pope to authorize Maximilian to communicate under both species. But the young prince was hardly to be satisfied with a liturgical privilege. Ambition and impatience obviously had their share in his thoughts. If, in 1553, he had criticized his uncle, the Emperor, and wished that Ferdinand would take a firm stand against him, he now reached a state of mind in which he envisaged an open rupture between himself and his father. On April 2, 1560, he dispatched his private secretary, Niclas Warnsdorf, to several German princes of Protestant denomination to ask them whether they would be willing to support him in case of an open conflict between him and Ferdinand.

Bitter disappointment, however, was in store for him. When Warnsdorf came back in July, he brought a heap of letters which were full of civil apologies but did not contain a single word of encouragement. Frederick the Pious of the Palatinate was the only one to promise Maximilian an abode in his territory; but he hastened to add that in such a case he would not be able to support Maximilian's candidacy for the imperial throne.

4

The youthful ambitions were gone. If Maximilian had ever been inclined to look upon the Protestant princes as heroes, he now had a bitterly different experience. But skepticism in matters of religion remained. Maximilian was now more prepared to participate in the conferences with Cardinal Hosius—to discuss the relations between religious and civil authority, in the first place—but he still recoiled from theology. "I am neither Catholic nor Protestant, but a Christian," he told Hosius in November.

Maximilian's conversations with Hosius quieted agitated minds in Madrid as well as in Vienna. The Count of Luna, Philip's new ambassador at the imperial court, gave a new turn to the course of events when he suggested, at the end of the winter of 1560–61, that the problem of the imperial succession should be taken up once again. According to the agreement which had been reached by the Hapsburgs at their family conference in Augsburg in 1551, Philip was to become Ferdinand's successor on the imperial throne. According to the developments which had followed, however, the King of Spain could hardly be expected to forsake his West European policy in favor of a revival of Charles V's original imperial program. Was it not time to come forward with a concept of policy which would reflect the changed situation?

Months passed and Luna was still waiting for an answer from Madrid. Was Philip contemplating a return to the career of his father, or was it just his incredulity concerning Maximilian's opinions which did not allow him openly to sanction Maximilian's candidature for the imperial throne?

In June, 1561, Maximilian suddenly returned to his former behavior in matters of liturgy. He refused to go through the crowning ceremony in Bratislava, at that time the capital of the Kingdom of Hungary. To accept the crown of St. Stephen, one was expected to fast, to confess, and to communicate according to the Latin rite, that is under one species only. The duty of a good Christian, Maximilian declared, was to accept not only the Body of Christ, but his Blood as well.

Even if we are unable to trace Maximilian's ideas back to their source, it is interesting to notice their historical affiliation. Communion under both species was certainly not one of the leading ideas of the Protestant reform. It was accepted by the Protestant protagonists because of its accordance with their reverence for the words of the Holy Scripture. But the actual reason for its popularity in the sixteenth century was the interest which some of the prominent medieval reformers had taken in it and which had impressed itself upon the opinion of the inhabitants of Central Europe. Was not the chalice—a red chalice on a black background—the symbol of the Czech religious movement of the fourteenth and fifteenth centuries? Did not the theologians who had founded that movement as well as the apostles of the "Devotio moderna" in the Netherlands preach the necessity of a "frequent and full communion" for the restoration of social justice? The chalice as a moral and religious symbol had certainly not been forgotten. Before his ascension to the imperial throne, Ferdinand I had tried to obtain from the Holy See a confirmation of the liturgical privilege conceded to the Czechs by the Council of Basel, the privilege of the laics to communicate under both species. And now Maximilian, his son and heir, took to the same idea. Several Czech noblemen were constantly among Maximilian's entourage. Vratislav Pernštýn, Jaroslav Smiřický, and Jiří Proskovský had accompanied him to Spain. We know, it is true, that, as early as the 1550's, Maximilian refused to take any interest in the doctrinal altercations of the Bohemian (Moravian) Brethren, a late-medieval religious society which was now seeking a *rapprochement* with the modern reforming trends. Nevertheless, he could have been influenced by the main tradition of the people whose king-elect he was.

To comply with the wish of his son, Ferdinand made another attempt to obtain a papal authorization for him to communicate under both species. Instead of sending another letter to the Pope, however, this time he selected an Austrian nobleman, Adam Dietrichstein, and dispatched him to Rome. Dietrichstein's instructions urged him to explain to the Pope secretly that if Maximilian did not get the authorization, his Catholicism might be at stake. And that, Ferdinand hastened to add, would fill his heart with sorrow.

But why was Dietrichstein's main mission a secret one? Officially, the Emperor's envoy went to Rome to ask for a few indulgences which could be attached to the private chapel of Maximilian's wife, Maria. After several months, all his petitions were granted, and in December, 1561, Pope Pius IV signed a letter permitting Maximilian to communicate under both species whenever the Emperor himself gave his consent. And again the Pope's letter and the privilege itself were secret. Was the whole affair considered dangerous for the Emperor's reputation among his Protestant subjects? Hardly. Ferdinand was rather inclined to see, in the "utraquist" Communion, a step toward religious pacification. His secretiveness had another source. In sending Dietrichstein to Rome, Ferdinand was afraid of what Philip, with all his conservative and uncompromising opinions, would think of his request. That was also the reason why he had chosen Dietrichstein, whose Spanish wife, Marguerita de Cardona, was a granddaughter of Aldonsa de Cardona, related by marriage to Philip's own ancestor, John III of Aragon. Dietrichstein's personal relations to Spain were expected to protect him against Spanish suspicions.

But somehow the secrecy was not preserved to the end, and the true reason of Dietrichstein's voyage to Rome was revealed. Vargas, the Spanish ambassador to the Holy See, heard some of the gossip and wrote about it to his king. This time Philip's anxiety for even the distant members of his family to keep to the intransigent line forced him to exceed the limits of family policy and to try other measures. He instructed his ambassador to approach Cardinal Charles Borromeo, who was then in charge of the papal Secretariat of State, and to ask him whether he knew that Dietrichstein had come to obtain a privilege for Maximilian. Borromeo, naturally, told Vargas quite frankly that he knew of no such mission. Philip's anxious conscience, nevertheless, was not yet assuaged. He inquired in Vienna, and the Count of Luna did his best to discover the truth, but without success. The Hapsburgs, who so often spoke of piety and of Christian charity in their official declarations as well as in their private letters, did not trust one another. They needed one another, but they were also afraid of one another.

Luna at last reported to Philip that, although some attempt had been made on Maximilian's behalf in Rome to obtain a liturgical privilege, the Pope had refused to comply with it and had told Maximilian to bring his petition before the General Council. Only after having received this assurance of his ambassador, did the King of Spain decide to give his official assent to Maximilian's candidacy for the imperial succession. Thus the final division of the empire of Charles V took place in an atmosphere of mistrust and narrow-minded secretiveness.

5

Speaking of a General Council in his report to Philip II, the Spanish ambassador at the imperial court meant the third stage of the Council of Trent. In 1561 it was only a dormant institution. Since 1552, when the second stage of the Council had been hastily closed—mainly because of the flight of Charles to Villach and also because of general uneasiness—there had been hardly a political negotiation at which the possibility of a new convocation was not mentioned. But the views about its aims and about the way in which it could be started differed as widely as did the hopes of the potential participants. The theologians, of course, had their own opinions, and even they were not identical. The King of Spain wanted it to accomplish its magisterial task, but hardly to touch the organizational reform of the Church. Ferdinand's views were different, and they were supported by four counselors, two of whom, Gienger and Seld, were Germans, and the remaining two, the Count of Luna and Francisco Córdoba, a Franciscan friar, of Spanish nationality.

The initiative finally came from the newly elected Pope Pius IV. It met with the unconditional approval of Philip II, expressed in a letter sent to Rome in June, 1560. The Emperor, however, had his doubts. It seemed as if the imperial court had inherited, to a much greater degree than the court at Madrid, the mistrusts and hesitations of Charles V. Reading, for instance, the notes which Adam Dietrichstein wrote during his stay in Rome in 1561, we have the impression of reading the diary of a diplomat active in the capital of an enemy. A basic lack of confidence permeates every word concerning the activities of the papal Curia and the preparations for a revival of the Council of Trent in particular. The reports which Diego Hurtado de Mendoza used to send to Charles V from Rome and from Trent during the first two stages of the Council could not have been more skeptical. And what Dietrichstein expressed in 1561 had been felt at the imperial court months before.

When Cardinal Hosius, acting as the Pope's personal envoy, had approached Ferdinand for the first time with the proposition concerning a new convocation of the Council, the Emperor answered with a memorandum, called "Scriptum in negocio concilii," in which he restricted the task of the Council to the solution of three problems: Communion under both species, the marriage of the clergy, and the reform of the property of the Church. The Pope, evidently, could not approve of such a limitation. But even before the Scriptum was refused in Rome, the Count of Luna had already written to his King, telling him, in the Emperor's name, that the Scriptum had not been based on Ferdinand's personal views. Whose views, then, did it represent? And why were the Emperor's apologies presented to Philip through the Spanish envoy at the imperial court and not through Martin Guzmán who at that time acted as the Emperor's envoy in Madrid?

But even if the Scriptum did not mirror faithfully the ideas of Ferdinand I, it was evident to any observer that there was a profound difference between the imperial and the Spanish policy as far as the General Council was concerned. Ferdinand remembered very well his late brother's disillusionment about the results of the first two stages of the Council. Consequently, deliberating about the possibility of a new convocation of the Council, he wanted it to be considered a completely new assembly which would achieve what had not even been discussed during the first two stages, namely, the reunion of Catholics and Protestants. Philip, on the other hand, had assumed a standpoint which differed greatly from that of his father. For Philip, the doctrinal definitions agreed upon by the bishops assembled at Trent and at Bologna during the first two stages of the Council meant an invaluable achievement and an evident clarification of the situation. What he wanted was a continuation, another and final series of sessions which would not only corroborate but also extend and bring to completion the work done in the preceding stages. He hastened to inform the Pope about these views of his, and Pius IV answered, in October, 1560, by an assurance that all the preceding decisions of the Council would be regarded by the Curia as valid and immutable.

Thus the leading representatives of the Hapsburg family found themselves opposing each other even before the third stage of the Council had started. In addition, the views of the imperial court were shared by many French. No one could expect, they affirmed, that the Protestants would participate if the Council which was to be convoked was not clearly marked as a brand-new affair. Zasius, one of Ferdinand's counselors, who had recently returned from a conference of the German Protestant princes in Worms, naturally upheld the same thesis.

In Rome, however, nobody saw any advantage in canceling the results of the first two stages of the Council. Had not innumerable discussions between Catholic and Protestant theologians been arranged in Germany, without reaching any positive conclusion? The main difficulty, evidently, did not consist in the divergence of various personal views on this or that theological subject but in the different opinions on authority.

On November 29, 1560, the bull announcing the new convocation of the Council was issued in Rome. The matter of contention was mentioned in it by three words only—*sublata suspensione quacumque* ("after the rescinding of all previous adjournments"). Ferdinand accepted it with evident resignation. But he still cherished some hope for the possible participation of the Protesants. A new conference in Naumburg seemed to have corroborated his views. For some time he even contemplated a diplomatic move which would bring the English to Trent. To Philip, the bull was not clear enough. A special envoy, Juan Ayala, was sent by him to Rome to persuade the Pope of the necessity of making a more explicit declaration. As a result of his mission, Raverta, a papal nuncio, arrived at Madrid, in May, 1561, with a special *breve* containing a full definition of the meaning of *sublata suspensione quacumque*. Philip, on account of this letter and also aware of the growing strength of the French Huguenots in the immediate neighborhood of his own dominions, finally authorized the bishops of his dominions to participate in the Council.

6

The ancient seat of the Bishops of Trent, situated in the border region of two great European languages, the Italian and the German, became once more the scene of an assembly of all the bishops living in communion with the See of Rome.

The participants were slow in arriving. Those among them who were Ferdinand's subjects—the Archbishop of Prague Antonín Brus, Bishop Drašković, and Sigmund Thun, the Emperor's ambassador—were the last to reach Trent. But, once there, they started—in accordance with the instructions they had received from Ferdinand—clamoring for a slowdown in the proceedings of the Council. Not only did they want to postpone the condemnation of the Confession of Augsburg, but they also asked the assembly to extend a special invitation to the Protestant theologians and to adjourn the second public session until the Protestants could arrive. The papal legates who presided at the Council—the Cardinals Gonzaga, Seripando, Simonetta, Hosius, and Altaemps—acceded to these demands as far as they were able to do so. They decided to hold the second public session only after more than three months, in May, 1562. When no Protestants appeared in Trent after a special invitation had been issued to them, the Emperor demanded another such invitation. But, as the issue was manifestly hopeless, the imperial ambassador declared at last that there would be no more protests on his side if the second public session was not postponed any longer.

As far as the dilemma between the concept of the Council as a continuation of the previous stages and as a means toward re-definition of the traditional doctrine, on the one hand, and that of the Council as a vague conference between Catholics and Protestants, on the other hand, was concerned, the policies of the two Hapsburg rulers still stood in sharp contrast. The Span-ish theologians in particular were much embittered against the indecisiveness of Ferdinand and his counselors. To the Span-iards the doctrinal tradition was the glory and the heart of civi-lization. Was it not the Spanish Jesuit Lainez who, during the first stage of the Council, in September, 1546, had delivered that famous speech, which defended the traditional concept of jus-tification against the Lutherans as well as against the papal legate Seripando, who had had some doubts about it?

Nevertheless, there were also matters concerning the Coun-cil in which the points of view of the two Hapsburg courts were almost identical. Two of them were of utmost importance.

First, the papal bull of convocation included an expression—actually, only two words, *proponentibus legatis*—which re-stricted the right of initiative at the debates to the legates of the Pope. Whereas in Rome the clause was regarded as necessary for smooth operation, both Philip and Ferdinand saw in it an un-just restriction of the bishops and also of the diplomats present at the Council.

Secondly, in Vienna as well as in Madrid, the opinion pre-vailed that the duty of the bishops to reside in their dioceses was of a divine, not of a human, origin. This abstract and seemingly unimportant theological tenet was of the greatest importance. To declare the duty of residence an obligation *iure divino* meant to affirm that a bishop is invested with jurisdiction at his consecration; in which diocese the bishop exercised his jurisdic-tion would then depend on various authorities, including the authority of a king. On the other hand, to declare the duty of residence an obligation *iure humano* meant to corroborate the monarchical constitution of the Church, according to which a consecrated bishop is given his jurisdiction only when the Holy See appoints him to rule this or that diocese.

The King of Spain clearly did not think much of the monarchical constitution of the Church. His almost Byzantine concept of the relations between the state and the Church made him rather suspicious of all tendencies which restricted the influence of the political power on ecclesiastical affairs. Curiously enough, many Spanish theologians sided with their king in this matter. Their reason for doing so was inherent in their anxiety for a spiritual reform. Had there not been many abuses among the bishops—most of them connected with papal dispensations from the duty of residence? There was, of course, Salmerón, one of the most prominent Spanish scholars, who, during the second stage of the Council, in December, 1551, made a sharp distinction between the consecration of the bishops and their power to govern a diocese. But Salmerón had not persuaded all his countrymen, and the character of the duty to reside loomed again on the horizon as a highly debatable subject.

7

The spring of 1562 was, for the bishops assembled at Trent, a period of endless adjournments. Several discussions had been initiated—the residence of the bishops, the definition of the present stage as a continuation of the preceding stages, and Communion under both species—but all of them were dropped again. Since the end of May, when the French official mission had arrived at Trent, the Council could amuse itself by observing the Spanish envoy, the Marquis of Pescara, entering and leaving the town at short intervals; the reason he had for his peculiar behavior was that no rule of diplomatic precedence had been established between Spain and France. The Spanish diplomat was therefore more anxious to avoid meeting his French colleague than to provoke a scandal.

The Marques of Pescara was actually a "locum tenens" for the Count of Luna, who had been appointed Spanish minister to the Council but had not yet been able to relinquish his post at the imperial court. Luna, whose interventions in the Hapsburg family affairs we have already mentioned, seemed at that time to be more and more influenced by the atmosphere of the Court of Ferdinand I. The reports he sent to Madrid now openly advocated the Emperor's point of view. Thus, for instance, he protested against Philip's endeavors to have the new stage of the Council declared a continuation of the preceding stages. He called such efforts a damnable disregard of the spiritual future of the Empire. Obviously, he was becoming much less Spanish than his King. But the time was to come when the men who succeeded him at his diplomatic post would be much more Spanish—in the imperialist sense of the word—than Philip II's successors.

The other Spaniard at the imperial court, Francisco Córdoba, who had reached Vienna only in 1559—sent there by King Philip to act as confessor to his sister, the wife of Maximilian—proved to be of an even more pliable nature. Some paragraphs of his letters written during the year 1562 read like an echo of the opinions which had been prevalent at the Council of Basel or in Bohemia of the fifteenth century. He was full of enthusiasm for the revival of the Communion under both species. But, on the other hand, his Spanish asceticism forbade him to accept the demand for the authorization of marriage of the clergy.

Supported, to such an extent, by Luna and Córdoba, Ferdinand I presented the Council, at the beginning of June, 1562, with another solemn letter, expressing once again his views on the way in which the reform of the Church should be conducted. His old demands, the Communion under both species and the marriage of the clergy, were not yet forgotten. From the "Scriptum in negocio concilii," however, this new memorandum differed in one aspect; it made no secret of the Emperor's total distrust of the Holy See. *In spiritualibus non videtur satisfacere officio* ("in spiritual affairs its activities are deemed unsatisfactory") was Ferdinand's verdict on the Curia.

But the lightning died as quickly as it had appeared. A *démarche* of the adroit papal nuncio at Vienna, Delfino, sufficed to persuade the Emperor to withdraw the memorandum.

Ferdinand's retreat opened at least one panel of the closed door which had prohibited the Council from embarking on its task. The other was opened when, in July, Philip announced his willingness not to insist on an immediate definition of the new stage of the Council as a continuation of the preceding stages and to agree upon a postponement of the definition of the espiscopal duty of residence. The only person who would not forget his opinions for a single moment was the Franciscan monk Córdoba. How could you, he wrote to the King of Spain, agree to the postponement of such an important business—the definition of the bishops' obligation to reside—on which the entire reform of the Church depends?

8

Finally, at the end of the summer of 1562, the Council was under way. Even the embarrassing problems of diplomatic protocol had been solved; Luna arrived at Trent not only as an envoy of the King of Spain but also in the capacity of an imperial ambassador, thus saving his precedence before the envoy of France.

The first two doctrinal questions which the Council now started to consider were the sacrifice of the Mass and the granting of the chalice to the laity. As far as the second of these two items was concerned, the Spanish theologians proved to be altogether uncompromising. They were not impressed by the support given to Ferdinand and to the Duke of Bavaria by the French delegation. Nor did they react to the Pope's repeated affirmations that there were no objections on his part against the granting of the chalice to the laity. The Bishop of Segovia told the Council that such a reform would destroy one of the oldest and most reasonable institutions of the Church. And another Spanish bishop did not hesitate to compare the partisans of the Communion under both species to the ancient Arians who tried to drop the expression *homousios* from the Credo. After a long discussion, the Council decided to classify the problem as a matter of liturgical discipline and to leave the decision to the Pope.

In spite of the purely theological character of this debate, however, the Council's ordeal, caused by political interference, was not yet at its end. In the winter months of 1562–63, another crisis started, provoked by new attacks of the Spanish, French, and imperial delegates against the exclusive right of the papal legates to determine the program of the Council. To make conditions even more difficult, two of the legates, Gonzaga and Seripando, died.

For a moment it seemed again as if the shaky structure of the Council would crumble under the incoherent but violent thrusts of Hapsburg rulers. It was at this juncture that Ferdinand came forward with the idea which had been refused by Charles V at the outset of his career as emperor—the idea of national councils which would regulate, in their own spheres, such matters as the General Council would not be able to decide upon. Luna, in his report to Philip dated March 31, 1563, supported this suggestion by taking up again the case of Bohemia as an illustration. A regional reform in that kingdom, he affirmed, would bring the utraquist clergy back under the jurisdiction of the Archbishop of Prague and pacify the country.

Philip refused to listen to such advice but persisted in his negative attitude toward the monarchical constitution of the Church. His resentment remained even when Cardinal Morone, who, together with Navagero, had been appointed papal legate to replace Gonzaga and Seripando, met Ferdinand at Innsbruck and weakened his resistance by skilfully playing up the papal recognition of Maximilian as Ferdinand's successor.

The Council then embarked upon what was to remain its chief glory: the redefinition of the Sacrament of Holy Orders, with which the whole problem of the education of the clergy and the establishment of seminaries in particular was connected.

It is interesting to observe how the two most powerful Catholic potentates of the time completely failed to grasp the importance of the decisions concerning these matters, decisions which were to be connected with the name of the Council of Trent for centuries to come.

Ferdinand's attitude, ever since his meeting with Morone, had been that of a politician who had had an idea but who had tried in vain to persuade others to adopt it. In his opinion the Council proved a complete failure. It had not fulfilled its original mission—that mission which Charles V had had in mind when he first tried to obtain its convocation. Therefore, the sooner the Council concluded its last session, the better for everyone. Let us forget the Council, which has turned into a mere impediment for practical religious policy, he said.

Philip, on the other hand, suspicious as he was of the intentions of the Holy See, could not dismiss the Council from his memory. At the time when the bishops at Trent were laying the foundations of a great educational revival inside the Church, he was much more anxious to have the outward relations of the Church settled—the relations which, to his mind, made the Church an integral part of the Christian state. Rumors were reaching him in those days that the legates were contemplating the introduction into the Council of a set of principles concerned with the relations between the Church and the state. Knowing the tendencies of the Catholic reforming trend, he feared a decision which would oppose his plans. He did not deny the authority of the Roman See in matters of faith. But as for social morals, could such a concept mean anything else than the ancient, traditional rights and privileges which would not suffer any innovation, not even such as might come from the Roman pontiff? And if the Pope chose to attack the power of a legal ruler, what authority other than the General Council would be able to stop him? The prerogatives which the Spanish kings had in the affairs of the Church in Sicily—and very peculiar prerogatives they were!—or the share to which they deemed themselves entitled in the various revenues of the Church, or even the Holy Inquisition, and many other privileges could be saved if the Council affirmed its supremacy above the Holy See.

Thus Philip embarked upon his last offensive against the proceedings of the Council. This time he was alone. His uncle, the Emperor, declared that he had a horror of all protesting. But also among the Spanish bishops at the Council—upon whose support Philip counted even now—there was a manifest change. Many of them were no more the "melancholy theologians," as they had been called in the preceding years, always very solemn in their patriotism and always very respectful of the wish of their King. When the Council, in the autumn of 1563, discussed the appointment of members of cathedral chapters and the interference of worldly rulers with it, many Spanish bishops profited by the secret ballot, introduced by Morone, and voted in favor of the idea of a completely free Church. Only Francisco Córdoba, the monk, remained faithful to Philip and continued sending him, from Vienna, extensive theological reports in which he denied the supremacy of the pope and his "plenitude of power."

Nevertheless, Philip's pressure on the Council, exerted mainly through the Count of Luna, was not altogether without success. The series of canons concerning relations between the Church and the state—if such a body of principles had been contemplated at all—dwindled into a general declaration against the unjust prerogatives of the rulers. And in November, in the next to the last session, which redefined the doctrine of Christian marriage, a statement was made, based on a special *breve* of the Pope, to the effect that the clause *proponentibus legatis* did not mean abolishing the ancient freedoms of the General Councils. But no pronouncement of the kind that the King of Spain would have liked to obtain was made. The assembled bishops and theologians knew very well what the real persuasion of the Church in these matters was. As they did not want, however, to exasperate Philip, they merely avoided the matter.

After having redefined, in its last session, the doctrine on purgatory, the invocation of saints, and the veneration of relics, the Council of Trent closed its portals forever on December 4, 1563 —in spite of frantic protests of the Count of Luna, who wanted an adjournment. The ambassador, who had been ailing for some time, died several weeks afterward.

It seems as if, with the death of the Count of Luna and with the end of the Council of Trent, two worlds had gone completely apart: the world of the living Church and the world of the absolutist state. No matter through what temporary estrangements they might have gone in the Middle Ages, no matter how great their mutual approach in the centuries to come would be, the achievements of the Council of Trent have set them far apart from each other. Medieval society, with its preponderantly Christian views of social duties, was disappearing fast. A new society came gradually into being, an individualistic society, which was to suffer much and learn less in the course of the coming centuries and of which the Church was no longer the soul.

The Hapsburg rulers were little aware of this change. They lived too near to it. Ferdinand was old and weak. Only half a year of life was in store for him. He used it, among other things, to secure papal approval of Maximilian's right to succeed him. On April 16, 1564, he also obtained papal confirmation of the liturgical usage of the Czechs to communicate under both species. Both things happened against Philip's will. The King of Spain wanted his cousin first of all to swear obedience to the Pope in matters of faith. He dispatched Martin Guzmán to Vienna to persuade him to do so. Cardinal Morone, however, selected a text of the oath in which the word "obedience" simply did not appear. As to the liturgical privilege for the Czechs, it came sooner than Philip had expected. Eight days after it had been granted, Philip still warned his uncle, in a letter dated from Valencia, not to grant a concession which, in his opinion, would make the Church in central Europe crumble. His prophecy did not come true. Nor did Ferdinand's expectations; a mere liturgical privilege proved incapable of stopping the religious disintegration in Bohemia.

When Ferdinand died, on July 25, 1564, six years after the death of his brother, Charles V, Philip was still at the beginning of his career. He never became an admirer of the work done by the bishops in Trent. When France, Poland, Portugal, Venice, and even Savoy accepted the decrees of the Council, Philip had them published with a clause affirming that they were to be considered valid only "without prejudice to the rights of the Spanish Crown." Even the skeptical Maximilian, who, in 1566, had the Tridentine decrees promulgated in the entire territory of the Empire, did not dare to restrict them in such a way. Philip, however, remained an enemy of the Catholic reformation and of the monarchical constitution of the Church up to the very end of his reign. As late as 1590, Luis de León, one of the prominent theologians in the University of Salamanca, had to criticize him because of his unwillingness to publish the papal bulls in Spain.

And yet, in the course of subsequent years, it was the King of Spain who, aroused in his deep feeling for the Christian tradition, pushed aside the political conception which he had inherited from his father and took to arms, trying by force to save Europe's spiritual unity.

THE REBELS

1

TWO-THIRDS of Philip II's reign, the years 1572–98, were spent in putting an end to the rebellion of the Netherlands and in defending the Spanish dominions against the forces united under the cause of the insurgents. Three-quarters of a year after the victory of Lepanto, the hitherto local troubles in the provinces where Charles V had been born and where he resigned his imperial office had suddenly assumed an international significance, and the whole military might of the Spanish empire had to be moved from the Mediterranean to the Atlantic.

Many historians have wondered about the major military event of the period, the naval expedition against England of 1588. The Spaniards appeared in the English Channel with large galleons, unable to cope with either the fast vessels of the Elizabethan navy or with the tempests of the Atlantic Ocean. This fact undoubtedly testifies to an unusual stubbornness and lack of perspicacity on the part of the Spanish. But it also has a profound symbolic meaning. The Spanish empire had been founded not as an Atlantic, but as a Mediterranean, power. Even its vast possessions overseas did not change this basic characteristic, impressed upon it by the past centuries of Pyrenean history as well as by Charles, the "builder" of the empire. The Spanish army and navy had been built as a defense against the Turks and against the North African pirates. They had not been meant to lay siege to Ostende or to fight the English ships in the Channel.

As it happened, the events of the last quarter of the sixteenth century assumed a major role in the story of Spanish preponderance in Europe. Philip himself could die with the belief that he had found a solution for the thorny problem in the declaration of the independence of the Netherlands under Archduke Albert. But in attempting to suppress the insurgents he had kindled a flame which then could not be extinguished by a mere act of diplomacy. Around the year 1600 the idea of a common European defense against the Turks was by no means dead, but it could no longer claim a predominant place in the minds of the Spanish generals and diplomats. Their attention was thenceforth attracted by another task which they thought an urgent one—the task of destroying the enemy inside Europe, the enemy who had attacked them from the rear. And the flame of hatred—a haughty hatred—remained glowing at the bottom of European hearts until it burst into the holocaust of the Thirty Years' War.

2

The insurrection in the Netherlands and the attempts to suppress it were legally an internal affair of one of the dominions of Philip II. But that does not mean that it was a clear business even from the juridical point of view. The sixteenth century knew little of the juridical positivism of more modern times. On the contrary, it criticized positivism and tried repeatedly to do away with it. In this particular field the Renaissance skepticism of a Montaigne worked hand in hand with the scholastic wisdom of a Vitoria. Only years later, after the end of the Thirty Years' War, did the positivist tendency win the upper hand in jurisprudence, affirming that there was no law above the ruler. But as long as Spain was considered the most powerful state of Christendom, the Christian doctrine of the law of nature lived in the minds of men, even if it was not liked by the Spanish kings themselves, who were as much inclined toward absolutism as any other ruler of the time. Consequently, the insurrection in the Low Countries and also the contemporary turbulent events in France occupied many a mind longing for ideal justice.

The interest in the essential principles of law was only

heightened by the occupation of the newly discovered countries overseas. The misery of the Indians, of which even the worldly minded Pope Leo X had to declare, "not only religion, but nature herself refuses to accept it," was getting worse and worse with every new step of the Conquistadors on the soil of America. The dramatic life of Bartolomé de las Casas as well as the inspired words of the lawyer Juan Lopez de Vivero testified in favor of the suppressed natives. What right had the conquerors to treat the Indians as slaves? Such was the question which kept ringing in the ears of soldiers and politicians, of priests and teachers.

The conquerors had their defendants, of course. Juan Ginés de Sepulveda, the most prominent among them, had perhaps less success with his book *Democratus secundus sive dialogus de iustis belli causis* than Bartolomé de las Casas had with his *Apologetica historica,* and he also had Charles V against him. Nevertheless, many of his readers shared his views, and a public discussion was arranged between him and De las Casas at Valladolid in 1550. And various political ideas assumed new importance in connection with this controversy.

There was, above all, a certain revival of regionalist feeling, opposed to any political centralization. A village or a town, affirms Bartolomé de las Casas, may certainly be considered one's fatherland. But what is the use of speaking of Spain, Germany, or England as fatherlands? Can they be considered, perhaps, as fatherlands of towns and villages? Listening to such arguments, we may have the impression of something unreal and anachronistic. Europe of the sixteenth century certainly did not resemble the world of the Greek city-republics of the fourth century B.C. The absolutist and centralizing tendencies of the kings were making rapid progress. Nationalist feeling—which has always been hidden somewhere at the bottom of human hearts—was also mounting. Nevertheless, a protest of this kind was as good an example of logical and clear thinking as it was rare and unusual.

Other new ideas, however, were of more practical impact;

some of them were connected with the "law of nations," others with the doctrine of tyrannicide.

Francisco Vitoria, the great renovator of the ancient *ius gentium,* quoted the verses of Virgil,

> Quod genus hoc hominum? quave hunc tam barbara morem
> permittit patria? Hospitio prohibemur arenae,

to show how old a doctrine it was. But the actual impulse under which this Spanish thinker began his studies was not reverence for an ancient discipline, but a very practical need of a solution of the basic problems of international politics. Are the natives entitled to close their countries to the discoverers? Is it lawful for the French to hinder the Spaniards from using the commercial routes in France? Such were the practical questions of the new era in which distances began to shorten and the field of international contacts to expand.

It was evident to Vitoria and his contemporaries that a guiding principle should be looked for rather in the sphere of rational constructions than in the sphere of ancient usages. The second sphere, illustrated by the activities of the *praetor peregrinus* in early Rome and by the ancient concept of international law in general, was amply exploited in studying and redefining such old customs as, for example, the immunity of envoys. But there were also traditional principles which conflicted with one another and which could not be clarified by mere comparison. Was *mare liberum*—the sea accessible to all— or *mare clausum*—the sea accessible to littoral countries only— the right principle? Were the Mexican Indians to be allowed human sacrifices if they considered them an ancient usage? Such deliberations led necessarily to the Christian concept of "natural law," according to which—as summed up in the most succinct way by Thomas Aquinas—right is that which is reasonable, the reasonable acceptance of the truth revealed by God included.

In the ultimate acceptance of the Christian explanation of the natural law, Catholics and Protestants of the sixteenth and seventeenth centuries were nearer to each other than a twentieth-century student of history would expect. Vitoria as well as the much younger Protestant scholar Grotius considered revelation the ultimate source of law. Grotius, whose treatise *On the Laws of War and Peace* was published in the eighth year of the Thirty Years' War, went so far, however, as to affirm that the relativity of laws was a "pestilential error"—which was certainly not in accordance with the Christian doctrine, because an absolute major principle does not exclude differences in detailed ordinances.

But if there was a legal order flowing from revelation and from human reason, then even a king was subject to it and was bound to obey it—quite in conformity with the best tradition of medieval Spain as expressed in *Las Siete Partidas* of Alfonso el Sabio.

Both the Catholics and the Protestants went far in evaluating the importance of the royal office. Juan Mariana, who was by no means blind to the dangers of absolutism, told his readers expressly: "If the fact of being Christ's disciples does not move us sufficiently to fulfil our duties, let the state step in and move us to do so." As to the Protestants, the high place given to the authority of the ruler by the Lutherans could hardly be outdone by the Calvinist theocratic communities, the influence of which now began to spread through the European west. In 1566 the painter Goeding was ordered by the Duke of Saxony to paint a "Last Supper" for the chapel in the castle of Stolpen; the Duke himself figured in the picture as Our Lord, his courtiers represented the Apostles; nothing could be more symbolic.

On the other hand, both sides stressed the obligation of the ruler to act according to the *ius divinum,* the revealed part of the *ius naturae.* From this statement only a short step was necessary to the affirmation that even the subjects of a ruler were entitled to resist his orders and perhaps to deprive him of his office if he did not act according to the natural and divine right. Martin Luther was the first to envisage the connection between this theory and the religious reformation; his pamphlets against

Charles V bear clearly in that direction. But Juan Mariana among the Catholic theoreticians of politics—in his book *De rege et regis institutione,* published in 1599—and Philip Duplessis Mornay, the French Calvinist author of *Vindiciae contra tyrannos,* went to great lengths to explain and corroborate this theory. The more popular it became, however, the more dangerous a doctrine it appeared to be. It could have been an excellent theory of political authority in a spiritually united Europe. With the deep contemporary division in matters of religious persuasion, it proved an argument that recoiled on its authors.

3

The first premonition of the coming troubles came from France, the native country of Calvin. Under King Henry II, successor of Francis I, Calvinism spread rapidly through the kingdom. The Huguenots—as its supporters there were called—had two advantages over the Lutherans: first, their enthusiasm was of a much purer, intellectual nature; and second, their leader was a born organizer. Up to his death in 1564 he worked indefatigably in Geneva, keeping in correspondence with hundreds of persons in different European countries. But the enthusiasm of the Huguenots was also of a more annihilating nature than that of the Lutherans. If their doctrine of predestination was inhuman, their hatred of art was something demoniac. In France they profited immensely from the death of Henry II. Under his three inferior sons, with their semipagan and selfish mother, Catherine de Medici, behind the throne, France quickly became a land of chaos. The "tumult of Amboise," organized by the Huguenots in March, 1560, with the aim of arresting some of the Guises, the leading Catholic family, met with failure; but the news of it sounded like an alarm in Madrid, as well as in Prague and Vienna.

There is a passage in Luis Cabrera de Córdoba's biography of Philip II which reads as if it had been written on the margin of some letters of the king. "Through apostasy," says the historiographer, "the ties between souls are loosened, and the union of communities which have professed one Catholic faith is destroyed; without such a union every government falls—in particular that of France; for such reasons the King was afraid that France, a large and well-united country, would become a victim of internal disorders and civil wars and that, to avoid them, it would seek salvation in conquests beyond its frontiers." Relating this, Cabrera de Córdoba was not trying merely to defend Philip; the king's real thoughts must have taken such a course. If, after all that had happened in France in the sixties and the seventies, he decided to help the French Catholic faction and to interfere in France's internal problems, it was because he had no other way left. Had he wanted to humiliate France or to conquer it, he would have done so in 1557, after he had defeated the forces of Henry II at St. Quentin. His plans, however, did not aim at conquest; they only attempted to save his empire from a danger which was perhaps best summed up in the political theory of the French humanist, Jean Bodin. The main difference between the Christian, traditional concept of policy and that of Bodin consisted in Bodin's identification of the absolute power in the state with the absolute power of the state. Such an absolute power of a state which was no longer affiliated to the international Christian community was precisely what King Philip was afraid of.

Both Philip II and Maximilian II, who, in 1564, had succeeded Ferdinand I as Holy Roman Emperor, observed the developments in France attentively. And they were able to communicate their impressions to each other.

The diplomatic service was, at that time, coming of age. The sending of regular or permanent envoys, as had been introduced into Europe's political life by the papal Curia, became gradually an institution. The two Hapsburg courts needed it more than any other. Legally, Spain and the Empire—not to mention Bohemia and Hungary—were now completely independent of each other. In addition, Philip resumed the old Spanish aversion to the imperial dignity; after some time, he even insisted that Maximilian should call him in his letters "Your

Majesty" and not just "Your Highness" as before. Thus the need was greater for mediating diplomats.

The old generation to which Martin Guzmán and the Count of Luna belonged was now dead. New people came into their places. Thomas Perrenot de Chantonnay—brother of Bishop Granvelle, an approved counselor of King Philip, first in Brussels and then, since 1579, in Madrid—went to the imperial court in Prague. After his recall in 1570, he was succeeded by Francisco Hurtado de Mendoza, Count of Monteagudo and later Marquis of Almazan. There were some extraordinary envoys, too: in 1564, the Count of Berlaymont, the Baron of Hierges, and Pedro Lopez de Ayala, Count of Fuensalida; in 1567–70, Luis Vanegas de Figueroa; in 1571, Bellido, a jurist; in 1572–75, Pedro Fajardo, Marquis of Los Veles. As to the imperial representatives at the Spanish court, the first of them, Adam Dietrichstein, arrived in 1564 and stayed until 1573. His place was then taken by another Austrian nobleman, Johann Khevenhueller, who, after a short stay in Madrid in 1571, remained there permanently from 1573 until his death in 1606.

The diplomats of those days were still called *honrados espiones* ("honorable spies"), but their service was not a lucrative one. Even Philip's envoys had to ask, from time to time, for a special *ayuda de costa* to cover their expenses. As to the imperial ambassadors, they were paid so badly that they had constantly to borrow money from one banking firm or another. Johann Khevenhueller even entered the service of the court to which he had been accredited and helped Philip II to build, in the years 1580–85, a new mint in Segovia which struck coins containing a lesser amount of silver than was usual.

But even such imperfect diplomatic channels met the needs of the Hapsburg family policy—or, rather, of Philip's unrelenting endeavors to make his cousin, the Emperor, share his own rapidly evolving fears and plans.

In 1559, Ferdinand I had willingly given his consent to Philip's decision to conclude the peace of Cateau-Cambrésis without asking the French to return Metz, Toul, and Verdun to the Empire. Maximilian's position was now much more difficult. The Calvinist action in the Low Countries, which started soon after the disturbances in France, was not so much a national as a religious concern. In matters of religion even Ferdinand had been more adamant toward Philip, refusing to do anything against the will of the Netherland nobles. When Philip had attempted to obtain from Rome an ecclesiastical reorganization of the Netherlands—a measure which, by establishing new bishoprics, aimed at religious progress as well as at affirming the king's influence—Ferdinand wrote to the Pope dissuading him from taking such a step.

Both the Austrian Hapsburgs, Ferdinand as well as Maximilian, knew well the peculiar attitude of the Netherland nobles toward the Empire. The utter failure of Charles V, who, in spite of being quite popular in his native country, had tried in vain to strengthen the ties between it and the other imperial provinces, was not forgotten. Had the Netherlands showed more interest in the defense against the Turks, the military situation in the southeast would have been much easier to handle. As things were, even the administrational reform of 1548, by which Charles had remodeled the constitutional relations between the Empire and the "Burgundian Circle," did not work. It declared the Netherlands free from the duty to obey any laws or ordinances of the Empire but kept them included in the "imperial peace" and bound them to pay three times as large a contribution to the defense against the Turks as any Prince Elector. The Low Countries, however, had ceased to pay in 1552. Ever since the resignation of Charles, Ferdinand and then Maximilian had demanded in their letters to Philip that payments should be resumed, but without result.

And now, despite all the disquieting news about the Calvinist disturbances in France and about the growing tension in the Low Countries, would there be any understanding in Vienna and in Prague for Philip's apprehensions and for his increasing inclination to reassert his legal rights and moral obligations?

4

On the five memorable August days, the fourteenth to the nineteenth, of 1566, on which hundreds of churches and monasteries and thousands of priceless treasures of art were destroyed all over the Netherlands by the looting mob led by Calvinist preachers, the abysmal cleavage between the Christian tradition and the new trends became more than apparent. Theological or philosophical disagreements were important enough, but their influence could reach the broad strata of society and modify their lives perhaps only after many years. The attack on art, however, was a fact of tremendous and immediate import. It divorced European man from what had been most human in the achievements of his fathers. And it was bound to shock many less conscientious than Philip II.

But even under such circumstances, Maximilian II, to whom the burden, if not the problems, of the imperial office was new, did not want to abandon the compromising line of policy of his father. There was a direct Dutch influence at his court, too. The Count of Hoogstraten, a close friend of William of Orange, had visited Prague in 1564, the year in which the discontented nobles had obtained the recall of Bishop Granvelle. Early in 1566, before the main troubles had started, Hoogstraten arrived at Augsburg to attend the imperial Diet there. On both these occasions he was the guest of Vratislav Pernštýn, the nobleman whose name we have already mentioned as one of those Czechs who had accompanied Maximilian to Spain in 1548. In Augsburg, as was natural, Hoogstraten avoided all contacts with the Spanish envoy, Chantonnay, Granvelle's brother. Nevertheless, Chantonnay was able to discover that a petition had been brought by Hoogstraten and, through Pernštýn, transmitted to the Emperor, to the effect that the Emperor should warn the King of Spain not to introduce the Spanish Inquisition into the Low Countries.

The story of the Netherlands' fear of the famous Spanish tribunal is curious. If we explain it by pointing to an anxiety to keep the door closed to any tool of absolutism—and the Holy Inquisition in Spain, in spite of its important share in the defense of the country, was such a tool—we have not yet explained the presence in the Netherlands of an extended organization, which, a few months later, was able to wreck so many values of art created by the Netherlanders themselves in their free past.

The role of Vratislav Pernštýn as Hoogstraten's friend does not seem a very clear one, either. Elected Knight of the Golden Fleece, at that time still a Burgundian order, in a chapter held in Antwerp in 1566, Pernštýn was undoubtedly well known to Orange, Egmont, Hornes, Montigny, Berghes, and the other prominent persons behind the turbulent events in the Low Countries. But his whole background was of a different kind. He had many friends among the Spanish courtiers of Maximilian's wife, Maria; Juan Alfonso Gastaldo; Francisco Lasso de Castilla, the *mayordomo mayor;* and Marco Spinola, Count of Tercerola, a Genoese and father of Carlo Spinola, one of the first Jesuit martyrs in Japan, were among them. Having visited Rome in 1552, he was sent to Spain again two years later and was present, on his way back, at Philip's marriage to Mary Tudor in Winchester. In 1556, he married Maria Manrique de Lara, daughter of García Manrique de Lara, a descendant of the Hurtados de Mendoza and Charles V's governor in Parma and Piacenza.

His marriage, it is true, brought Pernštýn a nuisance. Maria's mother, Isabella de Bresegno, an Italian, became involved in the activities of a Lutheran circle in Naples, a circle which had Juan Valdés as its initiator, Bernardino Ochino as its leader, and Giulia Gonzaga, Lucrezia Poggiola, Galeazzo Caracciolo, and Vittoria Colonna as the more prominent members. To evade arrest, Donna Isabella fled to Switzerland, where she remained until she died. Consequently, Pernštýn had to defend himself and his name against the suspicion of heresy. Not his Czech surrounding but his Spanish connections forced him to do so. It was according to the Spanish principle of *limpieza de sangre* ("purity of blood from heretical contamination") and perhaps also out of fidelity to the catchword of García Dey—

> ... cuya es sangre tan clara?
> de los Manriques de Lara—

that he finally, in 1569, asked the Pope himself, in vain, to stop the inquisitional process against Isabella de Bresegno.

Notwithstanding this, Pernštýn had a good name among the Spaniards. His knowledge of contemporaneous Europe was great. Well acquainted with Hans Jakob Fugger and with Chantonnay's predecessor, the Count of Luna, he represented Maximilian, in 1560, in Madrid at Philip's third marriage—with Elizabeth of Valois—and on that occasion he also paid a visit to Francis II at Blois. In 1568 we find him in Philip's own service, as his representative at the marriage of the son of the Duke of Bavaria in Munich. Was he or was he not on Hoogstraten's side in 1564? All that Chantonnay was able to learn from him in the spring of 1566 was a warning: it looked—so Pernštýn told the envoy—as if the King of Spain would have to send his soldiers to the Netherlands.

That such a step might become necessary also became Philip's own opinion at the end of the summer of 1566. He wrote to Maximilian and asked his authorization to recruit soldiers in Germany. The Emperor granted it only in November, after weeks of deliberation and after having dispatched to Madrid several letters counseling Philip to pay a personal visit to the Netherlands and not to take any soldiers with him. But even then the authorization included a clause affirming that Philip was bound to respect the imperial peace of 1555 and to recognize the freedom of the Confession of Augsburg in the Low Countries—which was not true because no imperial law was binding in the Netherlands after 1548. At the same time, the Emperor sent a letter—through Margaret of Parma, Philip's governor in Brussels, to the dissatisfied nobles, asking them not to push things to a climax. This letter—probably because it contained the same false affirmation concerning the Confession of Augsburg—was seized by Margaret and never reached its destination.

At the outset of 1567, Dietrichstein reported from Madrid about Philip's decision to appoint the Duke of Alba commander of an expeditionary force to be sent to the Low Countries. It aroused not a little consternation. Was not the Duke too old for such a task? Why did the King of Spain refrain from a personal visit to Brussels? The Emperor, without regard to the person of the commander, remained firm in his decision to restrict the trouble in the Netherlands as much as possible. Reluctantly, he extended to Austria the authorization to recruit soldiers that he had granted to the Spaniards in Germany; but he refused to extend it to Bohemia. At the same time, he did almost nothing to stop the German princes from supporting William of Orange and his associates.

All Maximilian's behavior in those days was of a perplexing character. Only a short time before, the so-called "Grumbach conspiracy," directed against the Emperor himself, had been discovered in Germany and its initiator, John Frederick, Duke of Saxony, was put in jail. No modern student of that rather strange affair—the documentary material of which is very inadequate—is able to tell with certainty what was its actual inside story. But there is one testimony which sends a piercing ray of light into those dark circumstances. It is an entry in Maximilian's own diary, dated June, 1567: "The two affairs, that of Grumbach and that of the Netherlands, are closely related to each other and a pretty mess has resulted from them...."

If that much was known to the Emperor, why did he not permit his cousin to act in the same way in the Low Countries as he himself had acted in Germany? Philip asked him to put at his disposal the small army which had been employed against John Frederick. Maximilian refused. Then, when Alba, using the route from Milan through the Franche Comté and Luxemburg, had reached Brussels and set up his "Council of Tumults," the Emperor himself told Chantonnay that some documents had come into his hands at the suppression of the Grumbach conspiracy which would bring several proud men in the Netherlands to the scaffold. Philip, having learned that, suggested that those documents should be placed at Alba's disposal. Maximilian again refused.

What was the sense of all that policy of trimming? Perhaps in answering this question we may also find the answer to another problem which we mentioned a while ago: What was the use of recommending to the King of Spain that he respect the Confession of Augsburg and safeguard its imaginary rights in the Netherlands, where there were almost no Lutherans? There is only one probable explanation: the Emperor wanted to strengthen the ties between himself and his Lutheran subjects and to avoid the establishment of a united Lutheran-Calvinist front. Perhaps he had some good reasons for such a policy. The revolutionary spirit of the German Lutheran princes had almost spent itself with the death of Maurice of Saxony. Its very last spark, the conspiracy of Grumbach, had been easily discovered and extinguished. Many years were to pass until it was revived again under the patronage of Gustavus Adolphus of Sweden. There was also recent evidence that the task of bringing the Lutherans back to political obedience might succeed. A noteworthy fact in this evidence was the behavior of August of Saxony, successor of John Frederick, who, having been asked by William of Orange for help, replied that first the Emperor and then Philip and Alba were the authorities to be approached.

5

If Maximilian was of the opinion that Calvinism could be contained and that a frontier could be drawn between the Empire and the west in matters of religious policy, Philip was soon to demonstrate the falsity of such a presumption. In the autumn of 1567, news came about John Casimir of the Palatinate, who, without bothering about any imperial authorization, had recruited soldiers for Condé, the leader of the French Huguenots. And then, at the outset of 1568, a great sum of money which was being transported by some Genoese bankers to the Duke of Alba was confiscated by the Palatine soldiers and never returned to its lawful possessors. At the conference of the Princes Electors in Fulda in 1568, the continuity between the Lutheran and the Calvinist action became quite apparent. The Protestant princes clamored for some action against Alba, who, they affirmed, had broken the imperial peace. Later, when Egmont and Hornes had been executed in Brussels, on June 5, 1568, even August of Saxony started supporting William of Orange. And the princes of western Germany, at a conference at Bacharach, joined the Protestant Electors in their opposition to the Spanish policy in the Low Countries.

Reading Maximilian's correspondence of those months is like reading the script of a comedy. After some hesitation, he published a letter of arrest against William of Orange—but did not care to enforce it. Then he sent to Madrid a protest against Alba's judicial actions and against his military units which had trespassed on the frontiers of the Bishopric of Trèves. To Alba himself he dispatched an admonition, copies of which were sent to the German princes. When Alba succeeded in August in ousting Louis of Nassau, one of the foremost rebels, from the province of Friesland, Maximilian—if we are to believe a report by Zasius, an imperial counselor—lost his speech; but that did not detain him from sending congratulations to Philip. When Alba asked him to punish a German prince, the Duke of Cleve, who had refused to help prosecute William of Orange, Maximilian rejected his petition very haughtily. But almost immediately afterward, in a letter to Madrid, he charged Alba with indifference to imperial authority. No wonder some of Philip's counselors—Bishop Granvelle in particular—suggested that the Emperor should be ignored and the western banks of the river Rhine be occupied by Spanish troops.

This diplomatic comedy reached its culminating point in October, 1568, when Archduke Charles, the Emperor's younger brother, suddenly set out for Madrid with a special mission concerning the uprising in the Netherlands. Two other envoys were dispatched simultaneously to the Duke of Alba and to William of Orange. The delegation which had been sent, a month before, to the imperial court by the conference in Bacharach had evidently persuaded Maximilian to put up a show. The mission was organized with utmost rapidity. Only Alba had time to remonstrate, pointing to its uselessness. Madrid was informed about Charles's task only when the Archduke had already reached Genoa. King Philip, usually a calm man, declared that his answer would be as vigorous as his cousin had been cocksure of his action. Perhaps the indignation of the Spanish King was further aroused by a memorandum composed by Maximilian's general Lazar Schwendi and sent to Philip's secretary, Pfitzing. According to it, the Low Countries should be given to Archduke Charles, who would then marry Elizabeth of England.

On hardly any other occasion did Philip II state his political program so clearly and concisely as in the two replies which he handed to Archduke Charles in Madrid, on January 20, 1569. In the meantime, the Emperor, having learned about Philip's indignation, started sending letters to Madrid in which he asked Philip not to take the Archduke's mission too seriously but rather send advice on how to answer the petition of the German princes. Philip ignored these letters. Of the two replies he gave to the Archduke, the first was a public one. It stated, first of all, that, according to the agreement of 1548, the Emperor had no juridical sovereignty over the Low Countries. It also stressed the moral obligation of every ruler before God to defend the liberty of revealed truth and of the tradition by which that truth is preserved. It ended with a defense of Alba, who—it said—had not done anything against justice; on the contrary, it went on to state, those who refuse to help him are acting against justice. The second reply, "El Recuerdo particular," had the character of a private letter. Its general purport was a reproach to Maximilian: How could the Emperor have any doubts about the righteousness of Philip's policy? Did he really believe that Philip was acting just for glory? Had he never heard about the duties of a ruler?

As the mission of the Archduke had been widely publicized and the Emperor, by sending his three envoys in such a solemn way, had assumed the role of a judge, Philip's answer was awaited everywhere. Expecting that the return journey of the Archduke would be a lengthy one—Philip had to lend him money to cover his traveling expenses—the King's secretaries sent the two documents to the Emperor by a special courier, who arrived at the imperial court in April. The first of the King's replies was sent in two versions, a Spanish and a Latin one, the Latin version being extended by two paragraphs in which Philip affirmed his good will toward the German princes. It would have been natural, had Philip asked Maximilian to give some sort of publicity to his answer. The King, however, ordered that, with the exception of the Pope, nobody should be given the text of the document until—and if—Maximilian himself decided to send it to the German princes either in full or in a summary.

Maximilian did neither. After a month had passed, he sent a letter to Philip telling him that he had to eliminate from his answer such sentences in which religion was mentioned and which would offend the Protestant recipients. Two documents which have been preserved to our own days show us the phrases in question, crossed out with red ink. If the King of Spain affirmed, for instance, that it was necessary to seek life and to accept death with faith, his words were suppressed. If he tried to demonstrate that no human decision can free man from his obligations to God or if he said that spiritual evil must not be allowed to spread, he was also silenced. Naturally he refused to be interpreted in such a way and, ignoring Maximilian's hesitations, sent a copy of his reply directly to the Bishop of Trèves and to the Bishop of Münster, so that it could be divulged in Germany.

After such an experience, little could be expected by the

Spaniards from an Emperor whose only ideal was the preservation of the status quo. Alba's troops in the Netherlands were victorious, but France, the center of disturbances, radiated unrest throughout Germany. The Duke of Saxony inclined more and more toward John Casimir of the Palatinate and his pro-Huguenot ideals. The Count of Monteagudo, the new Spanish envoy at the imperial court, succeeded in obtaining from Maximilian a few admonitory letters addressed to William of Orange and to the German princes, but he failed in obtaining the imposition of the ban of the Empire on the rebels. Whenever he asked for it, Maximilian countered by reminding him that Philip, as lord of the Low Countries, owed him the contribution toward the defense against the Turks—a debt of many years. The greater the disparity between the value of money in Germany and the value which the still very wealthy Netherlands were able to fix for their own coins, the more true that reminder was.

It was the wish of Philip in those years as well as that of Alba —whose units had in the meantime disposed of a new attack by William of Orange and his army, raised in Germany—to gain some friends among the German princes. Particularly in the summer of 1569, when the expenses of Alba's expedition began to be felt by the Spaniards, it became more and more clear to them that a major political and military action such as theirs required not only a sound moral and legal foundation but also some popularity among neighbors and other onlookers. Could not a sort of diplomatic union be achieved between the King of Spain and some German provinces?

The old Catholic Union of Regensburg, which had originated in the first tumults of the Lutheran movement, was now as good as forgotten. But another alliance was still in existence in Germany: the so-called "League of Landsberg," created in 1556 for the preservation of the Peace of Augsburg and including Catholic as well as Protestant princes among its members. King Philip had tried in vain to enter it, as lord of the Low Countries, as early as 1561. The Duke of Alba now renewed the attempts. But here again he met with the Emperor's opposition. In this case Maximilian's aims were even more evident than elsewhere. He did not want the League of Landsberg to become a preponderantly Catholic alliance; on the contrary, he wished that the Duke of Saxony would become a member so that the equilibrium in Germany would be strengthened.

For five years after the inglorious return of Archduke Charles from Madrid, Maximilian watched the developments in the west with a hesitating passivity. Perhaps he thought Spain too powerful, in spite of her recent difficulties. In the autumn of 1571, news came of the great naval victory at Lepanto—an event which in many ways can be considered the culminating point of Spanish might. It seemed also as if the Queen of England, who, counseled by William Cecil and using the expert services of Thomas Gresham, an international banker, had supported the Calvinist movement on the European mainland, would now change her policy in favor of Spain. She was evidently hesitating, seeing that the help given to the Huguenots meant actually helping the expansion of French influence. But then the trend of events suddenly changed direction. In April, 1572, a small fleet sailing under the flag of William of Orange seized the ports of Brill and Flushing, and the Calvinists were subsequently able to occupy a whole region in the northwestern Netherlands. The region, because of the canals and river estuaries which protected it, could not be seized by Alba without the help of the Spanish navy, which was still fully occupied on the Mediterranean. This new situation was not affected by the downfall, during the next summer, of the Huguenot might in France. There Catherine de Medici, guarding her personal power, ordered the assassination of Coligny, a prominent Huguenot; the French Catholics, embittered by Calvinist outrages—such as the massacre at Orthez, on St. Bartholomew's day in 1569—seized the occasion and resorted, again on the feast of the same saint, to fanatical killing, in which thousands of Calvinists lost their lives. But with the Netherlands rebels now firmly established behind the dikes and on the islands and with the rest of the Low Countries in virtual upheaval because of the rapidly increasing financial burden imposed upon it by Alba, the uncompromising policy of Philip reached a blind alley.

Once more, in 1574, Maximilian renewed his interest in the Netherlands. By that time, Alba had been replaced by Luis Requeséns y Zúñiga, son of Juan Zúñiga, whom Maximilian must have known as a prudent and discreet counselor of Charles V. His first steps in the Low Countries gave hope for a peaceful solution of the troubles. Pushing aside the discussions of the Spanish lawyers—whether the rebellion was a *rebellio absoluta* or a *rebellio mixta*—he persuaded Philip to grant a large amnesty. Siezing this opportunity, the Emperor sent two envoys, Schwarzburg and Hohenlohe, to the Netherlands and a third one, Wolfgang Rumpf, to Madrid. This time he carefully eschewed any remonstrances against Philip's principles. That notwithstanding, the envoys could do little more than await the result of the negotiations between Requeséns and the rebels. The unexpected death of the new governor, in March, 1576, preceded by Philip's second announcement of insolvency in 1575, plunged the Low Countries once more into chaos. The sending of Juan de Austria to take Requeséns' place, decided by Philip in the summer of 1576, met with Maximilian's strong disapproval, and Rumpf was dispatched once again, in August, to Madrid with a protest. That, however, was the Emperor's last action in that field; his life was near its end.

6

The relations between Philip II and his skeptical cousin had also thrown their shadow on the sunny landscape of Italy. Although in actual possession of the Milanese as well as of the Kingdom of Naples and Sicily, Philip, whose mind had a distinct legalistic tinge, still felt rather uneasy about the purely nominal authority which the Emperor had in Italy—as if the times of Frederick Barbarossa might return. As early as 1558 he had reminded Ferdinand—through a special envoy, Bishop

Quadra—of the family agreement made in Augsburg, according to which he was to be nominated as the Emperor's vicar in
Italy. The negotiations were kept secret; the German princes
would certainly have protested, had they heard about any sell-
ing-out of the imperial prerogatives. And the Emperor kept
postponing his decision until he died. After that, Philip ab-
stained from renewing his petition.

Maximilian recognized Philip's predominance in Italy not
only *de iure*—he accepted his oath of fealty on behalf of Milan
and Siena—but also *de facto*. Whenever he had, for instance,
any difficulty with Venice concerning the transportation of
grain on the Adriatic, he asked the King of Spain to interfere.
Nevertheless, there were other difficulties. First of all, Maximilian and his wife had inherited, by the testament of Charles
V, a revenue in the Kingdom of Naples. When they tried to
sell it, they did not succeed in obtaining a Spanish authorization. Second, there was the comic affair of Cosimo Medici.
The ambitious lord of Florence, who had married Maximilian's
daughter Joan, obtained, in 1569, the title of "Archduke of
Toscany" from the Pope. He had duly informed the Emperor
about his petition to the Pope, but after the Pope had conferred the title the Hapsburg pride suddenly felt offended.
Letters streamed from Prague to Madrid and back again, preparing a joint diplomatic action. But the Medici were rich and
the Hapsburgs needed money. Alba, in 1572, got from Florence
200,000 scudi to cover his expenses in the Netherlands, and the
King of Spain recognized Cosimo as Archduke. It took several
years more to gain the Emperor's approval. Cosimo died in
1574 and was succeeded by Francesco, but Maximilian still had
his doubts. At last, in 1576, he, too, obtained a loan of 200,000
scudi to cover his military expenses in Hungary, and he recognized the new dignity of the Medici.

The situation in Italy grew worse whenever the military interests of the Spanish generals were involved. Alba's actions in
the Netherlands were rather admired among the generals, and
they did not hesitate to affront even the saintly Archbishop of

Milan, Charles Borromeo. Maximilian knew the Spanish soldiers and respected them. When asked by Cosimo Medici to
authorize the occupation, by Florentine troops, of Corsica
where Sampietro de Bastelica, former lieutenant of the Florentine condottiere Giovanni delle Bande Nere, started another
uprising against Genoa, the Emperor consulted the King of
Spain and then refused to give his consent. The case of Finale
was a more complicated one. That small principality on the
Ligurian coast had been, until 1561, in the hands of the family
Sforza-Carretto. When the Genoese, with the help of an internal insurrection, seized the place, the Sforza-Carrettos asked
for help in Madrid as well as at the imperial court. Since the
Spaniards had excellent relations with the Genoese bankers,
they were not particularly anxious to re-establish the Marquis
of Finale in his lawful possessions. After many postponements
the Sforza-Carrettos were able to return to Finale, but in 1566
the Genoese incited another insurrection. This time Maximilian
sent his own commissaries to Finale, but, as he had to have
them accompanied by a Spanish protecting guard, the final
result was, in April, 1571, the occupation of the principality by
the Spanish governor of Milan, the Duke of Albuquerque.
Maximilian protested, but at last, in October, 1573, he reached
an agreement with Philip, which affirmed the imperial authority over Finale, but placed the principality under Spanish
"protection."

PREACHERS, DIPLOMATS,
AND ASTROLOGERS

1

PHILIP's solicitude for the spiritual well-being of his cousin Maximilian had survived all differences of opinion and halfhearted compromises. After all, the King of Spain and the Emperor were both members of the Hapsburg family. And the age of growing absolutism did not throw overboard the family relations, an old and approved political instrument. "Bella gerant alii, tu felix Austria nube" ("Let others engage in wars, thou, happy Austria, shall resort to marriages"). The wisdom of this adage was certainly not lost to the Hapsburgs of the sixteenth century. The elder of Maximilian's two daughters, Anne, was expected to marry Philip's son, Carlos. The younger, Elizabeth, had been promised to Charles, the second son of the late King of France, Henry II. In 1564, when Maximilian became Emperor, the grooms as well as the brides were coming of age, and the fourteen-year-old Charles IX had already ascended the French throne. To Maximilian's great surprise, however, Philip came forward with the suggestion that Elizabeth marry the King of Portugal, Sebastian. Perhaps this idea of the Spanish king was just a reflection of his estrangement from the land with which he had concluded the peace of Cateau-Cambrésis and whose princess, Elizabeth of Valois, he had marrried. But other surprises were in store for Maximilian. Rumors began to spread about the ill health of Philip's heir, Carlos.

It seems that great hopes were connected in Philip's mind with the name of his only son from his first marriage. He did not speak of them publicly, as, later on, he refrained from speaking of the sad end which annihilated them. But the Count of Luna, years before, did not hesitate to mention, in connection with Carlos, the possibility of a future *monarquia del mundo* ("monarchy of the world"). And Ruy Gómez de Silva, the king's most trusted friend, told Dietrichstein, the imperial ambassador, as late as 1565, that if Carlos was to marry Maximilian's daughter, the Emperor would have to make him his heir and successor.

Such dreams were soon to come to an end. The first symptom of "something rotten" in the state of Carlos' health was the journey to Spain, undertaken in 1563 by Rudolf and Ernest, the two sons of the Emperor. Philip had invited them. His sister, the Empress, prevailed upon Maximilian, who tried in vain to push the invitation aside. Vratislav Pernštýn was elected to accompany them, but, because of certain obstacles, Adam Dietrichstein and Marc Antonio Spinola became their governors— Dietrichstein serving, at the same time, as the imperial envoy in Madrid. The two princes lived in Spain until 1571. The strict spirit of the Spanish court, which surrounded them at every step, inoculated them with all the ideas among which their uncle himself had lived and worked. In 1566, for instance, they were asked by their educators to write a Latin essay on the contemporary events in the Netherlands, "Pro pacificatione Belgica." In vain did the Czech nobles protest in 1565 and again in 1567 against such an education of the heir to the crown of St. Wenceslas; they said the prince should be educated in Bohemia and not in Spain.

Giovanni Micheli, the Venetian envoy to Philip's court, was the first to say openly that the journey of the two princes was principally due to the ill heatlh of Carlos and, consequently, to the possibility of a future reunion of all the Hapsburg dominions. In November, 1567, Philip wrote a frank letter to his cousin, telling him about the "dementia praecox" which excluded his unhappy son from marriage and also from any share in government. Ironically enough, Maximilian did not trust the words of this letter and for half a year pondered about the possible reasons which made his cousin eschew the mar-

riage of Carlos and Anne. At last he decided to send his younger
brother, the Archduke Charles, to Madrid to inquire. But before
the Archduke could set out, the news arrived, on September 10,
1568, that Carlos had died. The Archduke then went to Madrid
with another misson, which we have discussed in the preceding
chapter. However, since Philip's second wife, Elizabeth of
Valois, also died at almost the same time, he could, after all,
make a definite arrangement of the family affairs. Elizabeth,
the younger daughter of the Emperor, married her original
fiancé, the King of France, and Anne, the elder, was married to
Philip II himself.

Maximilian was thus cousin, brother-in-law, and now even
father-in-law of the King of Spain. But their mutual relations
were, as we have seen, far from friendly.

The melancholy skeptic on the imperial throne seemed to
live in a world of his own. In his dominions, he at first attempted
to continue the policy of his father in matters of religion. He
renewed the efforts aiming at the authorization of the marriage
of clergy. Philip riposted. In July, 1565, he sent Pedro de Avila
to Rome, protesting against Maximilian's petitions. Pius IV
wondered why Philip and Maximilian did not attack each other
directly and sent Archbishop Marini to the imperial court to
tell the Emperor about the Spanish opposition to his wishes.
Philip then assured Maximilian that they would discuss their
ideas on the occasion of his, Philip's, trip to the Netherlands
which was then planned. Maximilian replied, in his letter of
November 20, 1565, that no one could charge him with any
deviation from the Catholic doctrine and that the unity of
Christendom was his only goal. To Chantonnay he even
affirmed that the negotiations concerning the marriage of clergy
was just a heritage left to him by his father which he was merely trying to bring to an end.

At least one of Maximilian's affirmations was true. He favored
a united, but "simplified" Christian doctrine. He did not like
the new sectarianism. In Bohemia, for instance, his religious
policy adhered to the old privileges authorized by the Council

of Basel; he repeatedly refused to sanction there any innovations, introduced by the partisans of the new trends, Lutheranism and Calvinism. In Austria he promised, in August, 1568, to authorize the Confession of Augsburg. Then, under Spanish pressure and also under the influence of the attacking letters which Alba sent him from Maastricht, he revoked his promise. Finally, in January, 1571, at a time when he had some trumps in hand against the Spaniards—because of the illegal occupation of Finale by their troops—he granted the authorization.

When Chantonnay was replaced by the Count of Monteagudo and a new confessor, Juan Espinola, arrived at the request of the Empress, the religious life at the imperial court assumed a new intensity. The work started by Peter Canisius in the fifties and the early sixties was now continued by other enthusiastic Jesuits. Some of these Jesuits were Spaniards, such as Hurtado Perez or Fernando Jaén, who later became a prominent member of the theological school at Salamanca. Others at least preached in Spanish, as did Lorenzo Magio. The court became a center of Catholic reformation. But there was a solitary figure in its midst, whose thoughts could not be reached by any Spanish influence.

When Adam Dietrichstein was leaving Spain for good, Philip granted him a special audience, the purpose of which he then summed up in a letter dated April 6, 1573. It was for the first time, the letter asserted, that the King of Spain spoke of the sorrow caused him by his cousin's behavior in matters of religion. Now, however, he was not able to remain silent any more. On the contrary, to speak was his duty as a relative. No matter what impression he made on Maximilian, Philip must insist. Maximilian confessed to a married priest, he did not receive the Holy Communion in his recent illness, he did not go to Mass, he employed Protestants at his court, and he authorized the printing of bad books. Either he really believed in a false doctrine, or he had some false reasons for not professing openly what he believed in his heart. In the first case it was up to the theologians to discuss things with him. But if Maximilian's behavior was merely political tactics, Philip had to warn him that no man was allowed to resort to tactics in such a serious matter.

Dietrichstein, having returned to Prague, tried to help the Empress Maria and her Spanish friends, but in vain. He could only restrict the Emperor's influence upon his children, including the two boys who had been educated in Spain under Dietrichstein's supervision. Complete runination of the Emperor's family life was the result. And his resistance was even more embittered than before. When Dietrichstein gave the boys a book— Eder's *Inquisitiones evangelicae*—Maximilian took it away from them. When the Empress exhorted them to participate in a particular devotion, Maximilian made her suggestion ridiculous.

The imperial court, which had always been moving from one place to another, was now more frequently in Prague. The capital of Bohemia was a city whose very stones testified to a troubled past, full of clashing ideas concerning religion and its impact on the organization of human society. Nor was that past altogether dead. From the reports of the Count of Monteagudo—who was much more interested in the life which surrounded him than Luna or Chantonnay had ever been—Philip was pretty well informed about the state of things in Bohemia. He knew about the Catholics of the Roman rite, represented by Vratislav Pernštýn and Vilém Rožmberk; he knew about the numerous Catholics of the Czech rite—the Hussites, as they were sometimes called—led by Jan Valdštýn; he also knew about the growing number of Lutherans and about the Brethren, who were now attempting to establish contacts with Calvinist Geneva. "The Bohemian heretics," wrote Monteagudo in March, 1574, "have declared several times that they would welcome even Turkish domination, provided that they would thus be able to get rid of the Catholics." And it was Monteagudo who, at an audience with Maximilian, declared that it was the wish of the King of Spain that Bohemia should return to a full obedience to the Church. Perhaps he felt encouraged by a sarcastic remark of Maximilian, to the effect that the Czech nobles who were claiming an authorization of the Confession of Augsburg had never set their eyes on that Confession.

But sarcasm was merely a sort of escape for Maximilian. In 1575, at the Bohemian Diet, he found himself between two millstones. On the one hand, a number of Czech nobles—joined by an equal number of Germans who had only recently settled down in Bohemia—asked for an actual extension of the Peace of Augsburg into Bohemia. On the other hand, not only the Czech Catholics of both rites but also the nuncio, the Count of Monteagudo, and even the French envoy were strictly opposed to any such step. Through the president of his treasury, Richard Strein, Maximilian made it clear to the petitioners that his own power to decide was restricted by what he called "the circumstances of the outer world." A few days later he authorized them to elect a small committee, the so-called "defenders." But on September 3 he revoked even that concession. Spanish influence had prevailed.

It did not, however, prevail over Maximilian's personal opinions. As skeptical as ever, the Emperor entered the last year of his life. Far from the quiet study of his rigorous cousin, the King of Spain, far from the busy discussions of the hidalgos on the stairs of San Felipe el Real in Madrid, but near enough to the thriving activity concentrated around the new college which the Jesuits were building in Prague under the patronage of "Doña Maria," wife of Vratislav Pernštýn, the Emperor was awaiting, in full consciousness, his last moment. Up to the end he protested that he was dying as a Catholic Christian. But up to the very last moment, on October 13, 1576, he refused to receive the sacraments of the Church. *"Mi bendita hora,"* were his last words; "Blessed hour; at last the Lord will set me free."

At his funeral, the brotherhood of Spaniards living in Prague participated, solemnly, in the procession.

2

However joyous and tranquil Philip's private life might have been—and the kind, loving letters he used to write to his daughters depict it as such—his political way was a solitary one. In the management of the affairs of state only Ruy Gómez de Silva, the companion of his younger years to whom he had granted the title of Prince of Eboli, and, for a certain period, Bishop Granvelle, whom he had summoned to Spain and appointed a member of the Council of State, remained his close collaborators. The Duke of Alba lost his confidence and never fully regained it. All the high offices were gradually filled by men of the younger generations, whose awe of the King and his political principles was certainly great but who never became his privy counselors.

As ruler of Spain and its dominions, he was even more isolated. The Holy Roman Empire was the only worldly power upon whose loyalty he could have been expected to count; but the Empire, as we shall presently see, became even more of a problem after the death of Maximilian II than it had been before.

This isolation, symbolized by the building of the Escorial, completed in 1584, was in sharp contrast to the task which Philip had inherited from his father: the organization of the common defense of Europe. He certainly had not forgotten that task. The treaty of Cateau-Cambrésis of 1559, aiming at the re-establishment of a durable peace with France, the naval efforts which culminated in the victory at Lepanto in 1571, as well as Philip's persistent attempts to come to an understanding with Elizabeth of England—all these facts testify that the leading political ideas of Charles V, including his concept of western Europe as basis of the defensive operations, were very much alive in his son's mind. But during the sixties the main presuppositions of that policy had, one after another, disappeared. The struggle of the three parties in France—the Calvinists, the "Politiques," and the Catholics—and the lack of power of its three royal brothers, the revolt in the Netherlands, and Elizabeth's enmity were the main factors in Philip's isolation. And what was more important was the influence of these factors on the strategic disposition of Spanish might. Up to 1573—the year in which Tunis was taken, only to be lost again a short time afterward—Philip went on, as we have seen, with his defensive task in the Mediterranean. But after that year he was forced to turn his back on the Turks completely and to face the north and the Atlantic. And there, naturally, he stood alone.

This complete change of front coincided with the inauguration of the pontificate of Gregory XIII, a Pope who was much less interested in defense against the Moslems than in political and military action against the Protestants. But, although the new Pope, who did not rule long enough to see the crushing defeat of the Spanish fleet in the English Channel, would have liked to see Philip at the head of a Crusade against the north, Philip's political and military strategy was as personal as it was cautious. Even in this respect he remained faithful to his pre-reformational concept of the Church and its role in politics.

The story of Philip's defense against the north can be summed up in a very simple statement: What he had lost in the sixties he never recovered again.

That was true, above all, of the developments in the Low Countries. Neither the Duke of Alba, deprived of naval support as he was, nor Luis Requeséns, who replaced him in 1574, was able to win back the provinces of Holland and Zeeland. The badly paid Spanish troops started revolting after Requeséns' unexpected death and increased the chaos. Juan de Austria, whom Philip transferred to the Netherlands from the Mediterranean at the end of 1576, reached an agreement with the insurgents, but several months later lost his patience with them. A general upheaval started, in the midst of which Juan died. Succeeding him in the command, the equally young Alexander Farnese of Parma—son of Margaret, under whose governorship the troubles had started—demonstrated real military genius but was forced to employ his troops in France and died at Arras, in December, 1592. After several other minor attempts to solve the problem, Philip resorted to a final diplomatic step, of which he perhaps expected too much: on May

6, 1598, he conferred the sovereignty of the Low Countries upon his nephew, Archduke Albert—who had been acting as governor of the province since February, 1596—and upon his own eldest daughter, Isabella, who was to marry the Archduke. Even with this, however, he did not cure the division of the Low Countries and the apostasy of its northeastern half.

The account of Philip's relations to France is another tale of frustration. Far from evolving from the treaty of Cateau-Cambrésis, they originated from the embittered struggle of the religious factions inside France. This struggle did not cease with the massacre of St. Bartholomew's day in 1572 but led to the formation of the French Catholic League in 1576. The Guises, who led this organization, contacted the Spanish court through their envoys in the autumn of 1577. After 1584, their agreement with the King of Spain developed into formal alliance, which culminated not only in the employment of Spanish troops—mostly troops from the Netherlands—in the French civil war but also in Philip's unofficial candidature for the French throne. Such developments, however, came to an abrupt end in the military and diplomatic victory of Henry of Navarre, who, in 1593, was generally accepted as King of France under the name of Henry IV. If the peace of Cateau-Cambrésis in 1559 had been a risky affair, the treaty of Vervins, which Philip, four months before his death, concluded with this energetic Frenchman, was equal to a mere truce of arms.

As to England, there Philip's affairs went from bad to worse until the very end. When finally—after Queen Elizabeth had supported the insurgents in the Netherlands and had attacked the Spanish ships on the high seas for years—the King of Spain decided to strike, he found himself lacking commanders who had experience and genius enough to bring an attack on England to a successful end. The "Great Armada," assembled in 1588, was lost because its commander stuck to his main mission—the transportation of Parma's army from the Netherlands to England—and did not dare to take any other step, no matter how obvious. Two other fleets, which Philip built in the very last years of his life, were equally dispersed and wrecked. Elizabethan England remained unconquered and an enemy.

The firm hold, however, which Philip had upon the immense administrative and military machine he had created only grew with the march of years and contributed much to the almost legendary fame of Spain in the minds of average Europeans. Even the financial situation of Philip's government did not alarm anybody. After the second forced conversion of debts in 1575—in which the expenses of the war in the Netherlands had their share—there followed a third one in 1596, two years before Philip's death. The wealth of the Milanese and of the Kingdom of the Two Sicilies were almost exhausted; the revenues from the Netherlands—the wealthiest European region of the late Middle Ages—were lost; amazing amounts of money were exacted from relatively poor Castile; and yet the belief persisted that almost anything could be paid by the King of Spain. The supply of bullion from across the Atlantic, which kept increasing throughout the second half of the sixteenth century, was undoubtedly the main pillar of this hall of artificial renown. But that fabulous source was, of course, hopelessly entangled with the net of private business interests of international financiers.

In 1580, after he had intervened in French religious disturbances but before the attack against England, Philip added Portugal to his dominions. King Sebastian had been killed fighting against the Mohammedans of Morocco, and Philip, having overpowered the French navy which attempted to instal another member of the Braganza family on the Portuguese throne, united the Pyrenean peninsula into one solid block. In Portugal and Portuguese colonies he respected the constitution and kept up a separate administration—a policy which won Spain the allegiance of the Portuguese for the next sixty years.

In Aragon, on the contrary, at almost the same time, Philip cut sharply into the feudal order of that country. Because of its constitution, Aragon differed from Castile. The feudal privileges of its higher nobility were perhaps best expressed by the formula with which the "Justicia Mayor," a nobleman, sitting in an armchair, crowned the kneeling king: "We who are as good as you swear to you who are no better than we, to accept you as our king and sovereign lord, provided you accept all our liberties and laws; but if not, not." Profiting from a clash between the Aragonese nobles and the Holy Inquisition—a clash which arose from the flight of Philip's secretary, Antonio Pérez, to Zaragoza—Philip had condemned and executed several Aragonese noblemen. He restricted the constitutional right of the nobles to summons to the Cortes as well as their right to spend an indefinite time on statements of grievances. He also abolished the principle of necessary unanimity for the enactment of a bill and made some other small changes in the constitution of the province.

The developments in Aragon showed distinctly that even Philip, with all his legalism and moral principles of policy, was not immune to the centralizing tendencies in contemporary political thought. It is true that the *fueros* which he abolished in Aragon were personal privileges of a few noblemen rather than liberties of all the inhabitants. But, even when abrogated in the name of a moral principle, they made place for the personal will of one person only: the ruler. And the time was soon to come in which the personal will of the ruler would be the only criterion of political morality.

3

The man who replaced Maximilian II on the imperial throne and who was now expected to collaborate with Philip and help him throughout his futile campaign against the north was Rudolf, one of the two archdukes who, as boys, had come to Spain with Adam Dietrichstein to be educated. Among the pathological offshoots of the Hapsburg family—and there were not a few of them, owing to constant marriages of close relatives—he was one of the queerest. His life reminds us of a phrase used by Juan Mariana to characterize a famous ruler of

medieval Castile, Alfonso el Sabio: "Dumque coelum consi-
derat observatque astra terram amisit" ("Contemplating the sky
and observing the stars, he lost the earth"). Only Rudolf was
certainly not a *sabio*. His interest in the arts and in astrology
sprang from a sick mind, upon which even a Spanish education was soon lost.

It is well known what a center of quasi-cultural commerce
Prague became under this emperor. Doctor Dee and his no less
famous "seer" Kelly had an important say in imperial affairs,
and even men like Tycho de Brahe or Johann Kepler were
unable to replace astrology by astronomy. An immense gallery
of works of art was assembled in the castle of Hradčany, only
to be dispersed and lost in the Thirty Years' War; and the
adjacent zoölogical and botanical gardens were equally fostered
by the volatile mind of the lonely and gloomy Hapsburg monarch. And, last but not least, the attractive art of alchemy found
abundant support not only at the court itself but also among
many nobles influenced by the Emperor's example.

Formally, Rudolf led a life more satisfactory to Philip than
that which Maximilian had led. But the split between his views
and those of the Spanish king was equally wide, if not wider.
His indifference to subjects deemed of greatest importance by
others—a variation of Maximilian's skepticism—became apparent, first of all, in personal and family matters. Rudolf seems
to have inherited, against all expectations of his Spanish educators, his father's aversion to the patronizing attitude of the
King of Spain. Was that perhaps a result of the family con-
tentions of which he had been a witness in his younger years?
When his mother Maria, Philip's sister, announced her wish
to spend her widowhood in Spain in a monastery of the Carmelite nuns whose reform had just been achieved by the great
woman, Theresa of Avila, Rudolf refused to let her go. A diplomatic wrangle resulted between him and Philip, whose last
wife, Rudolf's sister Anne, died in 1580 and who would have
liked to have the widowed Empress near his own residence.

At last, in 1582, the Empress prevailed upon her son and,

with a large suite, moved to her native country. Her solemn recession was one of the rare occasions—rare because of the almost monachal *permansitas loci* of the successors of Charles V, particularly of the builder of the Escorial—on which the splendor of Hapsburg might dazzled for a while the eyes of the world. Even young Luigi Gonzaga, the future hero of the Jesuit order, joined the Empress' suite on her way through Italy. Two daughters of Vratislav Pernštýn were also among the persons accompanying the Empress. One of them, Luisa, later entered the Carmelite monastery in Madrid and, as Sor Luisa de Llagas, became its prioress. The other, Joanina, who had for years acted as secretary of the Empress, celebrated, when the party reached Zaragoza, her marriage with Fernando de Aragón, Duke of Villahermosa. A tragic marriage: ten years later, Fernando, one of the leaders of the Aragonese noblemen's resistance against King Philip, lost his life in prison, and when, in 1595, he was granted a "post mortem" revocation of the charge and a monument was built in Veruela to celebrate his memory, only the signature of his wife, "Joannina de Pernestán," reminded the reader of the inscription of that solemn wedding in La Seo, the cathedral of Zaragoza. But years afterward, in 1608, one of the daughters of the unhappy pair, Maria Luisa, married Carlos Borja, son of Juan Borja, the former Spanish ambassador in Prague who had also been present at the fated wedding, and the two young people, having received again the title of Duke and Duchess of Villahermosa, became models for the heroes of one of the most pleasant chapters of *Don Quijote;* their seat in Pedrola was transformed, in Cervantes' imagination, into the castle where the *ingenioso hidalgo,* to his greatest surprise, found the fulfilment of his dreams, and the small near-by town of Alcalá de Ebro became the place where Sancho Panza went through the bitter experiences of people charged with political power.

Personal tragedies as well as dreams, however, are able to change more than the destinies of a family. What influence will the dreamy, incomprehensible character of Rudolf II have on

the course of events in central and eastern Europe? Such was
the question which rang constantly in the ears of Spanish diplomats such as Juan Borja, whose name we have just mentioned.

When he was leaving Prague in the suite of the Empress
Maria, Juan Borja y Castro, second son of St. Francis Borja, had
already gained much experience in representing the King of
Spain at the court of his nephew. He had arrived in Prague in
1578 as successor of the Count of Monteagudo and of two
envoys extraordinary, Ramiro Nuñez de Guzmán and Carlos
de Aragón, Duke of Terranova. He was an accomplished diplomat and author, whose *Empressas morales,* a collection of
proverbs and maxims with symbolical illustrations, published
for the first time in Prague in 1581, was republished again and
again throughout the subsequent hundred and fifty years. He
was also a tireless observer. Being genuinely interested in the
European east, he even ordered the publication, at Frobenius
in Basel, of a small Latin-Spanish-Czech dictionary for the use
of the Spanish colony in Prague. But the Emperor's personality
was, of course, his chief concern from the very beginning. In
May, 1579, he had sent his first report to Madrid about Rudolf's
indecisiveness, his melancholy and distrustful character, his
fears which made him call for his valet twenty times in the
course of a single night and confined him to his rooms during
the day, and his lack of interest in anything except art, science,
and the game of handball.

Rudolf's silent gloom grew increasingly worse as the years
passed. Borja's successor in Prague, Guillén de St. Clemente y
Centellas, a Catalonian who had started his career in the Spanish navy, found it even more difficult to gain access to the
imperial palace. And yet the ignorance of the principles of
heredity was such in those days that the very first suggestion
made by Philip to Rudolf was to marry him to his daughter
Isabella. During the subsequent years no other subject was discussed in so many reports and letters as this project. And no
other project was so completely frustrated. Only a year before
Philip's death, after two decades of waiting, it was decided to

give Isabella to Rudolf's brother Albert—as a part of the scheme involving the "independence" of the Low Countries which we have mentioned. To alleviate his anxiety for the cohesion of the Hapsburg family, Philip then resolved to marry his lately born son—the future Philip III—to a daughter of Archduke Charles, Rudolf's uncle. This marriage was effected only after Philip II's death, but it made the new King of Spain brother-in-law of the future Emperor Ferdinand II, a fact which, in the course of time, was to have its own significance.

4

What help could the King of Spain obtain from the "younger" branch of his family, represented by the dreamy and obstinate Emperor?

In Italy, the imperial authority fared no better than under Maximilian II. The various small territorial matters, such as those of Finale, Piombino, or Val di Tarro, were all finally arranged according to Spanish plans and with little regard to the wishes of the Emperor. In vain did Rudolf confer Finale once more upon the Marquis of Carretto by a solemn declaration, published in 1577, which recounted the entire history of that small town from the year 1162 on. The Marquis was finally forced to sell his possession to the Spaniards, who wanted to build a new port there. Spanish preponderance in Italy was now an accomplished fact, and the Spaniards carefully guarded their interests there as well as those of their allies. The Gonzagas of Mantua, for instance, could seize Monferrat without respecting the rights of the French branch of their family. And Charles Emmanuel, Duke of Savoy, whose territory was of much strategic importance, married the younger daughter of the King of Spain, Catalina; the preceding negotiations, however, were kept secret because of Rudolf's jealousy.

As for France, there Spanish interventions met only with a scrupulous neutrality from the Emperor, who avoided all steps which could stir the political calm of Germany. Nor was the Emperor's influence of any use in Switzerland, where the Span-

ish sway was at grips with the French. Direct Spanish negotiations with the Swiss had to be initiated in 1590. But the new
developments in the Low Countires were followed with much
interest—if not by the Emperor himself, then at least by persons near to him. Johann Khevenhueller, the imperial ambassador, characterized the insurrection in the Netherlands in one
of his reports as a small wound on the body of a strong animal
which does not heal but gradually saps all the animal's stamina.

But even Khevenhueller was rather surprised when, on November 5, 1577, he received the visit of Zayas, King Philip's
secretary, who had come to tell him that one of the Emperor's
brothers, Archduke Matthias, had left his usual residence in
Vienna for the Netherlands, having been invited by the rebels
to take over the administration of the country. The Emperor,
said Zayas, had approved the step, and Matthias, on his way to
Brussels, had already arrived at Cologne. Wild rumors started
circulating in Madrid. Matthias, people said, was to marry
Elizabeth of England and send a Protestant expeditionary force
to Poland, whose throne he wanted to occupy.

Rudolf's behavior on this occasion was typically like that of
his father. Almost a year later, in May, 1578, he admitted to
Juan Borja that he had discusssed everything with Matthias the
afternoon before his departure and that he had known that
some of the rebels, being dissatisfied with Juan de Austria, had
invited him to come to the Low Countires. But in the autumn
of 1577 he acted as if his brother had simply disappeared. Such
at least was the tenor of the letters which he sent out on October 4, the day after his brother's departure. Perhaps he was not
quite sure of the sincerity of his astrological advisers this time.
And astrology, as years passed, was becoming more important
to him than any legal or ideological instruction. In Madrid,
the Count of Monteagudo, former ambassador to the imperial
throne, now bearing the title of the Marquis of Almazán, called
the Emperor a liar. Ramiro Nuñez de Guzmán, an envoy
extraordinary who at that time was visiting the German
princes and persuading them to help Juan de Austria, received

new instructions: to oppose any diplomatic moves which Matthias or the Emperor might make in favor of the insurgents.

Philip himself shared the opinion of Bishop Granvelle—now in Madrid and member of the Council of State—that Matthias' action was a "boyish affair." At that time he had already approved of Juan de Austria's decision to use arms again and was sending him a large auxiliary force under Alexander of Parma. Among the counselors of the Spanish King there were—if we are to believe Khevenhueller, always anxious to please the Emperor—several who were inclined to accept Matthias as mediator. Among them was Antonio Pérez, the most influential of Philip's secretaries, who had his own contacts with the Netherlands nobles; soon afterward, on Easter Monday, 1578, he was to murder Escobedo, an envoy of Juan de Austria and thus to start his career of traitor and vilifier of King Philip. But after the victory of the combined forces of Juan de Austria and Alexander of Parma over the rebels at Gembloux, on January 31, 1578, opinion in Madrid turned wholeheartedly against the Archduke.

The Emperor, lacking probably any firm policy which he would be able to apply to the Low Countries, did not dare to intercede in Matthias' favor. Matthias himself tried to explain to the German princes—by letters as well as by personal envoys —that everything he had done had been done *aus deutschem Gemüt* ("from German conscience"). But all in vain, in spite of the important, but solitary, military action, taken at that time in favor of the insurgents by John Casimir of the Palatinate. Consequently, Rudolf refused to recognize Matthias as governor of the Low Countries and asked him, through a special envoy, Otto Schwarzenburg, not to receive any such office from the Netherlands nobles. After the death of Juan de Austria, in October, 1578, when Philip appointed Alexander of Parma as his successor as governor and when that talented soldier succeeded in dividing the Netherlands Catholics from their Protestant compatriots, Matthias was able to see for himself the fiasco of his self-imposed mission. After months of passive

waiting he left the Netherlands, at the end of 1581, as secretly
as he had arrived there.

And yet the Emperor's own point of view had not changed.
It seemed as if his Spanish education had been forgotten. He
was, of course, well informed about Philip's strict judgment,
which, under the influence of Granvelle, was only hardening
as months and years passed by. Juan Borja had explained to
him that Juan de Austria had the firm backing of his king.
In the autumn of 1578, a new Spanish envoy extraordinary, the
Duke of Terranova, arrived, and, although Rudolf succeeded in
directing him first to Cologne to attend a meeting with some
noblemen from the Low Countries, he had to receive him at last,
in February, 1579, in Prague. He learned from him that the insurgents would be treated as criminals. Answering him, he stated
very firmly that the Low Countries still belonged legally to the
Empire and that he, as Emperor, was competent to pronounce
the judgment in any controversy between King Philip and his
nobles.

Combined with his inactivity, such utterances of the Emperor made him a source of uncertainty which was not without
influence upon the decisions made in the Escorial. The more
anxious the King of Spain was to destroy Huguenot power in
France and the more frequently he used, on French soil, the
forces which should have been used in the Low Countries, the
greater were the fears of his counselors and diplomats that
neither the Emperor's authority nor his good will would be
sufficient to block an alliance between the Protestant nobles of
Germany, France, and the Netherlands. In 1581, Parma's troops
crossed the frontier of the Empire into the territory of the Free
Imperial City of Aachen to support its Catholic town council
against the Protestant part of its inhabitants. In 1582, when
Gebhard Truchses, Archbishop of Cologne, embraced the Lutheran movement, the Spanish troops from the Low Countries
came speedily to help his successor, a relative of the Duke of
Bavaria, to regain the territory of the archbishopric, although

the Bavarian ruling family was not on very good terms with Rudolf and his brothers. In 1586 the reports sent by Guillén de St. Clemente from the imperial court became so nervous and mentioned England so frequently that it is perhaps not an exaggeration to see in them one of the factors that influenced Philip's decision to send the Great Armada. From 1589 onwards, the small principality of Jülich-Cleve, whose Catholic duke had no sons but only sisters married to Protestant princes, was also frequently mentioned by St. Clemente.

Two ineffective diplomatic actions concluded the story of the mutual relations between Philip, Rudolf, and the insurgents of the Low Countires. In 1591, on the suggestion of a north German Protestant nobleman named Rhedt, an imperial mission was sent to Brussels to negotiate between victorious Parma and the rebels. Not to arouse any suspicions in Madrid, Rudolf appointed as its members Jan Pernštýn, Vratislav's son, who sometimes signed himself as Juan de Lara and was more Spanish than Czech, and Luis de Hoyos, whose father had come to Prague with Ferdinand I. Naturally, the semi-Spanish character of the mission was almost a guaranty of its failure. Then, in 1594, after Philip had appointed Archduke Ernest governor of the Low Countries, without having informed the Emperor about it, Maximilian Dietrichstein, son of Adam, was sent to Madrid by the Emperor to elaborate a point on which Rudolf and Ernest agreed, namely, that Philip should make peace with the new King of France, Henry IV. Even this step had no immediate results.

When Ernest died, in February, 1595, the debts in which he had involved himself in Brussels turned out to be another bone of contention; neither the King of Spain nor the Holy Roman Emperor wanted to pay them.

The plan which Philip thought final—the bestowal of the Low Countries upon the Archduke Albert and his wife Isabella—had been conceived and elaborated without the Emperor's help. Albert was perhaps the only one of Maximilian II's sons whose strict allegiance to the Spanish cause could not be doubted. In addition, he had been tried in Portugal and had satisfied the lord of the Escorial completely.

5

The same Empire which seemed to be a burden and an obstacle to Spanish policy in the west was still the gateway to the east—that east with which, in spite of the victory at Lepanto, there was so little contact on the Mediterranean. That the east was an immense and varied area had been known to the Spaniards for ages. But to contact it directly was—if we discount the sea route to India and the Far East—very difficult. In fact, the European east and the Near East seemed to be more distant from western Europe than the fairy island of Ceylon.

The Turkish Empire blocked the way. The walls of its fortresses closed the view. Only very little was known of the Persia of Shah Abbas or of the Abyssinia which the Portuguese sailors identified with the almost mythical "Country of Priest John" of the medieval legends. Since 1571, however, the Turks had slowly evolved into a "dormant danger." One felt more free on the Mediterranean, but no efforts were made to change the victory of Lepanto into the starting point of an offensive. On the contrary—as we have already observed—persuaded by Salomon Ashkenazi, an influential representative of the Jewish merchant community of Constantinople, Venice dropped out of the Holy League. Tunis and La Goletta were lost again by the Spaniards in the late summer of 1574, and, in the subsequent months, an evacuation of Oran and Mers el Kébir almost occurred. The attempts to win the Empire for the League had ceased with the unlucky mission of Pedro Fajardo in 1572. Spanish naval activities on the Mediterranean diminished so much in the subsequent years that in 1581 the Spanish bishops asked the King why they were expected to continue paying their contributions to the Turkish war if no such war existed.

The frontier in Hungary and on the Dalmatian coast, however, saw little peace. There, even after an agreement between the Turks and Maximilian II had been reached in 1574, local warfare had never been quite extinguished. Not only the regular Turkish army but also other forces were active in those regions. The Uskoks on the Dalmatian coast, recruited mainly from refugees from the territories occupied by the Turks, had no more respect for the imperial authority than they had for the Venetian Signoria. And all along great parts of the military line which divided Hungary, the Hayduks had established their nests of territorial piracy. A new large fortress, Karlovac on the Kulpa, had to be erected in 1578, and others, such as Györ, Komárno, and Nitra, followed. During the 1580's, nevertheless, there was some hope that the Turks would not be able to renew their pressure in the near future because of their difficulties in Asia and in northern Africa among the Berbers and also because of the exhaustion of their state treasury.

In the meantime the attention of the two Hapsburg courts was turned to another eastern state, to Poland. The last Jagielon on the throne of this vast country, in which Poles as well as Lithuanians, White Russians, and Ukrainians had found abode, Sigismund II August, died in 1572. Acting quickly upon the news, in September of the same year, Philip suggested to Maximilian II the sending of a special envoy to Poland with the task of persuading the Polish nobility to accept Archduke Ernest, Maximilian's son, as their new king. Either the Count of Monteagudo, Philip's ambassador at the imperial court, or Pedro Fajardo, the envoy extraordinary, whose presence in Prague at that time we have already mentioned, was to assume that mission. Maximilian did not show much enthusiasm about the project. Perhaps his sensitive mind had been influenced by the unhappy marriage of his sister Elizabeth to the late Polish king. Perhaps he was more of a realist than Philip and took into consideration the aversion of the Polish nobility to those absolutist inclinations for which the Hapsburgs had already become noted. In any case, when he had finally accepted the Spanish proposal, he chose, as his own representative to accompany Pedro Fajardo to Poland, Vilém Rožmberk, an ambitious Czech nobleman, who was more inclined to grind his own ax and in private talks warned the Poles not to trust the Hapsburgs. Henry of Valois, the youngest of the three sons of the French queen, Catherine de Medici, was then elected King of Poland —not without the support, it is interesting to note, of the Turks.

Two years later Henry decided to return to France, where his brother, the King, had died. He left Poland to its fate. In 1575—in spite of the secret efforts of Rožmberk, who this time proposed his own candidature—a part of the Polish nobles elected the Emperor Maximilian II himself. But the majority favored Stephen Bátory of Transylvania, and the conflict could have been solved only by a war. Monteagudo was all in favor of military action. The Emperor, however, preferred negotiations, which ended, naturally, with his death.

Ten years afterward, in 1586, when Stephen Bátory died, the Spaniards came forward once again with their suggestion. Not only St. Clemente but also Philip's ambassador in Rome, the Count of Olivares, were instructed to support the candidacy of a Hapsburg prince. As neither Rudolf II nor his brother Ernest, the candidate of 1572, showed any desire to figure as candidates for the Polish throne, the choice fell this time on Archduke Maximilian, another of Rudolf's brothers. Complying with the Spanish wish, the Emperor sent Stanislas Pavlovský, Bishop of Olomouc, to Poland. St. Clemente went there almost immediately afterward in the role of envoy plenipotentiary of the King of Spain. Their intervention, however, proved a failure. Only a minority voted in the Archduke's favor. The majority, led by Jan Zamojski, elected a Swede, Sigismund Vasa, who thus became Sigismund III of Poland. But that did not abate St. Clemente's enthusiasm. He urged the Archduke to invade Poland and wrote optimistic reports to King Philip, depicting, in particular, the nobles of Moravia as ready to support the Archduke's cause with their lives. Philip granted Maximilian a large subsidy—about 200,000 florins—and general expectations in the Escorial seemed to ignore the result of the Polish election.

But as soon as Maximilian was defeated at Cracow and, in 1588, for the second time at Byczina and was made prisoner of war, it was Spanish diplomacy again which came hurriedly with the advice to stop all hostilities with Poland. In a session of the Spanish Council of State, two of its members, Christobal Mora and Juan Idiaquez, asked an immediate revocation of the subsidy which had been granted to Maximilian. A special envoy, Vespasiano Gonzaga, Duke of Sabioneda, was sent to Prague to intercede for a quick peace. However, Spanish recognition of the new Polish king was postponed for a while—to save face. Perhaps no other instance than this sudden change of strategy gives us better insight into the uncertain character of Spanish eastern policy. The west—even the rebellious west of Elizabeth of England and of mutinous France—was still the axis.

The same principle prevailed in commercial contacts, as can be seen from the attempts to regulate the east-west trade in corn. Among the raw materials and goods which were imported to Spain in the sixteenth century—such as textiles, wood, copper, brass, and linen—corn was one of the most important.

It was repaid through export of vine and oil but, above all, by silver. Some of the corn came from Sicily, but great quantities were imported from Poland through the Hanseatic towns and through the Low Countries. Indeed, so large was this transfer that Rudolf II had to ask repeatedly—and without much success—for Spanish authorization to import corn from Sicily; he needed it for southern Germany and Austria, provinces which were not able to compete in Poland with the Hanseatic merchants and were too far away from the northern sea route.

Thus even in the importation of corn the Spaniards were dependent upon the European west. And, in spite of all the bitter fighting in the Low Countries, the merchant ships of the insurgents were continuing their trips to Spain and back again. Alexander of Parma asked the King to stop such an "infamous trade," as he called it. But that—as Khevenhueller promptly

remarked—would have been like making bills without having
been able to sell anything. Twice, in 1585 and again in 1598,
Netherlands ships were confiscated in all the Spanish and Portuguese ports. But both times they had to be released again
almost immediately afterward.

In May, 1582, a belated report came to Madrid from the Spanish ambassador in London, Mendoza, about the mission of Richard Chancellor to Moscow. It contained the suggestion that a
Spanish mission should be sent to Moscow via Prague to counteract the English success. Shortly afterward a Spanish cleric by the
name of Pedro Cornejo presented himself to St. Clemente in
Prague with another plan: the Spanish should buy the corn directly in the Polish ports of Gdańsk and Kralowiec, thus obtaining necessary food supplies and, at the same time, undermining
the economy of the rebellious Netherlands. The ambassador
received this suggestion with mistrust, not only because he had
his doubts about Cornejo's character but primarily because the
idea of governmental competition with private trade was rather
strange to him and his contemporaries. Had not the Austrian
Hapsburgs attempted several times, during the preceding decades, to take into their own hands the Spanish import of copper
from northern Hungary (Slovakia) and of quicksilver from
Istria? And did they not, in both cases, have to leave it to the
Herwarts and other private firms which were able to do it in
a cheaper way and to whom the King of Spain was bound to be
grateful because of this or that financial service?

Consequently, on St. Clemente's suggestion, a special agent,
Cornelius de Grootesvall, was sent by King Philip to Hamburg
and Lübeck, and another agent went to Gdańsk, both with the
mission of persuading the Hanseatic merchants not to sell the
corn they had bought in Poland in the Low Countries but to
ship it directly to Portugal and Spain. But the Hanseatic ships
were not armed. And very few unarmed ships would have been
able to escape the English pirates, always ready to hit an ally of
Spain. Even when a breach of peace transpired between Hansa
and England, so that the Spaniards could persuade the Hanse-

atic merchants to take the risk, the Spanish navy proved unable to protect their vessels. In such circumstances even a few solemn letters dispatched by Philip II to Fedor Ivanovich, the last of the Rurikids, to dissuade him from any commercial contacts with England, could not change the course of events. Nor could a new mission to Poland, undertaken in 1597 by Luis Enriquez de Cabrera, Duke of Rioseco, persuade the Poles to cut their commercial ties with the Low Countries. The northwest of Europe was rapidly rising to material preponderance, and Spain just could not do anything against it.

6

The northwest was also attempting, in the early 1590's, to provoke another conflict between Spain and Turkey. Since 1589, rumors had been spreading to the effect that the Turks were getting ready for another attack against Europe. English and French envoys in Constantinople expressed hopes that it would be a naval onslaught on Spain.

Perhaps it would have come to that, had it not been for the rather daring exploits of the defenders of the Hungarian frontier. A clash with the Turkish governor of Bosnia, in 1593, at Sisak on the Kulpa, sufficed to change the uneasy peace, which the Emperor had to pay for by an annual tribute, into another war.

Naturally enough, attempts were resumed at once to make the King of Spain interested in the developments in Hungary. Khevenhueller, who went so far as to send his own agent to Morocco to investigate the possibility of a revival of hostilities in Africa, got the support of two papal legates, dispatched to Madrid one after another in a period of only a few months: Camillo Borghese and Giovanni Francesco Aldobrandini. Also St. Clemente at Prague did his best to help the imperial cause, depicting the will to resist in Hungary and in Bohemia in terms which were more optimistic than true.

But all that the Emperor obtained, this time, from the Spanish King was financial support. In the spring of 1594 he was granted a subsidy of 300,000 florins' worth of silver from the next American cargo fleet. It is interesting to note that, although expert in financial transactions—let us remember his share in the building of the mint at Segovia in 1580–85—Khevenhueller found it difficult to transfer the subsidy. No financier was willing or able to pay so much cash in central Europe at such short notice. The ambassador had to wait until the arrival of the fleet from America, in May, 1595, and then to ship the bullion to Genoa and thence to Tyrol, where it was coined into Austrian money.

Spanish help arrived, however, at a most critical time. The green flag of the Prophet had been sent from Damascus to Hungary in 1595, and the Sultan himself arrived the next year to win the three-day battle at Keresztés over the imperial troops, commanded by Archduke Maximilian. The Emperor lacked allies, too. Venice, fearing the Hapsburg might in Naples as well as in Trieste, preferred to follow Ragusa (Dubrovnik), the other, smaller city-republic on the Adriatic, in the skilful game of neutrality. As for Poland, it was rather desperate to hope for help from there after all the differences which had resulted from the past elections of Polish kings. Sigismund III, a man of deep religious conscience, was not the main obstacle. The Polish nobles—Jan Zamojski in particular—were against any participation in the war; their line of policy was supported in Constantinople by French and English diplomats. The Emperor's appeals to the Dnieper Cossacks were futile. Even the combined influence of Pope Clement VIII and King Philip, who sent to Poland, in 1596, Francisco de Mendoza—"Almirante de Aragón," as he usually signed himself—were of little significance.

The only military aid came from the three Romanian principalities, Moldavia, Walachia, and Transylvania, which had been under Turkish dominance. Michael the Brave, Voievod of Walachia, started a particularly bloody uprising against the Moslems. Even the weak and indecisive Sigismund Bátory of Transylvania, protector of the Spanish Jesuit preacher, Alfonso Carillo—who was received by Philip, in 1596, at Toledo, in a special audience—joined his forces with those of the Emperor, thus risking the future of his throne.

It was to Sigismund Bátory that Philip, exceptionally, sent some few soldiers from Sicily. It was the war in Hungary also, which—together with a new attack against England—occupied his mind when his last days approached in the late summer of 1598.

The final weeks of Philip's life were, as is well known, an extremely sorrowful trial.

> Treinta agujeros tenía;
> por poco que le tocasen
> muy grande dolor sentía ... ,

people sang in a ballad composed after his death. Somewhere in the large palace of El Escorial, which he had built and where he had come to die, hung the picture on which El Greco had depicted him kneeling among the saints, but very close to the abyss of eternal damnation. The symbolism which El Greco had in mind was certainly of a religious nature. But was there not another, political, allegory in it, too? All Philip's political thought, since the very beginning of his political career, had been arranged around the central idea of the traditional order. To defend that order had been recommended to him by his late father. Having accepted that task in all earnestness, he had tried his best to fulfil it. It was not his fault that he had conceived the traditional order in a rather static way and did not understand its dynamic forces, the Catholic reformation perhaps even less than the enthusiasm of the Protestant reformers. But he certainly understood one thing: that Europe was in no less danger of Turkish imperialism now when he himself was dying than it had been forty years before. Should he dispatch a large expeditionary force from southern Italy across the Adriatic and strike at the heart of the Balkans? Such, at least, was one of the strategic plans to which he attended in the last days before his final illness. But, with that, the carefully calculated and largely unsuccessful stratagems of his life were exhausted.

ANOTHER EMPIRE?

1

THE King of Spain was dead. For half a century men had been accustomed to obeying his orders, admiring his glory, or hating him. Now he was no longer there, in his sober room in the Escorial. The vacuum which is felt at the death of every personality undoubtedly presented itself this time also. And those who concentrate on the study of rulers and their actions are certainly entitled to speak of Philip III—who was now twenty years old but whose health was poor and who was the exact opposite of his father as far as interest in the affairs of state is concerned—as of the first king to personify the dawning degeneration of Spanish might.

Not the King himself but his prime ministers, the *validos,* were now to become the actual chiefs of the Spanish empire. First among these was Francisco Gómez de Sandoval y Rojas, a grandson of St. Francis Borja. As Marquis of Denia, this man became the real ruler of Spain at the moment of Philip II's death. And under his new title, Duke of Lerma, he was to continue in his post, to advance the members of his family, and to enrich himself until October, 1618, when, only three years before the death of his King, he was replaced by his own son, the Duke of Uceda. The Spanish court at Madrid and at Valladolid no longer displayed the gravity of an administrational center governed by the most scrupulous ruler of the world but rather the joyous colors of a wealthy and powerful capital.

And yet, persuing the development of the relations between Spain and the Empire and Spanish foreign policy in general, we do not find much difference between the epoch of Philip II and that of Philip III. On the contrary, we are inclined to characterize the latter as the climax of the former.

174

There was no major change in Spanish policy under the Duke of Lerma. The idea of a western bloc, as it had been formulated by Charles V and pursued by his son, remained the leading principle. The peace with Henry IV of France, which had been concluded shortly before the death of Philip II, was ratified and preserved, even through the period of Henry's mounting ambition which preceded his unexpected death in 1610. As for England, another naval attack against it—as unsuccessful as the preceding ones—was prepared in 1601. Another followed in 1602, this time in connection with an uprising in Ireland. But then the death of Queen Elizabeth and the ascent of the compromising James Stuart to the English throne in 1603 solved this problem in such a way that a peace could be concluded in August, 1604, and Diego Sarmiento de Acuña, Count of Gondomar, was later able to resume, as Spanish ambassador in London, the old policy of permanent friendship with England.

At the same time, the seemingly interminable war in the Netherlands, which had been dragging on since 1572, finally ended in a truce of twelve years, signed at Antwerp in April, 1609. That this truce was not altogether humiliating for Spain was, however, due not so much to Archduke Albert and his wife Isabella, of whom Philip II had expected great things in the Netherlands, as to the military capabilities of a wealthy Milanese nobleman, Ambrosio Spinola, who had offered his services to Philip III and protected a number of important towns, including Ostende, from the insurgents.

As a whole—the new forced conversion of loans ordered by Philip III in 1607 notwithstanding—all these events seemed to the contemporaries, if not a victory, then at least a manifest proof of Spain's greatness. Philip II's fame, in some aspects, could be called legendary, but all the same it was real enough to become a political factor of the first order. The fabulous wealth of the Spanish territories overseas still seemed an infallible guaranty of permanent power. And the irresponsible character of many of the favorites of Philip III in financial matters, together with the sumptuous life of the Spanish court, even stressed Spanish glory.

In fact, Spanish fame seemed to exist almost apart from the realities of Spanish policy. And the spirit of national pride, visible in many a Spanish document of the epoch, was based rather on fame than on realities. We can see it, for instance, in the Spanish attitude toward the war, which was renewed in Hungary in 1593 and was concluded by the peace of Zsitva-Torok in 1606. In spite of the fact that the treaty of Zsitva-Torok was the first by which Turkey recognized a European power as being of a status equal to her own, it was not much of a success. The Turks had not availed themselves of the victory at Keresztés in 1596, because of their own difficult situation and not because of any strong resistance of the imperial troops. In addition to the obvious incapability of Sultan Mohammed III himself, troubles were arising everywhere for the Turkish Empire— in North Africa as well as in the Tatar khanates and on the Persian frontier. In Hungary the war dragged on, starting anew every spring and ceasing altogether in the autumn. Both sides lacked soldiers; the Turks resorted even to the transportation into Hungary of Tatar cavalry from beyond the Black Sea. Important towns, such as Esztergom, changed hands. In 1604 Stephen Bocskay, a nobleman from Transylvania, where Sigismund Bátory had proved of little help to the Emperor, went over to the Turks and, having proclaimed himself King of Hungary, granted freedom to the Protestant denominations. The peace of Zsitva-Torok left the military frontier almost unchanged. And, although Bocskay made a separate agreement with Archduke Matthias, who represented the Emperor in Hungary at the close of the war, his decree of toleration had to be renewed by the Archduke.

The Spaniards, St. Clemente in particular, were much dissatisfied with this course of events. But a curious disparity between their words and their deeds was becoming more and more apparent. With the exception of an expedition against Algiers, which failed altogether, and a diplomatic mission to Persia in

1602, which enhanced that power's enmity toward the Ottoman Empire, they had not taken any major step to help the Emperor in this last war. Their financial subsidies did not amount to much, and Johann Khevenhueller had to remind them constantly that the Bohemian treasury, from which the war had been largely financed, was exhausted. In his reports to the Emperor he even asserted that the Duke of Lerma had moved the Spanish court from Madrid to Valladolid just to stop the influence which the Empress-Widow Maria had on Philip III and which she used to remind him of his duty to help the Emperor against the Turks.

But, on the other hand, powerful anti-Turkish enthusiasm was spreading from Spain into other European countries in an unprecedented manner. In Spain itself, this resulted in the expulsion of all Moriscos in 1609. In France it inspired the "Grand Design" of Sully and also a brotherhood, founded by Charles Gonzague, Duke of Nevers. Jesuits and Capuchins echoed it all over Europe, as if another crusade was to be organized almost immediately. Nothing, of course, came out of all this. Three-quarters of a century were to pass before another blow could be directed against Turkish domination in the Balkans, but then the motives of the action were of a very different nature.

2

A factor which helped enormously to spread the glory of Spain at the turn of the sixteenth and the seventeenth centuries was the rapidly growing popularity of the absolutist system.

The absolutist tendencies of the kings, which had their roots in the medieval history of Europe, were by no means simple fruits of personal ambitions. There were not a few reasons which had made them generally acceptable and even popular. To those reasons the religious quarrels and conflicts of the sixteenth century added a new one. The number of people living in countries torn by religious strife who wished for a power which would be able to re-establish internal peace was constantly increasing. After all, was there not in absolutist centralization an attractive solution of all the internal difficulties of every community and every state?

The gradual rise of absolutist ideas in the political thought of the sixteenth century was also due to a cause which can be compared to the disinclination of the citizens of modern Switzerland to take part in a "referendum" or of the citizens of many a modern country to participate in a jury. Many nobles and burgesses regarded their participation in the sessions of Parliament as onerous and too expensive a duty. Had not the Castilian Cortes asked, as early as 1544, not to be assembled more often than once in three years "on account of the great cost and expense"?

When all that is taken into consideration, it is obvious that the system of administration created by Philip II had an attractive force which was still growing, even long after its author had closed his tired eyes. It tempted those who opposed the Protestant movement and were impatient for a solution, despairing of the powers of persuasion and doubting the possibility of a peaceful coexistence of two or more concepts of Christianity in one state. It lured those who, satiated with religious disputes and even more with religious warring, wanted peace and order. It attracted also the ambitious. There was, in the Spanish system, a number of promising careers for noblemen who, a century or two before, would have had their aspirations satisfied in organizing a seditious faction or similar outlet.

In a word, Spanish might, although its development was practically halted, continued to grow as a legend and an example—an attractive example, too. As such, it was viewed also by the people in Central Europe and led them to decisions which were to prove of tragic consequences.

3

The final descent of Spain from the pedestal of a great power started at the very end of the reign of Philip III with the outbreak of the Thirty Years' War. But the twenty years between the death of Philip II and the defenestration of Prague were to witness the culmination of Spanish influence, which we have just described. And perhaps nowhere was this development as remarkable as in Bohemia, the country where the war was to begin. In no other country was the contact between the Spanish sphere and that of its opponents so direct. In the Low Countries the military frontier functioned as a kind of barrier. In Ger- many the frontiers between the Protestant and the Catholic principalities were almost fixed, and the German Catholic princes, under the pressure of the nationalist trend in public opinion, more or less avoided any Spanish influence. But in the Kingdom of Bohemia, an ancient, but always rather independ- ent, member of the Holy Roman Empire, the two spheres of influence permeated each other.

On the one hand, ever since the twenties of the sixteenth century, the Lutheran reformation had been finding its way to the heart of the country. Its progress was not a simple process of ideological propaganda. It was much more than that. Wherever a Lutheran preacher had been appointed or a school given to a Lutheran teacher, the German language—the idiom of Luther's famous translation of the Bible—prevailed over the Czech idiom. All Silesia was thus Germanized, as well as many fron- tier districts of Bohemia proper and Moravia. German nobles were streaming into the country and settling down on its rich soil. Their political weight became greater and greater. In 1561 two German immigrants, Franz Thurn and Caspar Fels, were received by the Bohemian Diet among the inhabitants of the kingdom. In June, 1565, we find these same men among the noble members of the Diet; both their families were to play a prominent role in the history of the subsequent years.

On the other hand, the very presence of the Spanish ambassa- dor in Prague and the constant contacts between Spain and the imperial court were sufficient to give strong support to the Czech Catholics, both of the Roman and of the Czech rite, whose numbers had been diminishing, and to rally them into a group whose hopes were concentrated on Spain. St. Clemente was perhaps the best man that the Spanish king could have chosen for such a post. Of Catalonian origin, less proud and with more practical interests than the average Castilian nobleman, he was as accessible to the Czechs as he was to his own people, and he soon became an expert in the public life of the Kingdom of Bohemia. Not that he liked to live there too much: the older and the more ailing he was, the more he wanted to return to Spain and spend the rest of his days there. But Providence had another fate in store for him. He was to die in Prague and be buried in the Augustinian Church of St. Thomas, which he had helped to rebuild along the lines of contemporary Spanish style and in which he had constructed a tomb for Spanish citizens adorned with the following inscription:

> Salve Calcator Huius Marmoris
> Don Gullielmus de Sto Clemente
> Regis Catholici in Germania Legatus
> Eiusdem Regis Subditis
> In Sepulturam Perpetuam
> Hoc Conditorium Exstruxit
> Anno Christi MDXCVII
> Quisquis Legis Hic SS.B.P.
> Ave Maria.

Vratislav Pernštýn, the companion of the youthful years of Maximilian II, was the actual founder of the "Spanish group" in Prague. When he died in 1582, aboard a ship on the Danube near the city of Linz, his family was already connected by so many ties with Spain that his death was regretted in Madrid as that of a Spanish *grande*. With his daughters married in all parts of the Spanish empire and his sons serving in the Low Countries under Parma and elsewhere, he was considered "more of a Spaniard than a Czech," as one of the Spanish diplomats remarked. His wife, Doña Maria, was one of the first supporters of the Jesuit college in Prague—the oldest after Ingolstadt in Central Europe. But his political influence was inherited by one of his daughters, Polyxena—a very charming woman, if we are to believe her contemporaries, witty and learned, who may be compared to Francisca, daughter of the famous Spanish humanist, Antonio de Lebrija, to Lucia Medrano, Juana de Contreras, and other prominent Spanish women of her own or the preceding generation. She married Vilém Rožmberk, head of one of the wealthiest houses in Europe and a politician whose ambition we have mentioned when dealing with the Hapsburg interests in Poland. Vilém Rožmberk and Leonhard Harrach, an Austrian nobleman, were among the first members of the Order of the Golden Fleece nominated by Philip II after the original, oligarchical constitution of that order had been abolished.

When Rožmberk died, ten years after his father-in-law, the leadership of the pro-Spanish group in Bohemia and also the hand of Polyxena went—after another ten years, in 1603—to Zdeněk Vojtěch Lobkovic, a nobleman whose allegiance to the Spanish cause was unquestionable. Born in 1568, he went to see Italy and Spain before his twenty-first year and was received by Philip II in the Escorial. For the second time he saw the great monarch in 1595, when he had come to his court as envoy extraordinary of the Emperor to ask new pecuniary aid against the Turks, the sending of an auxiliary force from the Low Countries to Hungary, and the authorization of the import of corn from Sicily into Austria via Trieste. He had also been instructed to discuss the possibility of a Hapsburg alliance with Persia and Abyssinia. Thus, on this occasion, the entire international panorama of contemporary Europe was opened to him. Observing the difficulties which Philip II had in granting him what he had asked, he certainly was able to judge for himself how real the might of the Spaniards was. And yet in 1598, the year of Philip's death, we see him again in Spain. Such was the attraction which the unity and fame of that country exercised on a citizen of the spiritually and politically divided Kingdom of Bohemia.

Not only Catholics but others as well came under its sway. Karel Žerotín, perhaps the most prominent of the noble members of the Bohemian Brethren, a man of great experience, who had spent quite a time fighting in the army of Henry of

Navarre—later Henry IV—in France, was as enthusiastic about the political excellence of Spain as he was contemptuous about divided France. Remaining all the time a faithful member of his small religious community, he was in close contact with the "Spanish group" of Doña Polyxena. In a leter to Vilém Slavata, a former coreligionist of his who had recently become a Catholic, he recommended him to go to Spain to gather experience and not to France, "a disordered country and still in chaos because of the recent disturbances."

Another old friend of Spain, Adam Dietrichstein, having returned from his diplomatic mission in Madrid, settled down —although he was of Austrian origin—in Mikulov in southern Moravia and thus became a subject of the Bohemian crown. His four daughters married in Spain and two of his sons served in the Spanish army in the Netherlands; a third, Francis, born in Madrid and educated in Rome, became, in 1598, Bishop of Olomouc, the ecclesiastical center of Moravia. Even he was to become a pillar of Spanish influence.

Living among all these men and women who were true admirers of his country, St. Clemente was undoubtedly conscious of their importance from the point of view of Spanish international policy. High above his own residence in Prague— which stood in the vicinity of St. Thomas' church, on a site where, a quarter of a century later, the wary Valdštýn was to build his resplendent palace—in the cathedral of St. Vitus where gentlemen used to gather for the Mass in Spanish *capas* and *gorgueras,* as the contemporary fashion ordered them, there were painted on the side walls the emblems of Castile, Aragon, Leon, and Granada, reminding the citizens of the kingdom that their king was not only Holy Roman Emperor but also "Infans Hispaniae," member of the Hapsburg family and cousin of the powerful King of Spain.

But the Emperor himself was a man who could be trusted less and less as years went by. His lack of firm policy, the astrologers who surrounded him, his strange favorites, such as Wolfgang Rumpf and Lang, the valet who did not allow other people, even ambassadors, to see him—all that made St. Clemente think of one important question: Who will be the Emperor's successor? But as it was now evident that the Emperor's real authority was anchored in Bohemia and, in a lesser degree, in Austria and in the remaining strip of Hungary, the question was rather: Who will be the next King of Bohemia? Hence the importance of the Czechs in the eyes of the Spanish diplomat.

St. Clemente observed carefully the situation in Bohemia and registered every small development. The Bohemian silver mines as well as the regulations of the traffic on the river Elbe, but, above all, the ideological trends among the Bohemian nobles, interested him more than anything else. He knew that the Czech Hispanophile nobles were only a minority. Every year more and more Catholics of the Czech rite were joining the Lutheran church, in spite of the fact that the Jesuits in Prague and in Olomouc, profiting from the papal privilege obtained by Ferdinand I, administered Holy Communion under both species. Even many Bohemian Brethren sought friends among the Lutherans and Calvinists in Germany. And what was perhaps the most difficult problem for him was the question of the extent to which the Kingdom of Bohemia had already been changed into an absolutist state. Was the office of the kings of Bohemia an elective or a hereditary one? With Germany divided into two or possibly three camps of different religions, the future of the Holy Roman Empire depended entirely on the future of the Kingdom of Bohemia. If that kingdom could be held united, there was some hope that even the Empire itself could be held united. And, of course, if Bohemia remained in Hapsburg hands, the Empire would continue to be the eastern bulwark of the Spanish sphere.

The problem was even more complicated by the fact that, should Rudolf die, Archduke Matthias, his brother, would become his legal heir. Of the sons of Maximilian II, there remained now, after the death of Ernest, only four: Rudolf, Matthias, Albert, and Maximilian. Besides, there were also the

children of Charles, brother of Maximilian II, who had administered the Austrian province of Styria. But Matthias was in
some discredit because of his adventure in the Netherlands, and
there was a certain rivalry between him and his brother Maximilian. The latter, whose attempts to reach the Polish throne
we have discussed, had recently achieved some fame as commander of the imperial troops in Hungary and was making no
secret of his ambitions. His agent, a certain Westernack, was
canvassing the German princes. The Spaniards evidently would
have preferred Archduke Albert, whom Philip II had selected
for the "independent" Netherlands, to all his brothers. But to
support Albert and to deny the hereditary right of Matthias
would have meant to accept the thesis that Bohemia was an
elective kingdom and to place its future in the uncertain hands
of its nobility. Neither St. Clemente nor Lobkovic and his
friends saw any advantage in such an action.

4

In 1599, Lobkovic was appointed Chancellor of the Kingdom
of Bohemia. The *corona regni Bohemiae* was actually a loose
confederation in which Moravia and Silesia as well as Lusatia
had their own diets and their own laws. The Chancellor was
the only royal official common to all the provinces of the
crown. The appointment of Lobkovic to an office for which
there were prominent Protestant candidates meant a significant
victory for the Catholic, pro-Spanish group—*la facíon española,*
as St. Clemente called it.

Spinelli, the papal nuncio at the imperial court, had done
his best to help Lobkovic to the appointment. There had been
some doubts whether the Emperor would take such a step. The
older Rudolf became and the greater his seclusion, the less
understanding he had of the Catholic reformation. He criticized the Jesuits because of their alleged greediness, and he also
had several conflicts with the Order of the Knights of Malta,
whose Bohemian priorate was one of the most famous and best
endowed. As far as the religious legislation of the Kingdom
of Bohemia was concerned, it had required the utmost vigilance

of St. Clemente as well as of the nuncios active in Prague at the close of the sixteenth century to keep the Emperor from granting the Protestant nobles freedoms similar to those which they had obtained in France from Henry IV.

Lobkovic, taking charge of the Bohemian chancery, was thus assuming a post of outstanding importance. He was expected to face with energy and decision not only the attempts of the Protestants to legalize their doctrines but also the skepticism and growing irresponsibility of the Emperor. He had the full backing of the Spanish ambassador as well as of the nuncio. He decided not to make the slightest concession to the Protestants. And he went so far as to refuse to countersign—in 1601—an imperial decree expelling from Prague the Capuchin monks who had got into some trouble with Tycho de Brahe, the Emperor's astronomer. But all that would have been of little moment had his own ideas not been concentrated on a policy which, eleven years later, in a manifesto of the Protestant nobles of Bohemia, was called a "profound change of regime, directed against the old order."

In the castle of Roudnice on the Elbe, the building of which was accomplished by Lobkovic in the years following the battle on the White Mountain, we may find even today traces of the spiritual trends which molded the political thought of the Chancellor. The family archives preserve numerous letters which he and his wife constantly received from their Spanish relatives and friends. In the gallery and in the private rooms the walls are adorned with pictures by Antonis Mor, Alonso Sánchez Coello, Juan Pantoja de la Cruz, Andrés López Polanco, and other famous artists of contemporary Spain and of the Low Countries. But what interests us most is the library. There, bound in a way which almost always makes it easy for us to name the first proprietors, stand volumes of political, philosophical, and religious works as well as of fiction, frequently annotated by the hands of their sixteenth- and seventeenth century readers, including, in many cases, the hand of Zdeněk Vojtěch Lobkovic himself.

Various polemical treatises of Czech and foreign Catholic

writers and reformers had found their place on the shelves of
the Roudnice library, in close proximity to one of the first
editions of *Don Quijote,* whose sheer humor had reduced the
problem of good and evil to the presence—or absence—of love
in the human heart. Machiavelli's *Il Principe*—although condemned by Church authorities as early as 1559—is represented
by several editions, published in the time from 1540 up to the
first decade of the seventeenth century. His Italian admirers—
Guazzi, Sansovino, Guicciardini, and Paruta—are also there.
But so are his critics. The anonymous *Commentarii de regno,*
written probably by a Catholic Frenchman toward the close of
the sixteenth century; the rather naïve *De imperio virtutis* by
the Roman Oratorian, Thomas Bozio; and, above all, the *Tratado de la religión y virtudes que debe tener el principe christiano* by Pedro Ribadaneira. This last work—which Lobkovic
had not only in a Spanish edition, published in Antwerp in
1597, but also in a Latin and an Italian version—contained the
quintessence of Christian criticism of the famous Florentine.
Although he was an accomplished humanist and used profuse
quotations from various Greek and Latin authors, Ribadaneira
was able to discover Machiavelli's main mistake in his uncriti-
cal admiration of Cornelius Tacitus as well as of other pagan
authorities and to confront him with the Christian concept of
society, based on the natural and divine law.

The political situation, however, had changed considerably
since the time of Charles V, when Machiavelli wrote his famous work. The main problem of the time was not whether a
moral code should or should not be the veritable foundation
of every state, but which moral code should be that foundation.
Even the polemic of Fabio Albergati against Jean Bodin's
positivism, although published, under the title of *Discorsi po-
litici* only in 1603, was no more timely.

Ribadaneira, for instance, defining the difference between
a legal ruler and a tyrant as the difference between a monarch
who obeys the moral code and a monarch who does not, did
not hesitate to add that moral and religious principles should

permeate the social life to such and extent that the coexistence of people of different religions in one state would be impossible. Justus Lipsius, on the other hand, a German convert to Catholicism, whose *Politicorum libri, De constantia, Monita politica, Dissertatiuncula apud principes,* and other works Lobkovic evidently cherished, was of a different opinion: as long as there is peace in a country, he affirmed, the government should not interfere with the religious persuasions of the citizens.

Perhaps the Chancellor and his friends hesitated, not knowing which of these conflicting theories to choose. Perhaps, had they to decide between theories only, they would not have chosen the more radical one. But for them the whole problem was an immensely real one. On the shelves of the Roudnice library there were copies of Beza's *De iure magistratuum in subditos* as well as of the famous *Vindiciae contra tyrannos,* whose doctrines were closely connected with the Calvinist practice in France and in the Low Countries. And the Bohemian nobles who read these books lived in an atmosphere which gave little hope of a peaceful solution of the conflict between the different religious ideologies.

Did they know William Barclay's *De regno et regali potestate,* which—published in 1600—offered a theory of political power which differed completely from those of the Catholic as well as of the Protestant "tyranomachs"? They probably did, although in Roudnice we would find only later editions of Barclay's works. But the doctrine of pure absolutism which Barclay preached and which James I of England was to embrace and to defend in his dispute with Cardinal Bellarmin was hardly practical in Bohemia in the years preceding the Thirty Years' War. It could be practiced in England, where the Established Church had already in the past decades achieved a monopoly. It was, however, of no value in a Continental country whose citizens were sharply divided in their religious opinions. There, only two kinds of developments were possible: either an ideological pacification resulting in a common practice of religious tolerance or a religious kind of absolutism. The first being highly improbable, one had to decide for the second solution. Such was the idea which Lobkovic expressed in his own hand on the cover of one of the books discussing religious tolerance—*De autonomia,* by Franz Burghard—where he wrote: "Omni studio, universisque machinamentis, ferro ac igne abscindere a corpore morbum, a vita luxum, ab animo ignorantiam, domo discordiam, civitati seditionem oportet."

And yet it must have been known, through all those years, to the Czech Hispanophiles that the aims of Spanish religious absolutism were by no means identical with the wishes of the Church. When the new edition of the Roman breviary left out the legends concerned with the arrival of St. James the Apostle in Spain, the Spaniards protested. When, in 1604, one of their own clergymen, Diego de Torres, reported to Rome the scandalous way in which the Indians in South America were treated by the colonists, Spanish national feeling was offended. Such cases were discussed all over Europe, but none of them was given as much publicity as the dispute between the Spanish politicians and historians, on one hand, and the Italian historiographer Cesare Baronio on the other. In the new volume of his *Annales* which Baronio published in 1605, he criticized the prerogatives in ecclesiastical matters which the Spanish kings affirmed they had in Sicily. A veritable storm of indignation was the answer. In some places the works of the learned Italian Oratorian were publicly burned by Spanish officials. The same thing, and worse, happened to a Jesuit priest, a Spaniard this time, Juan Mariana, who, in his *Tractatus septem,* dared to criticize the monetary policy of Philip III—the constant deterioration of the material from which Spanish coins were minted. Mariana was imprisoned by the Holy Inquisition and his book confiscated. Although Baltasar Zúñiga, St. Clemente's successor at the imperial court, assured his king by a special report, dated March 6, 1610, that he had "collected" and burned all the copies of the incriminated work which he was able to find in Prague and elsewhere, one copy of it remained in Lobkovic's library.

The glorious cloth of Spanish fame was evidently not without its threadbare spots.

But perhaps the yearning for peace and order and the attractiveness of absolutist rule were stronger than any criticism. That could be the only reason why even the cheap answers to Baronio's *Annales,* based more on indignation than on scholarship, found their way into the Roudnice library. One of them, perhaps the most nationalistic of all, written by Juan de la Puente, a Dominican monk, and bearing the title of *La Conveniencia de las dos Monarquias Católicas,* compared the Spanish monarchy to the Church itself. The Spanish empire was, according to the argument of the author, also one, holy, catholic, and apostolic and therefore preordained to govern the world politically, as the Church was to govern it spiritually.

Of course, not all the Spanish political literature of the early seventeenth century was of the same quality. Some of the authors, such as Diego de Rojas, were approaching a concept of absolutism which Hobbes would have readily signed. Others, such as Juan de Santa Maria, a Franciscan friar, characterized the office of a king as an *imago fictilis et contrita* and, refusing democracy as a system opened too much to human ambitions, tried to revive the medieval concept of the moral order as superior to the will of the ruler. Still others, like Juan de Salazar and also the famous Campanella, a Spanish subject from Naples, engaged in fantastic plans, nearer to the "utopias" than to a real political theory. But all of them—in contrast to the preachers of "tyrannicide" of the preceding century—stressed the legitimacy of the Spanish kings. And legitimacy was an idea around which many worries of the supporters of an absolutist order in Bohemia and all throughout the Empire were to be concentrated in the coming years.

5

The problem of the succession in Bohemia and in the Empire was getting more and more urgent. In the autumn of 1600 the Emperor's health improved, but not for long. A year afterward,

Cardinal Dietrichstein, who had come to Rome to discuss the situation of the Church in Moravia, told the Duke of Sessa, Spanish ambassador to the Holy See, that King Philip III would have to make a grave decision. There was, in his opinion, a choice between only two possibilities. Either a candidate for the Bohemian, as well as for the imperial, throne was to be found at once among the members of the Austrian branch of the Hapsburg family, or the King of Spain would have to accept the candidature himself.

Thus, half a century after the resignation of Charles V, the idea of a personal union between Spain and the Empire was revived once again. Actually, it had never died in the minds of the Spanish statemen. The Count of Luna, at the time of his mission to Vienna in the early sixties, used to speak of a future "monarquia del mundo" ("a monarchy of the world"), thinking, of course, of Philip II's unhappy son Carlos. The same suggestion—as we have already reported—was once made to Adam Dietrichstein, the Cardinal's father, by Ruy Gómez de Silva. At the height of the French crisis, in the spring of 1593, when it was still uncertain whether Henry of Navarre or Philip II—supported by the French League—would predominate in France, the Duke of Feria, Philip's ambassador in Paris, came forward with a different plan: he wanted the French to elect Archduke Ernest as King of France; the Archduke, he said, could then marry Philip's elder daughter and become the ruler of the Empire as well as of France—and perhaps also of Spain if the ailing youth, Philip's son by his last marriage, the boy who later was to become Philip III, did not live long. At almost the same time, Pope Clement VIII—Hippolito Aldobrandini, who knew central Europe and also Spain very well—advised the King of Spain to secure the imperial dignity for his son.

According to the opinion of Cardinal Dietrichstein, the first of the two alternatives which he had suggested to the Duke of Sessa would lead to the candidature of the young Ferdinand of Styria, son of the late Archduke Charles and cousin of Rudolf II. Philip III, having been born of his father's last wife, who was Rudolf's sister, was a nephew of the Emperor and therefore a closer relative of his than Ferdinand of Styria was. Only one of the Emperor's three brothers who were still alive, Matthias, Albert, and Maximilian, would have a better right to succeed the Emperor than the King of Spain. Of the three, however, Albert was in Brussels and the candidacy of Matthias or Maximilian was not sympathetic to the Spaniards—for reasons which we have already mentioned.

The main difficulty, however, consisted in the undeniable right of the Czech nobility to a free election of their king. This fact remained in the center of discussions throughout the following years. The Spanish Council of State deliberated upon it in 1603 when discussing the general situation in the Empire. An anonymous memorandum, preserved in the Dietrichstein family archives, mentioned it but added that, as George Podiebrad, the famous King of Bohemia of the fifteenth century, had prepared his election by concentrating the military power in his hands, St. Clemente should also assemble, first of all, an army composed entirely of Czechs and then take care of the election of a candidate acceptable to the King of Spain.

But the Spanish ambassador was wiser than that. He knew well that not even all the Catholic noblemen in Bohemia were favorable to the Hapsburgs and that some of them would rather see a Czech or a Pole on the throne of St. Wenceslas. He also knew that the new policy, inaugurated by Lobkovic, had not been, so far, a great success. The decree issued under his influence by the Emperor in September, 1602, aiming at the protection of the Catholics of both Roman and Czech rite and at the suppression of all Protestant propaganda, was not respected. In addition, St. Clemente preferred not to do anything against the Emperor's will. In 1603 he attempted, with the help of the Archbishop of Mayence, to persuade him to co-operate in the election of his successor. Only in 1605, despairing of such attempts—the melancholy Emperor was by now almost intractable—did he make some allowance for suggestions such as that contained in the Dietrichstein memorandum.

In the meantime, Archduke Matthias, who had a clever adviser in the person of Melchior Khlesl, Bishop of Vienna, was able to show that Spanish mistrust would not stop him from having a say in the solution of the current problems. In April, 1605, he made an agreement with his brother Maximilian as well as with two of the young Archdukes of Styria, Ferdinand and Maximilian Ernest. Together, they all went to Prague and obtained from Rudolf the appointment of Matthias as new commander-in-chief in Hungary, where the war with the Turks was still dragging on and where, also, the insurrection led by Bocskay threatened to estrange the country completely from the Hapsburgs.

What followed was a rapid series of events in which the role of Spanish diplomacy did not show particular brilliance. Another meeting of the Archdukes in Vienna, in April, 1606, appointed Matthias head of the family—on the ground of Rudolf's mental illness—and declared him candidate for Rudolf's successor. The Spanish Council of State, informed about it, decided to drop the old grievances and to support Matthias. But almost at the same time, on June 23, 1606, Matthias, ignoring, for once, the advice of Bishop Khlesl, and with the help of a Hungarian nobleman, Stephen Illesházi, settled matters in Hungary by granting the Hungarian nobility not only administrative concessions but also freedom of the Protestant denominations. To that, not only the Spaniards but also the young Archdukes of Styria—whose sister Margaret had been married, since 1559, to King Philip III—reacted unfavorably. Even the peace of Zsitva-Torok, concluded in November, by which Matthias ended the long Turkish war, was not appreciated by them. On the contrary, as we have already seen, they criticized it as a sign of diplomatic weakness and insufficient statesmanship.

Also Rudolf, his personal pride hurt, now turned against Matthias and approached closer to the Styria branch. St. Clemente readily renewed his attempts to gain the Emperor's co-operation, and his hopes now concentrated on Archduke Leopold, the youngest brother of Archduke Ferdinand of

Styria, who, although not yet a priest, had become administrator of the bishopric of Passau and seemed now to have gained the Emperor's confidence.

Matthias, nevertheless, persevered in his course. During 1607 he entered into closer contact with a free association of noblemen who favored the grant of full freedom to the Protestants in all the Danubian countries; they were led by Stephen Illesházi in Hungary, Erasmus Tschernembl in Austria, and Karel Žerotín in Moravia. In January, 1608, he concluded an open alliance with them—with the aim of obtaining a ratification of the peace with Turkey and also of the religious settlement in Hungary; but at the same time he sent a diplomatic agent, Alexander Ridolfi, to Rome and to Madrid to defend his policy. In March, the Emperor, feeling his own weakness, started negotiating with him, through Cardinal Dietrichstein, who had tried to mediate between the two brothers as early as 1606. St. Clemente was rather surprised. He still could not imagine that the Emperor would be able to ratify the settlement in Hungary. He was even more surprised when Dietrichstein's efforts failed, and Matthias openly demanded Rudolf's resignation.

The events then started following rapidly in succession. Rudolf offered his brother the administration of Hungary. Matthias declared such an offer insufficient and, at the head of his army, entered Moravia. The Spanish ambassador, aged and ailing, decided to go and talk to him personally. But, before he was able to do so, Matthias was already in eastern Bohemia, in the town of Čáslav. There he was contacted by Pedro Montañana, St. Clemente's secretary, but nothing was accomplished at their meeting. Nor had St. Clemente himself any success when he finally contacted the Archduke in Kolín on the Elbe, a town even nearer to Prague than Čáslav.

At that juncture it looked as if the Kingdom of Bohemia as well as Austria and Hungary would be lost by the Emperor. Rudolf thought of seeking an abode somewhere in Germany, and St. Clemente was ready to follow him.

It did not come to that. The Protestant noblemen in Bohemia, now under the dominant influence of the German immigrés, did not look favorably on Matthias' successorship. They also resented the independent behavior of the Moravians, who were, after all, dependent on the Kingdom of Bohemia. They therefore sided with the Emperor. And when Rudolf promised them in May to consider, at the next diet, the grant of freedom in Bohemia to the Lutheran Church, the restriction of the authority of the Catholic Church in lawsuits concerning matrimony, the restriction of the activity of the Jesuits, and the appointment of Protestants to the leading posts in the administration of the Kingdom, they unanimously refused Matthias' demand to accept him as Rudolf's legal successor.

Protracted negotiations at Libeň near Prague followed, at which Montañana represented the ailing ambassador. Their result—the official cession of Hungary, Austria, and Moravia to Matthias and Rudolf's promise not to object to his being accepted as his successor in Bohemia, Silesia, and Lusatia also—could not now be reported by Guillén de St. Clemente to Madrid. The ambassador was sinking fast. He died in August, a few days after the arrival of his successor, Baltasar Zúñiga. Two men were standing at his bedside in his last moments: Zúñiga, the diplomat, and Baltasar Marradas y Pallas, a soldier in the Emperor's service, a native of Valencia and relative of the dying ambassador. Both these men were to play prominent roles in the dramatic events of the following years. In a way, they symbolized Spain's two strategic tools: diplomacy and the army. The army, however, was to prevail and to bring about the final failure.

6

Baltasar Zúñiga was a younger son of the fourth Count of Monterey, the Montereys being an old and prominent Salamantine family. As a young soldier he participated in the tragic expedition known as the "Great Armada" of 1588. Later, he served in the civil administration of Milan and then joined the diplomatic service, becoming adviser of Archduke Albert. As such he also participated in the negotiations with England, first at Boulogne sur Mer in 1600 and later, in 1603, in London. In this last year he was appointed Spanish ambassador to France and stayed in Paris for five years, observing cautiously the growing strength and energy of Henry IV. He was well acquainted, undoubtedly, with the activities of the Marchioness of Verneuil and the other spies which the clever Duke of Lerma maintained in France. Through them and from other sources he knew about the ever strengthening contacts between Henry and the Calvinist German princes. It was partially because of this qualification of his that he was transferred, in the eventful year of 1608, to Prague, to take care not only of the rapidly evolving situation in Bohemia but also of current events in Germany.

Indeed, if there was a feature which distinguished Zúñiga's diplomatic activity in Prague from that of his predecessor, it was his interest in the Empire as a whole. St. Clemente certainly did not neglect it, but his interest had been more and more absorbed by Bohemian events. Zúñiga's view of imperial policy was that of a man who had spent many years in the Low Countries and in France and therefore apprehended the German problems of the Empire as well as the Danubian ones. Even his wife, born De Clarehout, was a Belgian, and his secretary, Jacques Bruneau, came from Ghent.

The circle of friends of Spain in Prague remained basically unchanged. Zdeněk Vojtěch Lobkovic and his wife, Polyxena, Cardinal Dietrichstein, his young nephew Sigismund Dietrichstein—whom Zúñiga took into his own house and had educated in a way which made him *muy españolizado*—Vilém Slavata, Zdeněk Novohradský, who had married a Spanish gentlewoman, Eleonora de Rojas, and other noblemen were closest to the ambassador. Some new men were added, such as Karel Liechtenstein, who, like Slavata, had been converted to Catholicism from the creed of the Bohemian Brethren. The attraction exerted by Spain on central European nobility kept growing. Václav Budovec, a Czech nobleman who at that time was turning more and more toward the German immigrés, had to write long letters to persuade his younger compatriots not to travel to Spain and rather to avoid that "source of contamination."

Zúñiga had been instructed to keep two irons in the fire. On the one hand, he had to try to win Rudolf for a peaceful solution of the succession problem. On the other hand, he was to assure Matthias of Spain's support of his candidature. But, above all, he was to keep his eyes on Germany, where the Protestant Union, supported by Henry IV of France, had been established in May, 1608, while Archduke Matthias was proceeding toward Prague. Spanish policy in Germany, formulated and periodically adjusted in the sessions of the Council of State, would rather have avoided any split between the German princes. Especially the idea of a Catholic League, opposed to the Protestant Union, found little echo in Madrid. The Duke of Lerma—as far as he was interested in Germany at all—favored a dynastic policy. The Duke of Bavaria, who had suggested the formation of the League, was considered a dangerous competitor of the Hapsburgs. Therefore, his ideas were rejected, and an absolutist policy was preached to the Emperor as the only solution of his troubles.

During the preceding years, when Donauwörth, a small imperial town north of Augsburg, had already become a center of religious disturbances, St. Clemente's response—in spite of all the other troubles in which the Emperor was involved—was to send there a detachment of imperial troops. And when Rudolf, lacking the troops as well as the time to consider the affair properly, commissioned Maximilian of Bavaria to take care of the town, St. Clemente was dissatisfied.

The actual situation of the Emperor, however, was all but prepared for any absolutist move in Germany or elsewhere. Zúñiga was able to realize that almost immediately after his arrival in Prague. He also began to doubt the wisdom of the Spanish decision to promise support to Matthias. He could not shut his ears to the criticism of Matthias which he heard from many Catholics in Bohemia as well as in Germany. And gradually he accepted the opinion of his late predecessor, according to which not Matthias but Archduke Leopold would be the best man to succeed Rudolf.

But the Duke of Lerma still favored Matthias, in spite of the fact that in November, 1608, he had had to grant his agent Ridolfi a large allowance because the Archduke was not able to collect taxes in the provinces which he now administered. Restrained by this policy, Zúñiga refused to participate in the diplomatic move undertaken, in December, 1608, by the Emperor and by Leopold, who both asked Matthias to return Moravia and Austria. He merely watched the developments and was ready, as St. Clemente had been a few months before, to follow the Emperor into Germany in the event of an open conflict.

In the spring of 1609, nevertheless, relative calm spread through the Empire. The truce of twelve years, concluded in the Low Countries between Philip III and the insurgents, had a quieting effect. Zúñiga profited from the occasion to travel and to see people. He visited Styria and went to Passau to see Archduke Leopold. In Innsbruck he paid a visit to the old Archduke Maximilian. In Munich, in the absence of the Duke, he met his son, Maximilian Junior, and also the French Duke of Nevers, whose Catholic fervor and interest in international policy had brought him to Germany. Zúñiga's journey resulted in a certain modification of his ideas. He still indorsed Lerma's view about the disadvantage of a Catholic League in Germany; his motive for doing so was, of course, rather the insufficiency of the Catholic forces than the fear of Bavaria's ambitions. But he mitigated his negative attitude toward Matthias. Above all, he was now persuaded that there was really no hope for Rudolf in seeking abode in Germany.

Since his return to Prague, Zúñiga found it almost impossible to visit the Emperor and to discuss things with him. Rudolf's mental state was getting worse with each new day. And the Protestant nobles of Bohemia were now determined to use their numerical superiority. The Diet of Bohemia met in January, 1609, was dissolved by the Emperor in April, and met again at the end of May. At last, on July 9, the noblemen elicited from the Emperor the so-called "Letter of Majesty," according to which freedom was granted in Bohemia to the supporters of the "Bohemian Confession." The Bohemian Confession had been composed in 1575 by the Lutherans as well as by some of the Bohemian Brethren in an atmosphere of mutual mistrust between the supporters of the two denominations. The Letter of Majesty authorized the building of Protestant churches and schools by noblemen, knights, and cities on proper or royal domains. According to the constitution of the Kingdom of Bohemia, it never became a law because Lobkovic, the Chancellor, refused to countersign it. But, once in the hands of the Protestants, it became an important document.

Almost in the last moment before he signed the Letter, Rudolf sent Archduke Leopold to Zúñiga, to ask the ambassador for military protection. Zúñiga replied that he would have to hear such a demand from the Emperor personally. It may be doubted whether he was frank in giving this answer to Leopold. Probably he was well aware of his own lack of power. Only in the Capuchin monastery behind the Prague castle, where the Czech Catholic nobles met from time to time, did he dare to proclaim that "the Protestants will forget all their intentions and decisions as soon as they see a fire in the distance." But who would set that fire was yet to be decided.

7

Persuaded by the capability for action shown by the Bohemian Protestants and also by the arrival in Prague of Christian Anhalt—a German prince who had always been considered a close friend of the French Huguenots and of Henry IV—Zúñiga now revised even his opinions concerning the foundation of a Catholic League in Germany. In collaboration with the papal nuncio in Prague, he dispatched to Madrid an enthusiastic Capuchin priest, Lawrence Brindisi, the future saint, with the mission to explain the situation in the Empire to King Philip and to ask him to help the League if it came into existence. But perhaps the inspired words of the great preacher were unnecessary. The hopeless situation of the Emperor and the very possibility that the Kingdom of Bohemia would follow the Low Countries in their revolutionary way proved sufficient to change the course of Spanish policy. Before Brindisi's arrival in Madrid, in August, 1609, Philip III had decided to assemble a large force in Naples and in the Milanese, so that he would be able to dispatch it at once to Central Europe in case of need.

Thus, three-quarters of a century after it had come into Spanish hands, the ancient Kingdom of Bohemia was becoming the center of the last tragic chapter in the story of Spanish preponderance. Attracted by its romantic name and perhaps also by the news which, at that time, frequently mentioned it in connection with Spain, a country of seafarers, William Shakespeare located it, in his *Winter's Tale,* on the seacoast. And Baltasar Zúñiga, meditating in Prague upon the possibility of Rudolf's total desertion to the Protestants—a development quite conceivable in connection with a possible new attack by Matthias, supported by Spain—decided this time to take a course completely opposed to that which he as well as St. Clemente, his predecessor, had been envisaging only a short time before. If the Emperor, he wrote to King Philip, takes the side of the Protestants and perhaps even accepts a successor chosen by them, the Catholics may lose the office of the Holy Roman Emperor; but even in that case it will be much more important to hold Bohemia than to hold the imperial title.

And in Brussels Ambrosio Spinola, the soldier who had done so much to save Spanish prestige in the Low Countries, declared quite openly that Philip III should remind the world that his mother was a sister of the Emperor and declare himself Rudolf's heir and successor in Bohemia. Was the empire of Charles V, after all those years, to be revived?

THE BARTERED KINGDOM

1

THE year 1609, in which the discord between Rudolf II and his brother Matthias had reached its climax, assumed the character of a milestone in the story of Spanish preponderance in Europe. Of the two important decisions which then took place—that of Philip III to take certain military precautions in Italy and that of Baltasar Zúñiga to help the formation of a Catholic League in Germany—the second was the more momentous one. Whereas the policy of the King of Spain and his counselors was of a circumspect, tentative nature, the ambassador had now a very definite object: to defend the Kingdom of Bohemia, which he recognized as the pivotal point of the Holy Roman Empire. He did not know in what legal way Bohemia would be governed. He was not sure whether it would remain in the hands of the Austrian Hapsburgs or whether it would be better to include it among the Spanish possessions. But he knew that he was not going to lose it—and, in fact, he clung to this idea until, ten years later, a terrible war resulted from it. He wanted to organize the Catholic League in Germany in order to save Bohemia.

In Madrid, the Council of State still spoke rather in terms of a dynastic policy than in those of geography. Its main problem was the appointment of a commander-in-chief of the League; King Philip should support it only if a member of the Hapsburg family became its leader. But this wish naturally conflicted with the ambition of Duke Maximilian of Bavaria, who was not ready to participate in an association conceived merely to serve the absolutist aims of the Hapsburgs.

The negotiations were complicated by the young Archduke Leopold, who in the summer of 1609, almost immediately after the Emperor's capitulation to the Protestant nobles of Bohemia, embarked upon a daring military adventure by occupying, with a small army of no particular discipline, the small principality of Jülich in northwestern Germany. The Duke of Jülich-Cleve, who was a Catholic, had died in the spring, and his Protestant relatives were quick to seize his territories and to apply to them the famous principle "Cuius regio eius religio." Leopold in his enthusiasm wanted to make the Catholic League act before it was even created. He had the Emperor's authorization, and his agent at the imperial court, an astronomer named Tengnagel, furnished Rudolf with optimistic reports which Zúñiga and Ottavio Visconti, Archduke Albert's envoy, had to deny. For months during the winter of 1609–10 and in the following spring, the danger of an immediate clash between the Catholics and the Protestants was hovering over Germany. Strassburg, whose bishopric was also administered by Leopold, was invaded by its Protestant neighbors, and Henry IV of France showed increased interest in the situation, which offered him a good pretext for interference. Zúñiga wrote desperate letters to Madrid, asking for instant military help. But the men around Philip III were not even willing to promise a definite number of soldiers. Instead, they quarreled with the Pope, who, anxious to achieve a compromise between the Hapsburgs and the Duke of Bavaria, had suggested intrusting the papal general, Mario Farnese, with the command of the League's army. Only the Capuchin monk, Lawrence Brindisi, remained optimistic; he came back from Madrid persuaded that Spain will send three whole *tercios*.

Into this situation, very gloomy from Zúñiga's point of view, the news of the assassination of Henry IV of France—on May 14—by Ravaillac, a fanatic nurtured on the theories of the "tyranomachs," descended like lightning. And, curiously enough, only then, when the main danger of French intervention had passed, did the Catholic League come into existence. The final agreement, reached at the end of July, 1610, was mainly due to the willingness of young Ferdinand of Styria to compromise.

He and the Duke of Bavaria were appointed joint commanders of the League's army. The Emperor, the King of Spain, the Pope, and Matthias, now King of Hungary, did not enter the League, but Philip III promised to pay 30,000 guldens per month, for which price it was possible to sustain two *tercios*.

By establishing the Catholic League, however, Baltasar Zúñiga had not yet solved the problem from which the idea of the League had arisen—the problem of the imperial succession. As if ignoring the turmoil which surrounded it, the solitary figure of the Emperor stood in the center: between the Protestants and their French supporters, on the one hand, and the Catholics and their Spanish friends, on the other. Archduke Leopold was the only member of the family who was trusted by him. Queer companions: a prematurely senescent, almost insane, ruler of the oldest European state and an ambitious, irresponsible young man, full of enthusiasm but without discipline.

During the winter of 1609–10, when Henry IV was still getting ready to interfere in the Empire and nobody could predict his early end, the Spanish Council of State was strongly in favor of reviving the empire of Charles V by having their own king elected to the imperial dignity. Shortly before Christmas, Zúñiga received an energetic letter instructing him to prepare Philip's candidacy and to have the young Ferdinand of Styria in reserve. But, although the ambassador knew well of the French danger—which was the main reason for such a plan—he refused to obey and, on January 30, 1610, sent a long report to Madrid reminding King Philip of the late St. Clemente who, at the close of his life, had favored Matthias and also of the futile family strife among the Hapsburgs at the time of Charles V's resignation.

In spite of Zúñiga's adverse opinion and of his taciturnity, the Spanish plan had not remained a secret. Tengnagel, Leopold's agent in Prague, told the Emperor about it, and some Czech nobles—among others, Karel Liechtenstein, whom neither St. Clemente nor Zúñiga had trusted—came to the Spanish embassy to offer King Philip their support. But then, probably influenced by Zúñiga's report, the Council of State, on March 18, declared itself once again in support of Matthias. Informed about this decision, Matthias came to Prague in May; the Archdukes Maximilian and Ferdinand arrived in September, but no agreement with Rudolf could be achieved. On the contrary, a special envoy, the Marquis of Castiglione, was dispatched by Rudolf to Madrid in November to justify the Emperor's negative attitude toward his relatives and also toward Zúñiga, whose opinions were much deprecated by Archduke Leopold.

2

This stalemate found its eventual end in a wholly unexpected development. A small ragged army, consisting of five thousand infantry and two thousand cavalry which the foolhardy Leopold had assembled in Passau on the Danube and intrusted to the command of a colonel named Ramé, had suddenly, in January, 1611, invaded Bohemia and, on February 6, entered the left-bank quarter of Prague. Their presence in Passau, as well as their complete lack of discipline, had been the source of some anxiety during the preceding months. Zúñiga himself lent forty thousand guldens to the Emperor to pay them off. But nothing had been done, and now, spurred on by some unknown instigator, they arrived in Prague itself.

The Protestant nobility of Bohemia as well as a notable segment of the Catholics were convinced that the invasion had been arranged with Zúñiga's connivance or perhaps even suggested by him. In the right-bank quarters of Prague anti-Catholic riots and demonstrations of violence were organized, culminating in atrocities similar to those which the preceding decades had witnessed in France and the Low Countries. All the inhabitants of the Franciscan convent at Our Lady of Snows, for instance, were tortured for several hours and then slain. Even after Tengnagel, Archduke Leopold's agent in Prague, had been arrested by the Protestant nobles and after it had become evident from what he had told his interrogators that Leopold alone could be blamed for the invasion, anti-Spanish propaganda still persisted. The claim against the Spanish authorities was based on a confiscated letter of the Jesuit priest named Haller, confessor of the Spanish Queen and friend of Leopold, whose personal opinions had little to do with the official Spanish policy.

Actually, Zúñiga had warned the Emperor repeatedly of the danger inherent in the presence of Leopold's ill-disciplined army at Passau. But when the Emperor had done nothing and Colonel Ramé with his band of plunderers had entered Prague, the ambassador realized at once that it meant the end of Rudolf's authority in Bohemia. He offered refuge in his house to Václav Vchynský, a Czech Protestant nobleman who was trying to escape the invaders, and persuaded Baltasar Marradas, commander of the Emperor's guard, not to help Colonel Ramé in any way. On February 10, he dispatched a report to Madrid in which he stressed the necessity of supporting Matthias so that he might take hold of Bohemia at once because of the strategic and economic importance of the kingdom for anyone who would like to have any authority in the Empire. In conclusion he came forward with the suggestion that it would be of advantage to select Matthias' successor also. If this advice were to be accepted, he said, would it not be better to decide at once whether the young Archduke Ferdinand or perhaps one of the sons of the King of Spain should be chosen for that post? If, however, the second course be adopted, would it not be wise to teach the Spanish princes to speak the German and Czech languages? There is no doubt, he concluded, that they will remain true Spaniards even if such knowledge is imposed upon them.

The Duke of Lerma, however, and his associates had not much interest in what was happening in Bohemia. We would like to support Matthias, the Council of State replied, but, since our treasury is empty, let us remain neutral. Thus Zúñiga was left to act on his own responsibility. For some time he waited, seeing Matthias' troops approach the city from the east and Ramé with his soldiers flying back to Germany. But then he set out for Jihlava in Moravia to act as Rudolf's protector and to start negotiations with Matthias. He acted in this capacity even after the Emperor had resigned the crown of St. Wenceslas and Matthias had been crowned King of Bohemia, on May 23, 1611. It was necessary to put the finances of the half-mad Emperor in order. That task, of course, ended with Rudolf's going completely insane and with his death on January 20, 1612. But even then Zúñiga continued in his role of moderator. "No worse thing could happen to the cause of religion," he wrote in one of his reports, "than this invasion of Bohemia by Colonel Ramé which turned the Catholics into rebels and instigated hatred against them."

Once the Emperor was dead, things went more smoothly. Lobkovic remained in office, and Leopold was forgiven by Matthias for his foolhardy adventures. Even the Bohemian Protestant nobles managed to negotiate a loan with Zúñiga to pay and dismiss the army which they had hastily assembled in defense of Prague. Endeavoring to mitigate the tension between the Catholics and the Protestants in Germany, the ambassador also started recruiting the Lutheran Duke of Saxony for the Catholic League. In explanation he cited the precedent established by Charles V in his attempt to reorganize his original alliance with England, even after Henry VIII had broken away from Rome.

3

The next five years passed in relative tranquillity. Maria de Medici, the French Queen-widow, had made peace with Spain by marrying her young son, now Louis XIII, to Anne, Philip III's daughter. The young Bishop Richelieu, whom she was to introduce onto the political scene toward the end of 1616, was still busy in his diocese of Luçon. In 1613, James I, King of England and Scotland, married his daughter Elizabeth to the young and restless Count Palatine, Frederick, foremost of the German Calvinist princes. There was some apprehension in Madrid as to the possible political significance of this marriage, but the Duke of Gondomar, dispatched to London as permanent ambassador, was able to report after a period of circumspect observation that he could control the King's foreign policy. Even on the military border in the Low Countries peace prevailed.

The only spot of trouble was in Northern Italy, where the petulant Duke of Savoy, Charles Emmanuel, thought the situation appropriate for a small territorial extension. He seized the Marquisate of Montferrat, a territory situated between Savoy and the Milanese and bordering, in the south, on Genoa but belonging to the Gonzagas of Mantua. The legal pretext of the Duke—the affirmation that Montferrat, unlike Mantua, descended in the female line—did not satisfy the Spaniards, and a petty war resulted in which the Duke was defeated at Asti, in 1615. The ensuing peace, made by the indecisive Spanish governor of Milan, Hinojosa, offered anything but a permanent solution. More trouble was to come in that region, strategically so important for Hapsburg co-operation.

Castigating the Duke of Savoy for his greed, the Spaniards, of course, were not so sure whether they themselves would not like to step forward with a legal argument and win a new kingdom. Throughout the winter of 1611–12, Zúñiga concentrated all his efforts on assuring the imperial crown for Matthias. But as soon as Matthias had been elected—in June, 1612—Zúñiga's reports were once again preoccupied with the old problem: If Matthias dies, who will be the successor?

The problem was a difficult one, not only because one had to choose between at least three candidates—Ferdinand of Styria, the King of Spain, and now also the Spanish Prince Carlos—but because the atmosphere in Bohemia showed no signs of improvement. The Spanish ambassador knew very well that the selection of the candidate was dependent on the evaluation of the general situation in the kingdom. That situation, however, resembled the calm preceding a storm.

Pavel Skála, a Czech Protestant chronicler, writing during the first stages of the Thirty Years' War, characterized the years before the outbreak of the conflagration as a period of growing bitterness and enmity. He quoted Polyxena, wife of Zdeněk

Vojtěch Lobkovic, as having openly declared that the time would shortly come when either the Catholics would be able to tame the Protestants or be tamed themselves. Actually, it was by no means evident whether all Czech Catholics would be ready to fight against the Protestants and to ally themselves for that purpose with the Hapsburgs. In 1614, when Vilém Slavata, one of Lobkovic's closest friends and recently appointed president of the Bohemian treasury, had made an attempt to free his office from the control of the imperial treasury, he was rebuked and had to abandon his idea with much bitterness against Hapsburg absolutism. And there were probably others who did not share the intransigent policy of the Chancellor.

On the other hand, there were among the Protestants, especially among the Bohemian Brethren, many who openly refused the leadership of the German immigrants. Karel Žerotín, the cultivated gentleman on whose estates the Brethren had their best school and their publishing institute as well, resigned from the presidency of the province of Moravia in the autumn of 1614, refusing to govern the province according to the restless policy of the majority of the non-Catholic nobles in Bohemia, led by men such as Joachim Andreas Schlick, Henrich Matthes Thurn, and Linhart Colonna-Fels, whose families as well as ideas were German and strange to the traditions of the Kingdom of Bohemia and of its dependencies.

Informed about these developments from Zúñiga's reports, the Spanish Council of State hesitated. The Cardinal Archbishop of Toledo declared that, as even the late King Philip II did not consider himself inquisitor of foreign nations, there was no reason why his son should be interested in Central Europe.

Zúñiga nevertheless stuck to his persuasion that Spain should be interested. He was now more inclined to favor Ferdinand of Styria as candidate for both the Bohemian and the imperial crown. In the summer of 1613 he met Ferdinand's counselor, Eggenberg, in Linz and started discussing with him, first of all, the Bohemian candidature. True to the spirit of his age, which considered countries as the property of their rulers—property to which its possessor was bound by a legal obligation—the ambassador took it for granted that, if Ferdinand was to become King of Bohemia, a deal should be made with him concerning his and the Spanish King's hereditary rights to the crown of St. Wenceslas.

That such hereditary rights existed was, of course, by no means evident. But Zúñiga had a double end in mind. First, he wanted to corroborate the supposed hereditary character of Bohemia and perhaps even of Hungary by a solemn legal document, and, second, he wished to gain something for Spain and, for that purpose, he chose the district of Sundgau in Upper Alsatia, which at that time belonged to the Austrian Hapsburgs. This small district, important strategically because of its situation on the road from Milan to Brussels, was now to be exchanged for the Kingdom of Bohemia. Philip III, a grandson of the Emperor Maximilian II, had a greater right to the Bohemian throne than young Archduke Ferdinand, son of Maximilian's brother. Why should he not profit from this advantage?

With this plan in mind, in September, 1613, Zúñiga dispatched his secretary Bruneau to Madrid. The Council of State, however, reacted very slowly. Gabriel Trejo Panyagua, a famous jurist, was asked for an opinion. Finally, in June, an answer was sent back: the Council of State did not want a legal dealing but rather a political agreement. If the cession of Sundgau were included in such an agreement, military precautions should be taken, because there would be much resentment in the Empire.

New negotiations followed which were much more difficult and complex than those which had preceded Bruneau's journey. It was impossible to keep the plan a secret. And the greater the number of people who knew about it, the less easy it was to come to a conclusion. Matthias' chief adviser, Cardinal Khlesl, did everything to postpone it, motivated, probably, by the fear that, with Ferdinand's succession, his own might would come to an abrupt end. When no other argument was available, he announced that Matthias' wife was with child and that, consequently, there was hope for an easy solution of all the problems of succession. It took months before the falsity of this announcement was discovered. But even then the negotiations dragged on. The Spanish Council of State was so disgusted that in the spring of 1615 it accepted the suggestion of the Duke of Infantado, namely, to give up all hereditary rights to the Bohemian crown without asking for recompense of any kind. But Zúñiga refused to shelve his plan. He was too great a patriot to see his country lose. At last, in the beginning of 1616, when Zúñiga was already preparing his return to Spain, it was decided that the whole problem would be left for his successor to decide.

Thus, after eight busy years, during which he often had to work without instructions and to plan his policy for himself, the indefatigable ambassador left Prague without having accomplished his main task. The experience which he had gained, however, was not to be lost. He did not retire from the service of his king as his predecessors had done. As member of the Council of State in the years to follow, he was to have an important say in Spanish foreign policy.

In his reports to Madrid, Zúñiga used to distinguish between the dominions of the Austrian Hapsburgs, which included Austria, Bohemia, and Hungary, and the German principalities, in which the authority of the emperors was only nominal. Thus, without saying so expressly, he distinguished the German area of the Holy Roman Empire from what was one day to become the Austrian Empire. He wanted the Catholic League to safeguard Germany. But the League, in the meantime, proved to be a stillborn child. One infantry regiment and one cavalry battalion, commanded by Marradas, were all her forces. Spain had ceased to pay its contributions in 1613. And the danger of an internal conflict in Germany was again imminent. For some time after 1613, Zúñiga had hoped that even France would become a member of the League. In 1614 France was actually able to help to achieve a peaceful solution of the Jülich-Cleve problem by dividing the disputed territory between the Catholic Duke of Palatinate-Neuburg and the Protestant Duke of Brandenburg. In 1616, however, conditions deteriorated rapidly. In the instructions which Richelieu, who had only recently started his political career, gave to Schomberg, a diplomat whom he sent to the German princes, it was stated explicitly: ". . . it is necessary to point out to them that we do not favor any extension of the Spanish might and that we are willing to help the princes, albeit clandestinely, against the plans of the King of Spain, who wants to obtain for his son, in course of time, the Bohemian as well as the Hungarian and the imperial crown."

At the very close of Zúñiga's stay in Prague—where he remained in spite of Matthias' decision to move the court to Vienna—the conflict with Duke Charles Emmanuel of Savoy flared up again in Italy. The Duke had obtained private support from the French Huguenots, whose force, commanded by Marshal Lesdiguières, came to his aid. In spite of this, he was defeated in 1616 by the new governor of Milan, Pedro de Toledo, Marquis of Villafranca, at Apertola and in the following year had to accept the peace of Pavia and renounce all claims to Montferrat. The fighting, however, spread to the frontier between Venice and the Austrian province of Carniola, administered by Ferdinand of Styria. Venice, there is no need to explain, sympathized with the Duke of Savoy. Zúñiga had to divert to Carniola all the money which he obtained from Madrid for the League. Two Spanish officers, Marradas and Dampierre, went to take charge of the defenses on the Isonzo River. A third one, the Count of Buquoy, had been invited to come, but, for the time being at least, had not been set free by Archduke Albert, under whom he served in the Low Countries.

4

After months of waiting, Zúñiga was finally able to welcome to Prague, on February 1, 1617, his successor, Iñigo Velez de Guevara y Tasis, Count of Oñate, a man full of dynamic energy but of lesser diplomatic skill. Having served for some time as

Spanish envoy at the court of the Duke of Savoy, Oñate had had some experience in Italian affairs. According to the instructions which he had received in Madrid, he was expected to stop in Venice and arrange a peace between the Signoria and Archduke Ferdinand. He failed to do so and went straight from Milan to Prague; but his son, who accompanied him, went to Styria to meet Archduke Ferdinand.

There was behind this refusal of Oñate to act according to the instructions much more than the influence of the Marquis of Villafranca, Milan's bellicose governor, who favored peace with Venice even less than he wished to come to a peaceful settlement with the Duke of Savoy. A third generation of Spanish imperialists was rapidly gaining ascendancy on the political horizon. Both Villafranca and Oñate belonged to it. The Spanish ambassador at Venice, Alfonso de la Cueva, Marquis of Bedmar; the inscrutable Viceroy of Naples, Pedro Tellez Girón, Duke of Osuna, who was to die in prison under the Count Duke of Olivares; and Ambrosio Spinola in the Low Countries, along with hundreds of others, both diplomats and soldiers, formed part of it. Theirs was neither the compromising spirit of Charles V nor the spirit of strict discipline which Philip II had imposed upon his administrative and diplomatic apparatus. Nor did they think much of the Turkish danger. They were fully occupied with the Calvinists and with their possible French or Venetian allies. All of them—the Duke of Osuna perhaps more than the others—were individualists who liked to set a goal for their policy in an independent way. Such men were now the actual lords of the Spanish dominions. Power was their main aim. They could be almost sure that they would make the gods of fate jealous.

Upon his arrival at Prague and especially after Zúñiga's departure, Oñate did not show much caution in adapting himself to his new post. He quarreled almost immediately with Baugy, the French envoy at the imperial court and a good friend of Karel Žerotín, very critical of the activities of the German immigrants.

As the indecisive but unintermittent war in Carniola, on the

Venetian frontier, was still going on, Oñate continued to support Archduke Ferdinand financially as Zúñiga had done before
him and even obtained an official authorization and enlarge-
ment of the support from Madrid. He also tried to induce the
Duke of Osuna to undertake a major naval offensive against
Venice. In this, again, he differed from the Duke of Lerma,
Philip III's all-powerful minister, who at the same time, in
collaboration with the Venetian envoy in Madrid, tried to reach
a peaceful settlement. Oñate evidently counted on the intransigent policy of the Marquis of Villafranca, at whose instigation
the negotiations with Venice had been bound to those between
Spain and Savoy. As the concepts of policy of Lerma and Villafranca clashed, however, no final settlement was forthcoming.
France entered the stage in the late summer and succeeded in
arranging a treaty between the belligerents, dated October 9,
1617. But even this did not bring an end to hostilities. The governor of Milan spent almost half a year before he decided to
fulfil the conditions of the treaty with regard to his province
and the Duchy of Savoy. As to the frontier on the river Isonzo,
another regiment, recruited in Alsatia with Spanish money,
was sent there as late as January, 1618. Only in February of that
year was a real agreement between Venice and Ferdinand of
Styria—at that time already King of Bohemia—finally reached
in Wiener Neustadt.

In the meantime, the atmosphere of general uneasiness in
Bohemia and in Germany had increased again. It is very difficult, even for the most assiduous student of documents, to grasp
the almost imperceptible fibers of developments which were
rooted in fear as well an in hatred. Perhaps the main source of
apprehension was the revived activity of Frederick, Count Palatine and leader of the German Calvinists. Perhaps Frederick's
own restlessness was at least partially due to the behavior of
Spanish diplomats and officers such as the Duke of Villafranca.
In any case, Frederick's Heidelberg—where his two poor satel-
lites, Christian Anhalt and Joachim Ernest Hohenzollern, also
lived—again became the focal point of Spanish anxiety.

Until the spring of 1617 there existed several important free cities in Germany which still did not belong to the Protestant Union, although their population was predominantly Protestant. Oñate, faithful to Zúñiga's opinion that a good Spanish diplomat should avail himself of the enmity between the Lutherans and the Calvinists, hoped to be able to win them for the League. At the congress of the Union at Heilbronn, however, in the summer of 1617, the cities entered the Union. Only the Duke of Saxony was still available. Forgetting easily what fears the Lutheran Saxony had inspired in the Spain of Philip II, Oñate did not lose any opportunity to attract its ruler into his own sphere of influence.

In one respect, at least, Oñate proved as quick a negotiator as his actions were wilful. He solved the problem of the Bohemian succession in a few weeks after his arrival. His son, whom he had sent to Styria while on his way to Prague, brought him Ferdinand's promise that, if he became King of Bohemia and Emperor, he would appoint the King of Spain lord of all the imperial fiefs in Italy. But Oñate wanted Sundgau, in spite of the fact that the Council of State persevered in its decision not to ask for it and despite the fact that the Emperor and his brother Maximilian were opposed to such a demand. He sent Bruneau—the secretary he had inherited from Zúñiga —to Styria to propose again to Ferdinand the marriage of his son with the Spanish princess Maria, although he knew well that the Duke of Lerma and the Count of Gondomar would have liked her to marry the Prince of Wales. And in March, when Ferdinand himself had come to Prague, the negotiations were concluded by a secret treaty, dated March 20, 1617, which completed the barter.

The document, supposing the future renouncement of Philip III's rights to the Kingdom of Bohemia, stated that the male successors of the King of Spain would always have a greater right to the Bohemian crown than Ferdinand's own female descendants. It also contained a clause promising that Ferdinand, if elected Emperor, would appoint Philip to all the

Italian fiefs which would become vacant and that he would turn over to him the district of Sundgau consequent upon the death of Matthias. An official ratification of the agreement was promised by Ferdinand after Philip's renouncement had been published. Actually, the document bears a ratifying signature of Ferdinand, elected King of Bohemia, dated in Prague on July 29, 1617.

5

Archduke Ferdinand's sudden and unexpectedly peaceful election to the Bohemian successorship was an event which surprised even Oñate himself. His influence upon the Czech Catholics was much more restricted than that of his predecessors. He lacked the tact of a St. Clemente and the experience of a Zúñiga. The dissolute life of his son—an excellent and feared fencer—did not recommend him to the Czechs. And Cardinal Khlesl, Matthias' rather self-centered minister, did not like him either.

But Matthias fell dangerously ill in May, 1617, and Khlesl had to authorize the convocation of the Bohemian Diet for recognition purposes.

The fears were great. Under the circumstances of the moment, anything could happen. The Bohemian nobles could refuse to accept Ferdinand. They could ask for a confirmation of Rudolf's famous Letter of Majesty. They could also ask for the convocation of a common Diet of all the provinces of the Crown, in which Moravia, Silesia, and Lusatia would participate and which would easily become the center of a potential revolution. That nothing of this sort happened—except for an attempt of Schlick to enlarge the Diet—was obviously the work of Zdeněk Vojtěch Lobkovic.

Since 1599, the Chancellor of the Kingdom of Bohemia had not rested a moment in his assiduous efforts to preserve the constitution of the country and defend its tradition against the influence of the immigrants. He did not hesitate to oppose the combined efforts of the Spanish ambassador and of the nuncio, both of whom wished to do away with the Czech Catholic rite, and confirmed repeatedly the rights of the so-called

"Lower Consistory," which headed the parishes of that rite —as opposed to the Upper Consistory and the Archbishop of Prague, who led the Catholics of the Roman rite. He directed, with a firm hand, the central offices of the Kingdom and it was with the help of the other officials—with the exception of Henrich Matthes Thurn—that he now prepared the recognition of Ferdinand of Styria as Matthias' successor.

True to his belief in the value of the monarchical system, dependent on the law of nature and opposed to unnecessary changes founded on the ambitions of various noblemen, he asked for a recognition, not for an election, of the Archduke. His thoughts were similar to those of William Shakespeare in *Troilus and Cressida*.

> How could communities,
> Degrees in schools, and brotherhoods in cities,
> Peaceful commerce from dividable shores,
> The primogenitive and due of birth,
> Prerogative of age, crowns, sceptres, laurels,
> But by degree, stand in authentic place?

When Adam Sternberg, one of the officials of the Kingdom, questioned the members of the Diet one after another, only two Germans, Thurn and Colonna-Fels, voted against the recognition. All the others present—including prominent Czech non-Catholics, such as Václav Budovec—were in favor of Ferdinand. The session had a tragicomic aftermath. When it came, as was usual after such a solemn event, to the reappointment of the officials of the Kingdom and Heinrich Matthes Thurn was given a higher but less remunerative office than before—the office of the Judge of the Royal Court—he protested, declaring explicitly that "he did not know the customs of the Kingdom nor its laws."

It was, however, the same Heinrich Matthes Thurn, who a year later, on May 23, 1618, brought a group of his friends into the chancery of the Kingdom of Bohemia in the Prague castle and, in Lobkovic's absence, seized two Catholic officers of the Kingdom, Martinic and Slavata, and had them thrown out of the windows. "Edle Herrn, da habt ihr den andern," cried he pushing his second victim toward the wall. He little knew that his clenched fists were dispensing the first blows of a war which was to last thirty long years.

What happened in Bohemia during the twelve months between the recognition of Ferdinand II and the May defenestration of 1618? Nothing of importance, other than the fact that the new king, following the advice of his Jesuit confessor and pushing aside Oñate's remonstrances, had recognized the validity of the Letter of Majesty. The Catholics, nevertheless, were not willing to go beyond the concessions contained in the Letter. On the contrary, acting according to the principle "Cuius regio, eius religio," on which the Letter was based, Lobkovic had extended the power of the governors of the royal cities and issued strict ordinances against the spread of Lutheranism. On the same ground the Archbishop of Prague and the Abbot of the Benedictine monastery of Broumov had forbidden their subjects in the villages of northern Bohemia to build Lutheran churches.

There was nothing in these steps of the Church dignitaries which would have been contrary to the Letter of Majesty—as Thurn and his associates tried to insinuate. True to the spirit of the time, the Letter authorized the building of Protestant churches by those in authority, not by their subjects. The churches in Hroby and Broumov had been built by the commoners without authorization of any kind. Nevertheless, the German leaders of the Bohemian Protestants, instigated by the Count Palatine, who only recently had reached an agreement with the Duke of Bouillon, the new leader of the French Huguenots, saw a good opportunity and were not slow in seizing upon it. Within a few weeks all the vital centers of the Kingdom of Bohemia were in hands of the insurgents.

The defenestration took place when Matthias, Ferdinand, and Lobkovic were absent. Matthias had spent the preceding winter and spring in Vienna while Ferdinand and Lobkovic were in Hungary. Oñate was in Vienna when news from Slavata and Martinic—both of whom had escaped with slight in-juries—reached him. His reaction was that of a soldier rather than a diplomat. "I would be well satisfied," he wrote to Philip III on June 6, "but it seems to me almost impossible that the nobles who have been so far very successful and who are well armed would now ask for less than a complete surrender of all political as well as religious affairs into their hands; to accept such a demand would mean to lose everything." It really meant war.

But some time was necessary before Oñate succeeded in per-suading Matthias that no compromise was possible. Not until the ailing Emperor had seen Oñate's "Memorandum on the Events in Bohemia," composed on Lobkovic's demand and dated May 30, a week before the first report to Madrid, did he decide which course of action to take. But then his letters, ad-dressed to King Philip and to Archduke Albert and dated May 30 and June 1, reflected almost verbally the ideas of the Spanish ambassador. Oñate wanted war, and the Emperor duly wrote for help. There is no doubt that this decision of his was attacked at first by several partisans of a more diplomatic plan of action, such as Karel Žerotín, who had come from Moravia to Vienna, and Adam Valdštýn, who had sent a report from Prague. On June 21, Oñate had to hand the Emperor another memorandum to counteract their suggestions. Finally, he won his cause.

But did he really gain completely what he desired? In his first memorandum to the Emperor he voiced the opinion that some military help from Bavaria and Saxony would be suffi-cient; he also wanted the services of Tserclaes de Tilly, a native of the Netherlands who now served as general of the Bavarian troops. On these accounts Matthias, in his letter to Philip, asked merely for financial help. But in his report of June 6, Oñate went far beyond this. He wanted soldiers, ten or twelve thou-sand infantrymen, who could be recruited in the Kingdom of Naples and shipped to Trieste. Should Venice oppose such a move, there were other ways: from Milan to Innsbruck and from the Low Countries via Alsatia to Bavaria.

It is rather interesting to observe Oñate's references to Italy. At the moment he was sending his report to Madrid he prompted the Emperor to send a letter directly to the Duke of Osuna in Naples sketching the plan for transportation of troops to Trieste. He knew very well that no one would welcome a new military adventure in Central Europe more than the leading Spanish officers in Italy. The Duke of Osuna had spent his youth in the France of Henry IV and in England almost as an exile, because of his rash and impetuous character. Ever since he had come to Sicily in 1612, he had wanted to start an offensive against Turkey. He could now be expected with certainty to grab any occasion which would give him hope for a conflict with Venice. To Matthias' letter he reacted by reports dispatched from his seat in Pozzuoli to Madrid and to the Marquis of Bedmar, Spanish ambassador in Venice as well, declaring his readiness to participate in the undertaking. Only a few weeks before, the Signoria had announced the discovery of a plot in which Osuna and Bedmar, as well as the Spanish novelist Quevedo, were involved. The purpose of this plot, it affirmed, was to arrange an armed rising in Venice on Ascension Day, when all the inhabitants were out of the city celebrating the traditional "Wedding of the Sea." Whether the Spanish viceroy of Naples did or did not share in such an undertaking may be a matter of discussion among historians. He certainly was ready to start a conflict with Venice. "If they resist," he wrote to Bedmar, "I shall settle things with them once and for all." And to King Philip III he enumerated all the superfluous infantry units totaling about ten thousand men which he had assembled in his territory during Villafranca's war with Savoy and which he was now ready to send to the Emperor.

6

In spite of the readiness of the Spanish officers in Italy, however, Oñate found the transition from ideas to action long and tiresome. While Thurn rapidly fortified the south of Bohemia, placing about four thousand infantry there, the danger that the uprising would spread to Moravia increased. Matthias spent his time negotiating with Buquoy, Archduke Albert's general, whom he wished to take over the command of the imperial troops. In the meantime the Spanish Council of State took up the Bohemian affair at its meetings on July 6 and 14. Its conclusions proved to be unfavorable to the ambassador's plans. Baltasar Zúñiga, now a foreign-policy expert of the Council, stressed the absolute importance of Bohemia for the maintenance of Hapsburg influence in the Empire, but even he was against any employment of Spanish or Italian soldiers. The Duke of Lerma, whose power was rapidly declining, was against any sort of help; he even insisted that Oñate dismiss troops which he had been paying in Carniola until now.

But Oñate was not the man to wait for the decision of his superiors. Before the King of Spain could even consider the conclusions of his Council, Oñate had already persuaded King Ferdinand and the old Archduke Maximilian to arrest Cardinal Khlesl on July 20 and to remove him from the Emperor because of his indecisiveness. He also fought with Ferdinand's counselor Eggenberg because of his defeatism. He transferred the troops available in Carniola closer to Vienna, paying them partly from his own treasury and partly from funds obtained in the meantime from Brussels. When, in August, Buquoy finally reached Vienna, he found some twelve thousand men awaiting him.

Nevertheless, the situation of the Spanish ambassador was by no means enviable. When in September he had received about 150,000 guldens for the pay of the troops fighting in Carniola, very little was left to him, since he owed about 130,000 guldens to one of the regiments now under Buquoy's command. His inability to obtain any more substantial help was criticized at the imperial court. There a pessimistic atmosphere prevailed, as is evident from the contemporary correspondence of the Czech Catholics, who, fleeing for their lives, went to Bavaria rather than to Vienna.

Oñate himself would at that moment have favored a complete subordination of the forces of the Catholic League to the young

Duke of Bavaria, Maximilian, son of the Duke of Bavaria who
had participated in its very establishment. But there were other
obstacles besides Spanish passivity and the Emperor's indecisiveness. Count Frederick of the Palatinate had been able, in July,
to stop the military preparations of the Bishop of Spires, and
consequently not only the timid Archbishop of Mayence but
also other partisans of the League hesitated to take up arms.

At this juncture, Oñate revived an old idea of Baltasar Zúñiga
and approached the Duke of Saxony, John George. He even requested King Philip to send him a letter, wanting evidently not
only to play up the Lutheran enmity toward the Calvinists but
the Duke of Saxony's jealousy against Frederick of the Palatinate as well. In this he was indirectly supported by the directors of the Prague insurrection, who, although mostly Lutherans, looked to Frederick as their best ally and had already
obtained a regiment of infantry from him under the command
of Ernest Mansfeld, a regiment which was actually paid by the
ambitious Duke of Savoy. Two other things which helped
Oñate were the death of Archduke Maximilian and the rapid
fall of the Duke of Lerma. The first of these events, which
occurred in November, made possible a definitive arrangement
of the command of the League troops; from that moment on,
Archduke Albert had the command in the north and Maximilian of Bavaria in the south. The decline of Lerma's influence
also allowed Zúñiga to send Oñate some badly needed financial
aid.

Nevertheless, the situation did not look favorable for Oñate
until the end of 1618. The Emperor, impatient and mistrusting
the Spanish envoy as well as his own ambassador in Madrid,
Francis Christopher Khevenhueller, nephew of Johann Khevenhueller, dispatched Cesare Gallo as new envoy extraordinary to
Madrid, to clarify the problem of Spanish aid. Nor were the
military developments satisfactory. Buquoy made an incursion
into southern Bohemia, only to retreat again. One of his best
lieutenants, Colonel Creange, lost his life on November 9, in a
rear-guard action at Lomnice, while Mansfeld, to the contrary,

was able to take the city of Plzeň, which had remained faithful to the Emperor. Buquoy decided to spend the winter in Budě-jovice, the capital of southern Bohemia, leaving Vienna almost defenseless. Thurn seized the opportunity; he left only a part of his forces, commanded by Hohenlohe, another "guest" from Germany, to check Buquoy and marched with the bulk of his army against the capital of Austria. It looked like a catastrophe. Only the sharp onset of winter forced the leader of the Bo-hemian rebels to stop and turn back to the north.

7

The upheaval in Prague aroused a great deal of interest in the capitals of the European west. In France the news reached the royal court at a moment when the Spanish envoy, Hector Pigna-telli, Duke of Monteleone, was about to leave his post but still had to spend whole days in settling dissensions between King Louis XIII and the Spanish ladies-in-waiting of the Queen. Times had certainly not improved since the days of Maximilian II, at least not so far as Spanish ladies-in-waiting in foreign courts were concerned. For a long time Monteleone had no in-structions concerning the developments in Prague. The Spanish Council of State as well as Oñate hesitated to approach France because of fear of the Huguenots. In the autumn of 1618, how-ever, Louis XIII himself interfered by asking the Duke of Nevers to arrange peace between the Emperor and the rebels.

The Duke of Nevers was a religious enthusiast, but never a fanatic. He had made himself prominent not only through his participation in the struggle for Montferrat but also through his "Christian Militia," a new crusading order which he had founded in 1612 and propagated with the help of Joseph Tremblay, a Capuchin, who later, as aid of Richelieu, was given the surname of "The Gray Eminence." The Duke of Nevers was now going to Vienna and elsewhere to meet some noblemen who were interested in the "Militia" and gladly under-took the king's mission. In Vienna, however, his enthusiasm clashed with Oñate's suspicions. We do not know exactly why

Oñate rebuked the Frenchman, who had quickly assumed the Emperor's point of view and even offered to bring him some troops from France. But it is more than probable that Oñate did not take the enthusiastic Duke seriously.

The news about the Prague defenestration which had reached England was colored by the knowledge of the close contacts between the rebels and the Count Palatine, King James's son-in-law. Yet, in spite of all the anti-Hapsburg feeling among the English citizens, the Count of Gondomar, Spanish ambassador in London, remained optimistic. He was now well acquainted with King James, author of *Triplici modo triplex cuneus.* So sure was he of James's legitimist views and of his loyalty to Spain that he did not wait until Sir Walter Raleigh—an old enemy of the Spaniards who was imprisoned on charges of piracy—was condemned and executed, but went rather, in July, 1618, to visit Spain.

Gondomar was not mistaken. In August, word came from James through Cottington, his envoy at the Spanish court, that he did not approve of the Prague upheaval. And when the Prague "directors" addressed to London a list of grievances against the Emperor, James sent it quietly to Madrid on September 3, accompanied only by mild advice that the religious freedoms of the Bohemian noblemen should be respected. The Spanish Council of State, in this case, showed no hesitation and asked James, on September 5, 1618, for mediation. The result was a letter by Buckingham, James's first minister, dated September 30, in which Gondomar was assured that the King of England would see to it that no help should come to the rebels from Germany.

It was this international atmosphere more than anything else which gave hope to Oñate that no compromise would be necessary and which also strengthened Zúñiga's position in the Council of State. For the first few weeks of 1619 Oñate had still to take into consideration the indecisiveness of the ailing Emperor Matthias, who had not ceased attempting to establish a committee of mediation composed exclusively of princes of the

Holy Roman Empire. But then, on March 20, 1619, Matthias died, and Oñate and Zúñiga were able to shape, between themselves, the future not only of Bohemia but of the whole of Europe.

Baltasar Zúñiga had by now obtained a position of paramount influence in the Council of State. Even the King's confessor, Luis Aliaga, who had always had a rather wary eye for any new military commitments, gradually accepted his opinions. Also the Duke of Villafranca, who in the meantime had taken his seat in the Council, did not oppose the core of Zúñiga's policy, although he was at times skeptical as to the military preparedness of Spain. At first, before Christmas in 1618, Zúñiga suggested that two infantry regiments and one thousand cavalry should be sent to Bohemia. But then he rapidly increased his demands to three regiments of Spanish infantry, two others from Naples, and one from the Low Countries. He warned, however, against any concentration of troops in Alsatia, since he wished to avoid any revival of fighting in the Netherlands. In that he differed, at that time at least, from Archduke Albert, who not only supported all Oñate's demands but also presupposed a new clash in the Low Countries as soon as the truce concluded in 1609 expired. To any concentration of troops in Alsatia, Zúñiga preferred to pay larger and larger subsidies, for which he wanted Oñate to recruit soldiers in Austria or in its neighborhood. Osuna's willingness to ship troops to Trieste was not welcomed by the Council of State; any trouble in Italy, especially a conflict with Venice, was to be avoided.

But the need was pressing. Only a few soldiers could be recruited in Central Europe. Therefore, Oñate paid little heed to Zúñiga's farsighted strategy and exacted help from the Netherlands. There at least he met with full understanding. At the end of April six thousand infantry—among their Walloon officers was young René Descartes—and one thousand cavalry, commanded by Captain Gauchier, set out from Luxemburg for Alsatia. There they were taken over by Baltasar Marradas, who, in addition, also took command of one regiment of German infantry recruited at the same time by a German prince, the Count of Nassau. It was just in time, for the Prague rebels had in the meantime registered a new and important success in extending their influence to Moravia. There with the help of the dissolute Ladislav Velen Žerotín and aided indirectly by the passivity of Karel Žerotín—who did not approve of the rebellion but did not want to fight against his coreligionists either —they began expelling the Catholic noble families and confiscating their property. Among the expellees was Albrecht Valdštýn (Wallenstein), the future commander-in-chief of the imperial forces in the second and third stages of the war; fleeing to Vienna, he took with him the military treasury of the province— a deed which helped the imperial cause considerably.

At the beginning of June, Thurn appeared again under the walls of Vienna. But, although circumstances favored him—the expeditionary force from the Low Countries had not yet arrived —he met with another failure. The arrival of Dampierre at the head of a very small contingent forced him to retreat. In the meantime, Buquoy succeeded in surprising Mansfeld, who had left Plzeň and was moving southward, and defeated him decisively at Záblatí in southern Bohemia.

These two events hastened developments in the political field. At almost the same time, the Princes Electors, at their meeting in Frankfort, chose Ferdinand II as Holy Roman Emperor; and the Count Palatine—who was not present at Frankfurt but whose representative there did not protest against Ferdinand's royal title and even voted in Ferdinand's favor—was asked by the Bohemian rebels to come to Prague and accept the crown of St. Wenceslas. Few other periods had witnessed so much political inconsistency. And more was to come. How many times during the previous months had the leaders of the Prague rebellion declared that the office of the King of Bohemia was an elective and not a hereditary one? And yet, a few months after Frederick's ascent to that throne, they were to guarantee him and his posterity its hereditary character. How many times had Václav Budovec, the closest Czech collaborator of Heinrich

Matthes Thurn, affirmed that he was a good patriot? He now finished his career by helping to place on the Bohemian throne a stranger, whose first step was to destroy all the treasures of art accumulated in the Prague cathedral through many centuries and to celebrate this "purge" by a German Calvinist service.

8

Seen in historical retrospect, Ferdinand's election to the imperial dignity and Frederick's ascent to the Bohemian throne can be regarded as the culminating events of the year 1619. For the Count of Oñate they were important steps toward the final decision. Alone at the center of events, he often had the disadvantage of seeing their meaning in another light than that of his compatriots. Thus, when the Count of Benavente, chairman of the Spanish Council of Italy and member of the Council of State, came forward with a plan to raise money by selling estates and various revenues in the Kingdom of Naples and to employ it in the Bohemian affair, the whole project was almost wrecked by the news of Thurn's second march against Vienna—news which was received by the majority of the members of the Council of State with pessimism and despair.

Again, when the Neapolitan expeditionary force was finally approved and assembled—about seven thousand infantry, commanded by Guillermo Verdugo and Carlo Spinelli—the Duke of Osuna, having received news of Ferdinand's election to the imperial throne, regarded it as a victory of such moment that he ordered the soldiers already on their ships in the Bay of Naples to disembark. Only several days later were they allowed to embark again and to proceed by sea to Finale and thence by way of Milan and the upper valley of the river Adige into Tyrol. But even then Oñate had to ignore the authorities in Madrid, who wanted to send the whole force to Alsatia for the winter and then to dispatch more than half of them to the Netherlands. He simply directed all the forces to Austria.

The situation in the autumn of 1619 was again a precarious

one. Frederick of the Palatinate, self-styled King of Bohemia, seemed to have gained ground in France, where Fernando Girón, an ailing and not very intelligent diplomat who had succeeded the Duke of Monteleone, had less and less influence upon Louis XIII and upon Puysieulx, his minister of foreign affairs. The French envoy in Heidelberg, St. Catherine, on the other hand, seemed to pull his king toward Frederick. King James of England had published, in February, 1619, a new treatise defending the absolute power of the rulers against Cardinal Bellarmin. But it was not altogether clear whether he would continue to remain where the Count of Gondomar wished him to remain. In June he dispatched the Viscount of Doncaster on a mission to Vienna and Prague. Doncaster arrived at Vienna—after a short stop at Brussels and Heidelberg— before the election at Frankfort took place and before Frederick had accepted the Bohemian crown. His views, conciliatory to the rebels, clashed with those of Oñate, with whom he conferred several times. After the two above-mentioned events had taken place, his mission, of course, failed to make any headway at all.

Even after the arrival of the troops both from the Netherlands and from Naples, Oñate's goals were not yet realized. Through the constant efforts of Zúñiga he had obtained the means necessary for sustaining twelve thousand men who were to supplement the relatively small imperial forces. Another twenty-four thousand were expected to be provided by the Catholic League and perhaps by Saxony as well. A few months were still needed to complete these numbers, and then the offensive would be under way. It was to be a many-sided offensive: political and religious as well as military. "When traveling in the Low Countries," wrote Vilém Slavata to a friend of his in Spain, "I have noticed how the Calvinists there had quickly wrung the necks of the Lutherans; only in Bohemia we have been constantly preaching tolerance because, we used to say, tolerance begets peace; but now experience has taught us otherwise."

The military plans were almost ready in November, 1619. They provided for a double attack: from Austria and Bavaria against Prague and from the Duchy of Luxemburg—the most southern province of the Netherlands—against the Palatinate. One aspect of the plan was constantly stressed in Oñate's reports to Madrid: that the entire action would be of a thoroughly Spanish character. Oñate was persuaded that neither Maximilian of Bavaria nor Emperor Ferdinand II would participate in it personally. Consequently, the command of the southern army would be in the hands of Buquoy, a citizen of the Spanish Netherlands. Ambrosio Spinola was expected to command the northwestern army. It could not be otherwise; Oñate and the great power which he represented were the only hopes of the Holy Roman Empire. The words which Ferdinand II uttered to Doncaster, describing Oñate as "the man with whose friendly and frank help all the affairs of the Hapsburg family are being managed," were completely true.

For a brief time, in November, 1619, it seemed as if Oñate's plans would have to be employed immediately, before the completion of mobilization. The Prague insurgents had succeeded in establishing friendly contacts with some nobles of the free, northwestern part of Hungary, led by Gabor Bethlen, and persuaded them to attack the imperial troops from the east before the winter set in. From the imperial point of view, such an attack could not be treated lightly. Oñate wrote urgent letters to Munich and Brussels, asking that the general attack on the enemy should begin at once. But before the troops began to move, the danger passed. Bethlen was attacked from the rear by the Cossacks, who had crossed the Carpathians from the north and forced the Hungarians to return home.

Curiously enough, the arrival of the Cossacks in Slovakia was not the result of any official alliance between Poland and the Hapsburgs. There existed a secret agreement between the Hapsburgs and Sigismund III of Poland, who was a fervent Catholic, but it was void of any political significance, if for no other reason than because, in oligarchic Poland, the king had hardly any authority. In addition to that, Zúñiga had warned the Council of State against any alliance with Poland. He regarded the Polish claims to Silesia as dangerous. When, of course, at a later date the Duke of Saxony claimed not only Silesia but also Lusatia, there were no protests forthcoming from Madrid. Thus the Cossack action against Bethlen had nothing to do with the Hapsburgs. It was arranged by Adolf Althan, a German nobleman who had been sent to Poland by the Duke of Nevers to propagate there the "Christian Militia." It certainly spared Oñate a very serious setback.

THE "WHITE MOUNTAIN"

1

THE war had started. The whole Kingdom of Bohemia, the wealthiest member of the Holy Roman Empire, was at stake. Everybody knew that this time the two parties engaged in the conflict—the Catholics and the Protestants—would fight each other to the bitter end. But the main question was: Would the war remain restricted to Bohemia, or would it spread into a general conflagration? Military plans were ready for a Spanish attack on the Palatinate, the German principality belonging to Frederick, the usurper of the Bohemian throne. Would Spain decide to use them?

At the end of December, 1619, the Spanish Council of State met to listen to a long and well-prepared speech of Baltasar Zúñiga. The former ambassador to the imperial court concentrated on one effort: to make it clear that the situation was to be dealt with in an energetic, decisive way. The Turks, who gave their support to Bethlen, Frederick of the Palatinate, the Dutch, and the English had all joined hands to undermine Spain's position. The Bohemian conflict was only a beginning. A revival of hostilities in the Netherlands would follow. Was it not possible to imagine a combined attack of the English and Dutch navies on Lisbon? That city would be an easy trophy, being inhabited by so many foreigners whom the Inquisition was unable to control. One had to be prepared for the worst and to remember the energy with which Charles V and Philip II had met similar dangers.

Zúñiga did not refer directly to Charles's conflict with the League of Schmalkalden in 1547, in which Bohemia was also involved, but it was clear to all who were present that it was that particular event which, above all, he had in mind. This

229

time, it was more evident than ever that the loss of Bohemia would mean "great changes in all the four parts of the world."

No final decision was made by that particular meeting of the Council. But the scales were now weighing more and more in favor of Spanish intervention against Frederick. When, in January, 1620, Emperor Ferdinand II made a truce with Bethlen, who had had to retreat because of the defeats suffered at the hands of the Cossack expeditionary force, the Spanish Council of State was more than disturbed. It informed the Emperor that, if a similar step was contemplated between him and Frederick, all Spanish support would be withdrawn.

The Council of State was also in some doubt as to what to think about Buquoy's hesitating strategy. Seen from Madrid, his inability to bring things to a head during 1619 looked rather suspicious. Because of his dilatory policy, even Oñate, the Spanish ambassador, did not defend him without reservations. We have, however, to admit that to organize the forces which the Emperor had at his disposal was by no means an easy task. Relations between the commanders of the regiments were strained. One of them, Carlo Spinelli, a very rich "condottiere," quarreled with Baltasar Marradas and contemplated resignation. The most difficult problem of all, however, was the co-ordination of the Spanish units with those of the German Catholic League, commanded by Maximilian of Bavaria. Oñate's original idea of making them a part of the Spanish forces under the command of Buquoy had proved impossible. Maximilian was an exacting ally. He wished the Emperor to give him assurance that, after the completion of the war, he would be made one of the Prince Electors, that all the territories he would occupy would be incorporated in Bavaria, and that Bavaria's autonomy in the Empire would be increased. No wonder that for some time the Spanish Council of State thought of asking the Pope to appoint the commander-in-chief of the combined forces.

There were also difficulties of a technical nature. Scarcity of gunpowder was a serious handicap to the troops located in Austria. It proved impossible to have it transported from the

Netherlands. And as to transportation from Milan, across the Alps, few tasks could require more time. Even money, which Oñate was now able to obtain regularly, had to be sent by the way of the Alpine passes and the Tyrol. The Nuremberg bankers who, until then, had willingly served the interests of Spanish foreign policy, now, under the influence of Frederick, refused to continue to honor Spanish money orders. However, sending money directly across the Alps had the advantage of placing in Oñate's hands Spanish and Italian coins which he had melted and reminted into the much cheaper coinage current in Central Europe.

At the same time, the Spanish statesmen did not underrate their enemy. Aware of his strength, they wanted to insure themselves on all sides. They were ready to make territorial concessions on the left bank of the river Rhine to gain the help of Louis XIII of France. Everything was done, especially by Oñate, to insure the collaboration of Maximilian of Bavaria also. It was because of Maximilian's argument that he would not be able to leave his own principality unprotected that Oñate stressed again and again, in his reports to Madrid, the necessity of attacking the Palatinate directly by a Spanish expeditionary force from the Netherlands. In the middle of February, 1620, the Council of State finally decided to finance such an operation. To obtain the necessary 1,600,000 guldens, several large estates belonging to the Spanish crown in the Kingdom of Naples and in Sicily had to be sold. But, even then, there were prominent Spaniards —the Duke of Feria, the new governor of Milan, was among them—who criticized the whole project, pointing to its danger to the general peace of Europe.

Nevertheless, that the Duke of Bavaria did come to help the Emperor was the result not of the good offices of the Count de Oñate but of an event of a quite different nature: the French diplomatic mission which, quite unexpectedly, concluded a pact of nonaggression between the Protestant Union and the Catholic League in Germany.

2

The story of the French mission to Germany in 1620 started
in the autumn of the preceding year. At that time the attacks
against Spain by the Palatine and Savoyard diplomats had already lost much of their original vigor. A congress of French
Huguenots in Loudun reminded Louis XIII and his ministers
that France itself might face a Protestant revolt, if the rebels in
Bohemia were to achieve a victory. In addition, a special envoy
of the Emperor, Vratislav Fürstenberg, grandson of Vratislav
Pernštýn, the Czech statesman whose career we have followed,
arrived at the French court with a demand for help. This demand was supported not only by the papal nuncio, Bentivoglio,
and by the king's confessor, the Jesuit Arnoux, but also by the
Duke of Nevers, who, forgetting Oñate's adverse opinion of his
diplomatic mission of 1618, was once more ready to make his
services available. Perhaps he would have liked to earn some
fame on the battlefields. The Huguenots, of course, were not
inactive. The Duke of Bouillon, their leader, sent the King a
letter, asking him to help Frederick.

The result was a double decision of the King. After Christ-
mas, 1619, he started assembling a certain number of military
units in the Champagne. According to current rumors, it was
expected that these units would be placed at the disposal of the
Emperor as a private army, probably under Nevers's name. The
Spanish statesmen in Madrid were more than eager to use this
"French auxiliary force," as they called it. At the beginning of
February, 1620, the Spanish Council of State gave its approval
to the suggestion to intrust Nevers with the occupation of
Baden, one of the Protestant provinces of southern Germany.
But then, probably also because of the bad impression made
upon the French by Buquoy's slight activity, Louis XIII put his
second iron in the fire; it was a step which he had already contemplated when ordering the gathering of troops in the Champagne region and which found wholehearted support on the
part of Jeannin, the old, conciliatory representative of the "Poli-

tiques" movement and councilor to the late Henry IV. In March, the King of France announced that he was going to send a diplomatic mission to Germany, and he nominated the Duke of Angoulême as its head.

It was evident that the prevention of any war in Germany was the chief interest of the French. This idea gained even more ground in April, when a diplomatic agent of the German Protestant Union, Buwinkhausen, who had already visited England, came to France. Louis XIII received him at Orleans and, from what he heard from him, came to the conclusion that the Union also had its fears and that a general civil war in Germany must not be regarded as a necessary outcome of the rebellion in Bohemia. Consequently, Luynes, the king's minister, invited Boisschot, the agent of Archduke Albert, to a conference, and told him that Angoulême had been given a definite mission: to persuade the Union not to support Frederick. Thus, he said, the French would be able to help to preserve peace in Germany.

Angoulême's mission met with complete success. It found Maximilian of Bavaria with his troops near the city of Ulm, on the upper Danube, facing the army of the Union. Between these two camps, the French envoys arranged a peace. For the time being, the danger of a conflagration in Germany was averted. And what was more, Maximilian's troops were now free to go to Bohemia.

Most of the Spaniards were not very quick in grasping the advantages of this arrangement. Archduke Albert also was completely confused by what had happened at Ulm. He thought that the agreement served just one purpose: to make an attack on the Palatinate impossible. Accordingly, he persuaded the Spanish Council of State to change its decisions once more and to make the army stationed in the Netherlands available for use in Bohemia. The attack on the Palatinate, it was resolved, would wait until a settlement could be reached in Bohemia.

But Bentivoglio, the papal nuncio at Paris, and also Oñate, saw the full significance of the arrangement at Ulm, and they considered it a great advantage for the Emperor's cause. Even when accepting the postponement of the attack on the Palatinate, Oñate stuck to his persuasion that the Spanish army in the Netherlands was to be reserved for that task, and he did not allow it to be sent to Bohemia.

3

Oñate had still another reason to believe that total punishment of Frederick was possible without putting the Emperor's small authority in Germany in danger. He now knew for certain that England would not come to Frederick's help.

Indeed, King James's court in Greenwich differed more and more from the court of Queen Elizabeth which had delighted only in "singeing the beards" of the Spaniards. The King himself, a great lover of political theory, preferred endless discussions to action. Listening to the Spanish arguments as well as to those which were put before him by the supporters of his son-in-law Frederick, he was able to postpone his decision from day to day and thus to keep both sides engaged without engaging himself.

During the winter of 1619–20, Frederick's agents in London were unhampered. Gondomar, the Spanish envoy, was still absent. He spent his leave in Madrid, arguing with the Council of State and defending his realistic policy against those who, because of religious reasons, shunned every suggestion of friendship with non-Catholic England. The Council listened to his expositions with much patience, but, at the same time, it deliberated upon the possibility of starting a Catholic revolution against James under the command of a Scotch nobleman of the "clan of Argyll."

One of the arguments which the directors of the Spanish policy used against Gondomar was the inadequacy of James's influence upon his own subjects. Gondomar himself was well aware of the shadows around the English throne. New proofs of James's weakness came in almost every day. The English diplomats who had been sent to the mainland proceeded in their missions according to their own opinions, neglecting the instructions which they had obtained from the King. Doncaster, who had been sent again to the Emperor in the autumn of 1619 to congratulate him upon his election to the imperial throne, had stayed a longer time in Heidelberg than elsewhere and then, for some unknown reason, went to the very frontier of the city-republic of Venice—probably to meet a Venetian notable. The other English envoys, William Trumbull in Brussels and Sir Edward Herbert in Paris, acted in a similar way, defending rather the interests of Frederick than those of their own monarch.

As to the disparity between the opinions held by the King of England and Scotland himself and those of the nobility and wealthy merchants of his realms, the Spaniards were fully informed about them from the interesting reports which were regularly sent to Brussels, to De la Faille, Archduke Albert's secretary, and by William Sterrell, an agent, who, although serving the Spanish cause, made no secret of his own Protestant persuasions.

It was therefore no wonder that Gondomar had recently lost much of his former enthusiasm for a permanent alliance between Spain and England, a plan which seems to us almost reminiscent of the young years of Charles V and Henry VIII. Since his departure from London, a year and a half before, the insurrection in Bohemia had given him ample occasion to reexamine his ideas about a possible collaboration with James I.

In London, in the meantime, a literary "conflict" was raging between the Palatine agents and Van Male, the official representative of Archduke Albert. The weapons were mainly defamatory pamphlets. Frederick's propaganda did not stop short of charging an opponent with what could be said, with much more truth, of Frederick himself. According to such affirmations, Ferdinand had been elected King of Bohemia in an illegal way, and his main fault had been that he had obstinately introduced foreigners into the kingdom. Van Male was perhaps not a very bright polemicist. But he knew a lot about Czech constitutional history, and he used this knowledge to the best advantage. King James was ready to accept and even to read every new pamphlet. But whenever someone asked him for a judgment, his reply was always that he had not yet grasped the complete truth.

In January, 1620, Christopher Dohna, Frederick's chief agent in London, was joined by his brother Achaz. Together, they started a financial crusade among wealthy and influential Englishmen. They found men like George Abbot, Archbishop of Canterbury, and the Earl of Dorset willing enough to cooperate. They were not so fortunate, however, with the rich merchants of the city of London, who obviously had little sympathy for the son-in-law of their king. In vain the Dohnas showed them intreating letters bearing the signature of Elizabeth, Frederick's wife—a signature which, according to Van Male's affirmation, they had forged. What the merchants wanted was nothing less than a signature of their own king. James, however, refused to issue such a guaranty; nor did he allow Buckingham to sign one in his place. The only step in Frederick's favor which he decided to take was the permission granted to Buwinckhausen, the agent of the German Protestant Union, and to a certain Captain Gray, a "condottiere" in Palatine service, to recruit professional soldiers.

The Prague rebels dreamed, of course, of other things. Rumors spread among them, at that time, of twenty-four tons of gold which had been gathered in London to be sent to Frederick. It is true that in the latter half of March, 1620, King James I paid a visit to the City of London and asked the merchants to follow the example of the dignitaries of the Church of England, who had already started collecting money for Frederick. But that was all he did. It had proved impossible to persuade him to any active interest in Frederick's cause, especially since the return of Gondomar to London on March 18.

Altogether, three collections to aid Frederick were arranged in England during 1620. The first of them, organized between March and June by Achaz Dohna with the help of some of the members of James's court, had some success among the clergy.

About 13,000 pounds were collected and were all spent by Captain Gray for recruiting soldiers. It cannot be said with certainty how many soldiers he finally succeeded in assembling. In London itself he failed altogether, if we are to trust Sterrell, who was usually quite objective in his reports. Perhaps he met with better success in Scotland, where he went from London. What we know is that Philip Burlamachi, an Italian merchant who had settled in London and whose agents used to take Dohna's reports to Heidelberg and to Prague, sent a bill to Dohna—a copy of it reached Van Male's hands—charging him for two thousand soldier's jackets, but for the transportation from Gravesend to Hamburg of only twelve hundred men. It is also known that the expedition, which sailed from Gravesend on June 5 was transported on five ships—a fact which corroborates Van Male's conclusion that it did not consist of more than two thousand men.

The even more scanty information which we possess concerning the fate of Gray's expeditionary force on the European mainland tells us about further mishaps. In July the Duke of Saxony forced Gray out of Lusatia. In August the force finally arrived in Bohemia and was reviewed by Frederick in Brandýs on the Elbe. But then, according to the Czech chronicler Skála, who numbered the men at four thousand, it quickly disintegrated because of lack of discipline and various illnesses.

What else could have been obtained at the court of James I, where the King himself was busy reading pamphlets and where Gondomar, the Spanish ambassador, living comfortably at Hatton Garden which the King had prepared for him, was still an influential person? A certain uneasiness, however, was now apparent between the King and the ambassador. Had the King not spent a whole audience questioning Gondomar as to why he had shaken Buckingham's hand with so much strength that the latter's thumb had been damaged?

In June, nevertheless, things began to move in England. It became evident, from reports arriving from the Continent that a Spanish attack on the Palatinate was not just an empty threat.

The Palatinate was not Bohemia. It was Frederick's legal property and therefore could be defended even by such a staunch legitimist as James. The King of England was certainly not ready to admit that the Spaniards were moved by any necessity of a military nature. On the contrary, he openly declared that the Palatinate was the property of his daughter, *filiae nostrae fundus dotalitius.* He now also showed more benevolence toward Dohna, who, in June and July, organized another drive for money and this time collected about 17,000 pounds. Following the suggestion of an influential member of the Privy Council, the Earl of Southampton—Shakespeare's well-known patron —the money collected was used for the sending of a new expeditionary force to help Frederick. This force numbered about two thousand men and was sent to Rotterdam.

Because of its small size, the Spaniards were not to disturbed by this expedition. Besides, they knew that Dohna, who gave its command to Sir Horace Vere, had made a grave mistake by neglecting the wish of Buckingham, who had favored Sir Edward Cecil. What disturbed the Spaniards much more was the sudden decision of the English to send a few ships to the Mediterranean against the Moslem pirates. Only a few months before, Gondomar would have appreciated such help. But now it was as if the ghost of Raleigh had suddenly appeared before his eyes, the ghost of that Raleigh around whose condemnation Gondomar had concentrated all his activities at the time of his first stay in London. With James's son-in-law in Prague, the presence of English ships in the Mediterranean seemed rather a danger to him. He tried, therefore, to persuade King James to keep them at anchor in Plymouth. At last, however, they sailed in spite of his protests.

Gondomar's influence, nevertheless, combined with James's indecisiveness, was still sufficient to keep England out of the war and to make her policy one of appeasement. In June, James announced the sending of new envoys to the belligerents. Sir Henry Wotton, who was to go back to Venice as regular envoy, was ordered to make a call in Vienna. At the same time, Francis

Nethersol, who had already participated in Doncaster's mission, was to see Frederick in Prague. They were empowered to offer a new plan to both parties: Frederick was to keep the title of King of Bohemia for life, but Bohemia should go back to Ferdinand, who, in his turn, was to confirm all the privileges of the Bohemian nobility and recognize Bohemia as an elective kingdom.

The acceptance of such an offer would probably have meant peace. But such a peace was not Oñate's aim. Nor was it now the aim of Ferdinand himself, who, almost on the day of Wotton's arrival at Vienna, wrote to Gondomar exhorting him to continue his work because "Frederick was already beginning to feel the wrath of God."

4

The "wrath of God" was rather Oñate's wrath. The budget of the Spanish embassy at the imperial court for the first half of the year 1620 rose to 555,000 gulden, of which 525,000 went to military preparations. Not a small amount was required, for instance, to pay fifteen hundred newly arrived Cossacks, who were nominally in the service of the Emperor but were actually paid by Oñate. Out of their pay, the Cossacks supported another thousand of their comrades; together they proved the scourge of every region which they visited.

In the diplomatic field, Oñate now gave the finishing touch to the agreement with the Duke of Saxony. That this Lutheran prince should help the Emperor to save the provinces of Bohemia and Moravia from the hands of the Protestant insurgents was itself a paradox. That, as a reward, he should receive under his patronage Silesia and Lusatia, the other two provinces of the Crown of St. Wenceslas, was a condition hardly in the spirit of those who, only a generation earlier, prized the "purity of blood from heretical contamination" above many other things.

The help offered by Saxony was, however, not nearly so important as that which could be expected from Bavaria. And

Bavarian help would now materialize, having been set free by the French diplomatic mission. It was an altogether unexpected event. Up to the day when the news arrived about Angoulême's success at Ulm, the outlook had still been dubious. Reading the letters sent by Francis Cardinal Dietrichstein to Italy and to Spain, we are confronted with a picture of persecution, the end of which was not then to be seen. The correspondents of the Cardinal shared his fears. Some of them were interested in the martyrdom suffered by the Catholic clergy in the regions occupied by the insurgents—especially in the heroic death of Jan Sarkander, pastor of the Moravian town Holešov, who had been tortured to death by the German Calvinist invaders and some of their Czech associates in Olomouc. Others, such as the Cardinal's sister, the Marquise of Mondejar, were already looking for an abode for the Cardinal in Spain or elsewhere. To live amid all that despair and yet to be sure of a future victory was not an easy task for Oñate.

When the French envoys, continuing their journey from Ulm, arrived at Vienna, they found Oñate not only all-powerful but also very sure of himself. Angoulême and his companions had come to repeat what they had already done in Ulm: to arrange a truce or perhaps even a peace. But immediately upon their arrival they saw that Oñate—who, according to their opinion, was doing much more than his superiors in Madrid were expecting him to do—would not allow them to complete their mission.

To distract the French from their task and, at the same time, to profit from their presence, Oñate decided to employ them in Hungary. He sent one of them, de Sigogné, and, later on, the whole deputation to Bethlen, who, in August, reached the summit of his revolutionary career by declaring himself King of Hungary. Oñate had now no use for any attempts to conclude a peace. How sure he and his aids were of their victory may be seen from a wager made during the summer between Polyxena, the wife of Lobkovic, and Oñate's secretary Bruneau: before Christmas our troops will be in Prague—such was Bruneau's conviction. Indeed, a direct attack on Bohemia's capital, an old and cherished idea of Oñate, the advantages of which he had tried to demonstrate to Buquoy a year before, again became the center of all his thoughts and actions.

There were now about twelve thousand imperial troops in Austria and in southern Bohemia, including Gauchier's cavalry, all paid with Spanish money. During the month of July, Oñate paid a personal visit to some of those units, and he also went to see Buquoy in his headquarters. At the beginning of August, Maximilian of Bavaria crossed the Austrian frontier, bringing with him the forces of the Catholic League, about ten thousand men. The Emperor's second army, which was much smaller—about six thousand men only—was still busy, under the command of Dampierre, on the Hungarian frontier. Oñate's main strategical idea was a risky one: to keep Bethlen in check and, at the same time, lead a quick, concentrated attack against Prague itself. Bethlen, although now declared King of Hungary, had not yet decided to arrange for his own coronation. Thus there was always a chance for a peaceful settlement. About eight thousand Hungarian cavalry had been sent to help Frederick, but a regular attack against the imperial forces was probably considered by Bethlen too risky. Oñate's clever decision to send the French envoys to Hungary resulted in another imperial triumph. The small army commanded by Dampierre would hardly have had strength enough to resist Bethlen's onslaught. Dampierre himself found unexpected death in a skirmish near Bratislava in the first days of October. But, once the French diplomats started negotiating with Bethlen, Austria's and Moravia's eastern frontiers were safe. The negotiations lasted until the second half of November. And then, of course, Prague was already liberated and Bethlen isolated.

In the meantime two events took place in western Europe which made the Spanish aims clear enough to all those in France and in England who still had doubts as to whether the Emperor would really be supported by the King of Spain.

The first of these events was the occupation of the Valtelline during the month of July. The significance of this event can be appreciated by anyone who consults a map of Europe of that time. Two small territories, Sundgau, the southern part of Alsatia, which had belonged to the Austrian Hapsburgs, and Valtelline, the upper valley of the river Adda in northern Italy, were of the greatest strategic importance to the Spaniards. We have already discussed Oñate's negotiations concerning the exchange of the Crown of Bohemia for Sundgau. The Valtelline was of even greater moment for the Spanish strategists. It gave them a corridor from the Duchy of Milan through the Stelvio Pass into the County of Tyrol, so that troops using it were able to avoid Venetian territory as well as that of the Swiss, who were always ready to protect their independence against any territorial encroachments. But, although the inhabitants of the Valtelline proper were Catholics, they lived under the military domination of the Swiss canton of Grisons (Graubünden), the inhabitants of which were Protestants. The Spanish governors of Milan had, for many years, managed to live on good terms with the Swiss. Some fortifications built on the shores of Lake Como by the Count of Fuentes de Valdepero, who became governor of Milan in 1600, was all that had been done, so far, to protect this vital connection with the lands of the Austrian Hapsburgs. An attempt, made at almost the same time, to occupy the Valtelline, had been given up, because the France of Henry IV was too strong and it had not been advisable to provoke her. In the autumn of 1619, when the troops from Italy were to cross the Alps into the Tyrol, large amounts of money had to be spent in order to obtain permission of the Swiss to use the valley which they dominated. Then, in July, 1620, the Spanish governor of Milan declared himself protector of the Catholic inhabitants of the Valtelline and his troops occupied the valley. Neither France nor Venice did anything to oppose this step.

The second development, an event of even greater weight than the occupation of the Valtelline, was the Spanish attack against the Lower Palatinate. Seen from London, this move was a surprise, in spite of all the suspicions concerning its possibility. Even when Ambrosio Spinola, the commander of the Spanish army in the Netherlands, had finished his preparations and had assembled enough troops in the southern part of the territory under his command—the Duchy of Luxemburg— the King of England was still waiting for some more evident proofs. Trumbull, his ambassador in Brussels, was most uncertain in his reports. Several letters of his, asserting that the attack on the Palatinate would not take place, were suddenly, on July 10, contradicted by a new report, affirming that the attack was imminent. Then another letter arrived, affirming again that troops had been assembled in the Luxemburg area as a mere threat which would not be carried out. But James, alarmed at last, had already reacted to the news of July 10 by immediately sending another diplomatic mission, led by Sir Edward Conway and Sir Richard Weston, to Brussels, Dresden, and Prague. The main object of this mission was to stop any military action which Spinola might undertake. But its entreaties had not the least influence on Spinola, and, in the first days of, September, his army crossed the border into Germany. The news of this development made the English outlook more bleak than ever. According to Sterrell's reports to Boisschot, the authorities in London were convinced that Spinola was intent on occupying even the free city of Nuremberg, the banking center where the Prague insurgents kept their financial reserves.

5

Besides the threat to their Nuremberg deposits, the situation of the Prague insurgents was endangered by other factors. Frederick was becoming less and less popular in his new capacity of King of Bohemia. Infectious diseases were ravaging the country, and in many districts armed farmers were resisting the rebellious nobles.

The men who had organized the Prague insurrection knew well that Spanish power was the greatest danger facing them.

They had, in the autumn of 1618, published a Spanish-written leaflet—*Questión si la causa de los Estados de Bohemia es justa o no*—trying to influence the opinion of the statesmen in Madrid. Then, as the ineffectiveness of such propaganda became evident, they took an openly hostile position. On the occasion of a banquet given in honor of Mehmed Aga, the Turkish envoy, and of the envoy of Bethlen, one of the insurgents declared that the Hapsburgs, "following the immoral practice of the Spaniards, had sold the Kingdom of Bohemia to Spain and had thus changed its freedom into servitude and its free citizens into slaves." And pictures of Spanish strongholds in non-Spanish countries, such as those of Milan or Antwerp, each guarded by a fortress in its center, or of Naples, watched by two fortresses on the seashore and a third one high above the city, were now evoked as means of anti-Spanish propaganda.

The number of Protestant troops in Bohemia had diminished since the beginning of the insurrection; it amounted now to twenty-five thousand men. It included about nine thousand infantry, thirty-five hundred cavalry paid for from the treasury of the Kingdom of Bohemia, about four thousand men who had been recruited in Austria, an equal number of infantry from Silesia, several thousand cavalry from Hungary, and about three thousand men from Moravia, who arrived at the beginning of September.

The Moravian nobles had assembled, all together, about twelve thousand men, but the commander of these troops, Jiří Náchod, son-in-law of the wise Karel Žerotín, let his men encamp in the surroundings of Jemnice in western Moravia and went alone to Bohemia to see for himself what Frederick's regime was like and whether the directors of the revolution were really working for the good of the country. What he saw was much worse than what he had expected. Lack of discipline and disturbances prevailed everywhere. It could be reasonably presumed that any major mishap would mean the beginning of total disintegration. There had been serious discord among the commanding officers ever since Frederick had confirmed Thurn as commander-in-chief and had subordinated to him the more experienced Mansfeld. Thurn himself had one chief interest: to fill his pockets. He was reappointed to the most remunerative office of the Kingdom—the governorship of Karlův Týn. He also continued confiscating the estates of others and making them his own. Jiří Náchod was able to observe all that. He decided to stay in Moravia, with all his troops. This decision undoubtedly influenced the eight thousand cavalry recently sent by Bethlen to help Frederick and proceeding slowly across Moravia toward the west. Consequently, they progressed even more slowly and finally, having received the news of Frederick's defeat on the White Mountain in Kolín on the Elbe, turned back to Hungary.

Spinola, in the meantime, had crossed the river Rhine and was making his way into the very heart of the Lower Palatinate. The Protestant Union reacted by sending another envoy to London. But Gondomar was still able to hold James I in check. He even sent his chaplain, De la Fuente, to Rome, as if sending him for papal permission to celebrate the nuptials of the Prince of Wales and the Infanta of Spain, although he well knew that the conditions under which the English were willing to authorize such a marriage would not be acceptable in Madrid. Thus only one precaution was taken in England: a third collection of money. The Prince of Wales, the members of the Privy Council and the City of London collected 28,000 pounds; from the rest of England and Scotland came 6,000 pounds.

In the meantime, in August, Maximilian of Bavaria came to Austria. He was not accompanied by all his forces, because, even after the agreement of Ulm had been signed, it was necessary to leave some troops to protect Bavaria itself. The Protestant nobles of upper Austria surrendered to Maximilian without fighting; the small amount of troops which they had sent to Frederick remained, nevertheless, in Bohemia.

Maximilian, who had intrusted Tserclaes de Tilly, a Netherland soldier, with the actual command of the troops, proceeded according to the prepared plan, the chief aim of which was the liberation of Prague. For that purpose he had sent a detach-

ment directly from Bavaria in the direction of Furth im Walde-
Domažlice to secure the main pass leading from Bavaria into
Bohemia through the Bohemian Forest; other passes of the
same region had already been secured by Baltasar Marradas.
As the main body of Frederick's forces, commanded by Anhalt,
was at that time in lower Austria, in the vicinity of Eggenburg
and as it was dangerous to ignore it, Maximilian, after a short
incursion into southern Bohemia, returned to Austria. When
Anhalt, however, retreated toward Moravia, Maximilian refused to follow him and again crossed the Bohemian frontier.
On September 17, his and Buquoy's troops started their march
toward Prague.

Thurn, Frederick's commander-in-chief, was a poor strate-
gist. From the very beginning he was at a loss, not knowing
whose advice to follow. First of all, he refused to act according
to Anhalt's counsel—to leave a few units on the Moravian
frontier and to attack Vienna itself. Then he decided to put up
a defense in the region of Tábor in the center of southern Bohemia and to send Mansfeld, who was hardly able to hold the
southwest of the kingdom, into Lusatia against the Duke of
Saxony.

But the imperial forces quickly proceeded toward the northwest, in the general direction of Plzeň. There a sort of negotiation started between Buquoy and Mansfeld. It seems that
Mansfeld, a "condottiere" without ideals, tried to change sides.
Thurn himself, when asked whether he knew about it, affirmed that it was a ruse. In any case the negotiations were
without result. Another attempt to negotiate, made by Frederick himself, was equally frustrated. A defensive line, built up
by Frederick's forces at Rokycany, was then avoided by the
imperial army, which proceeded northward toward Rakovník.
Anhalt, who in the meantime had been summoned with his
troops to Bohemia, tried in vain to stop them there. They made
a tentative attack on his position but then eluded his stratagem
and, by way of Nové Strašecí, hastened toward Prague, approaching the city from the northwest. Frederick's generals
had the choice of shorter but much more difficult ways, if they

wished to reach the capital before Maximilian and Buquoy.

Thus it happened that during the night of November 7–8, 1620, Frederick's army, tired and spiritless, arrived at a plain near Prague, which hardly deserves its name, the "White Mountain." Although situated much higher than the city of Prague, which lies, hidden in the deep valley of the river Vltava, some five miles away, it is only a slope, gradually descending from the Hvězda Park to the village of Motol. In the small hours, before dawn, the imperial forces also reached the place from the northwest. This time there was no escape. A battle had to be fought, which ended Thurn's ambitious insurrection, but which could not stop the spreading conflagration of Thirty Years, the longest continuous war in the history of Christian civilization.

Thurn, although not relinquishing the supreme command, put two other German immigrants in charge of his line of defense. Anhalt took over the right wing, protected by the high wall of the Hvězda Park against any attack from the side. Hohenlohe commanded the left wing. Units of infantry and cavalry were employed by them side by side. There was some artillery on both flanks. German soldiers constituted the majority of the infantrymen. Among the cavalry, there was a large group of Hungarians, commanded by Colonel Kornis.

The imperial army had only a small number of Germans and Czechs in its ranks. The majority, more than three-quarters of the total number, were Italians from the Milanese and from Naples, Frenchmen from Lorraine and from the Netherlands, and Flemings. The army's chief chaplain, the Spanish Carmelite monk, Domenico Ruzzola, from Calatayud, used to preach in Italian and French. Among his listeners there still was a young officer by the name of René Descartes.

The forces of the Catholic German League, commanded by Tilly, took a position on the left flank of the imperial army, opposite the units commanded by Anhalt. To their right were the units furnished or financed by Spain—the cavalry commanded by Philip Areyzaga, the regiments of Preiner and Tiefenbach, the cavalry of La Croix, the units of Montecucoli and

Verdugo, then Buquoy's own infantry, and, on the right wing, the cavalry of Gauchier. The reserve consisted mainly of the regiment of Spinelli.

The battle itself did not last long. It started with an indecisive attack by Gauchier. Then Frederick's forces attacked and succeeded in pushing back the imperial center, consisting of the infantry of Preiner and Tiefenbach. Their attack, however, was soon stopped by the imperial reserve and also by the cavalry of La Croix, who was killed in the action. Immediately afterward came a fierce attack by the imperial right wing. The whole line of battle turned as the troops commanded by Hohenlohe gave way and fled. The right wing of Frederick's forces defended itself for some time, but then also started running away. The last unit to hold its position close to the wall of the Hvězda Park was a company which had been sent to Prague by some Moravian nobles.

Frederick himself, after having received the first news about the progress of the battle, left Prague for the battlefield. He had, however, to turn back before he reached the White Mountain; the streams of soldiers running for their lives made his visit to the battlefield void of purpose and even impossible. Frederick returned to the Prague castle, where he had been entertaining Conway and Weston, the envoys of his father-in-law, and then hastily left the city for Silesia.

The day of November 8, 1620, ended as it had started, in mist and drizzle. Many of Frederick's soldiers had lost their way and drowned in the marshes on the left bank of the Vltava. The next day the victors entered the castle of Prague. In a solemn procession, Domenico Ruzzola, the chaplain, entered the cathedral, carrying a picture of Our Lady, which he had found in Strakonice in southern Bohemia, in a church devastated by the Protestants. The moment of his entry was later depicted on a solemn-looking fresco in the Carmelite Church of Santa Maria della Vittoria in Rome. In reality, the entry was not at all solemn. Plundering and looting was going on in the city, and worse things were to come.

ON THE WAY TO ROCROI

1

WARS should not get such a prominent place in history as they usually do. Even if a conflict meant a milestone on mankind's way to the fulfilment of time, it should be remembered that a milestone would be useless without a path, whereas a path can always exist without milestones. The Thirty Years' War can certainly be regarded as a boundary between two epochs; the enthusiasm of preceding years was slain on the battlefields by the initial skepticism of a new age. But the catastrophe itself did not add anything to what had been achieved by the preceding decades. It only consumed and destroyed.

It also destroyed the family alliance upon which the relations between Spain and the Holy Roman Empire had been based since the days of Charles V. It almost destroyed Spain and the Holy Roman Empire themselves. Two wars were actually fought in the decades which followed the rebellion of Prague: the ideological war in which the existence as well as the Catholic character of the Holy Roman Empire was at stake and the war for military and political preponderance in Europe, in which Spain was challenged and defeated by France. The two conflicts started together and ended separately; in their division perished the idea of traditional policy which had molded the age of Spanish preponderance.

Two aspects were prominent in this development. The first was the lack of rulers filled with religious enthusiasm. Ferdinand II, who died in 1637, two years after the final stage of the war had begun, was the last of such monarchs. In his son the conciliatory inclinations of the Austrian branch of the Hapsburg family prevailed once again, and there was no Spanish corrective this time. Second, Spanish military art and army declined. And again not only the lack of material resources, which overshadowed the last days of Ambrosio Spinola, but the growing lack of military leaders characterized this decline. The Cardinal Infante Ferdinand, the younger son of Philip IV, was rather a poor man to be last in the series of prominent generals which Spain and its dominions had produced; under his command the Spanish forces won their last major victory, at Nördlingen in 1634; after his death, in 1641, the way to the disaster of Rocroi stood open. Perhaps it might be noticed, in this connection, that in the battle of Rocroi, in which young Condé routed the Spanish army under Francisco de Melo, the non-Spanish, German, and Walloon troops turned their backs on the enemy and fled, whereas the Spanish core of the army had to be massacred. The indifference to the nationality of the demoralized mercenaries was paid for dearly. But this indifference itself was a sign of an estrangement between the spirit of the Spanish nation and the now almost mechanical imperialism of the Hapsburgs and their ministers.

Mechanical imperialism had outgrown its formative years in the first two decades of the seventeenth century. St. Clemente, Zúñiga, and Oñate had been its main Spanish cultivators on the soil of the Holy Roman Empire. They provided it with strategic plans. In doing so, they had acted as representatives not only of a great power but also of a glorious tradition. The suppression of the Bohemian rebellion and perhaps also the renewal of military actions in the Low Countries—urged by Ambrosio Spinola and decided by Zúñiga—were the last and final issues of this die-hard but purposeful policy. What followed was almost purposeless; it had not been planned, it was just accepted. And, with the gradual disappearance of the traditional enthusiasm, it amounted to a disaster.

2

It was not so easy to stop the avalanche which the rebellion in Bohemia had set in motion. On the one hand, those who opposed Spanish imperialism on the European mainland attached their hopes to the Bohemian adventure. They found it difficult to accept the imperial victory on the White Mountain as fate's final verdict. Mansfeld held Plzeň for some time. The town of Kladsko in eastern Bohemia was surrendered by Thurn's son only in October, 1622. The German Protestant Union stuck to its decision to defend the Palatinate up to the early spring days of 1621, and only then, but still reluctantly, it abandoned the country and declared itself dissolved.

On the other hand, the ambitions of the victors grew with their successes. Oñate came forward with a wholly unreasonable suggestion to form, out of the Lower Palatinate and the Sundgau, a new principality which might be given to Philip III's second son, Carlos. The situation in the Protestant Netherlands seemed propitious for the renewal of the war there; the Dutch Protestants had been divided since the beginning of the century by doctrinal strife between those who believed in the terrible Calvinist dogma of predestination and the followers of Jacob Harmensz, who did not. This ideological struggle had just ended, in the spring of 1619, through the declarations of the synod of Dordrecht. The ensuing persecution of the milder faction culminated in the execution, by his compatriots, of Jan Oldenbarneveldt, the most venerable of the anti-Spanish revolutionaries, and left many bitter memories.

Nor did the Hapsburgs feel themselves secure. Gabor Bethlen renewed his rebellious campaign in Hungary in the spring of 1621, and Gustavus Adolphus, King of Sweden, started a war of conquest against Poland. It was decided, therefore, to continue the military efforts. Even Maximilian of Bavaria refused, early in 1621, to accept the advice of some members of the German hierarchy to put an end to the League. Shortly afterward, Spinola was recalled to the Low Countries by Archduke Albert, and the actual command of the Spanish troops in the Palatinate was intrusted to Gonzales Córdoba. In June, 1621, the war in the Palatinate, which had come to a standstill in the preceding autumn, started again, and, half a year later, it spread even to Alsatia. By the beginning of 1622 Mansfeld, who in the meantime had left Bohemia, had assembled quite a large army at Germersheim on the Rhine. He was joined by Frederick himself and also by troops levied by two other Calvinist princes, Duke Christian of Brunswick-Wolfenbüttel and the Marquis George Frederick of Baden-Dürlach. Only the military genius of Tilly, who had now united his forces with those of Córdoba, was able to dispose of this force in the battles of Wimpfen and Höchst. By the spring of 1623 the whole Palatinate was in the hands of Maximilian of Bavaria, recently appointed its administrator by the Emperor. Mansfeld and his associates fled to the Low Countries to help Maurice of Orange against Spinola.

While it was simple enough to leave the Kingdom of Bohemia at the mercy of Ferdinand II, it was not so easy to decide what to do with the Palatinate. Oñate's idea of a new German principality consisting of a territory on the left bank of the Rhine as well as of the lower Palatinate, was refused even in Madrid. The members of the Council of State were anxious to retain the friendship of King James I of England, Frederick's father-in-law, and favored the establishment of Frederick's son as new Count Palatine. It was decided to postpone the ultimate solution and, in the meantime, to recognize Maximilian of Bavaria as Prince Elector to replace Frederick. The problem was finally solved only in 1648, by the treaty of Westphalia, which gave the Upper Palatinate, together with the electoral dignity, to Bavaria and restored the Lower Palatinate to Frederick's son Charles Louis, for whom it created a new electoral office.

The ideological controversies were still raging. The Palatine war was accompanied by a wave of polemical pamphlets, in which two publications played the lead. One was the *Anhaltische Kanzlei,* published by a counselor of the Duke of Bavaria; the other was the *Cancellaria hispanica,* issued by a secretary of Frederick. Whereas the first, using some papers of Christian of Anhalt, attempted to prove that the Calvinist movement was opposed to any legal order, the other, quoting a letter written by the papal nuncio in Vienna, tried to demonstrate that the German Catholic princes were acting as dumb tools of Spanish imperialism.

With the occupation of Heidelberg, the conflict which had started with the defenestration of Prague was, to all purposes, ended. It had not ended, however, in the Low Countries, where Mansfeld and his associates had now taken refuge. There, even during the years of 1624 and 1625, which had brought a temporary peace to Central Europe, the guns continued to boom incessantly, and Breda, an important stronghold of the Protestants, opened its gates to Spinola in May, 1625. Nor had the Protestant onlookers been reconciled with a Hapsburg victory, which, they thought, threatened their own freedom. The opinion of the English nobles and merchants turned decisively in favor of the defeated husband of King James's daughter, and James, as well as his successor, were finally forced to enter a virtual alliance with the Protestant Low Countries and thus to commit themselves to war with Spain. Gondomar's efforts were forgotten. And the efforts of the Count Duke of Olivares, who attempted to carry Gondomar's policy forward, met with a failure.

3

The policy of the Count Duke of Olivares, son of Philip II's ambassador to the Holy See and nephew of Baltasar Zúñiga, has been all but identified with Spain's rapid decay. His name is mentioned more frequently in the historical studies concerning Spain's participation in the Thirty Years' War than that of Philip IV. His character has been analyzed and found deficient. He certainly helped much to debase the efficacy of the already cumbersome bureaucratic apparatus of the Spanish administration by atomizing its central offices and councils. And he placed his personal interests too high.

It should not be forgotten, however, to complete the picture and bring it as close to reality as possible, that Olivares was not a revolutionary. No matter how divided his efforts were between the service of his country and the advancement of his personal welfare—which he promoted by providing amusements for the lighthearted king—his main lines of policy did not deviate from the great Spanish tradition. There were many chances for a change at the time when he was assuming his new responsibility, after the death of Philip III on March 31, 1621. Archduke Albert, another witness of the glorious past, died in the following June. And Baltasar Zúñiga, the man who carried the torch of the traditional foreign policy into the reign of Philip IV and who made the most important decision of all—the decision to revive the hostilities in the Netherlands—died in October, 1622. And yet there was not the slightest attempt on the part of the Count Duke to change either the principles or the tactics.

In a memorandum dated November, 1621, and written for the new king, Olivares reminded him that being the "greatest monarch of the world" and "the main support and defense of the Catholic religion," he was morally bound to "defend himself against the rebels of the Low Countries and the other enemies of the Church and to attack them." The succeeding paragraphs of the memorandum stressed, of course, the sad state of the royal treasury and the need for a sound economy. In this document as well as in other similar records, written in 1629 and even later, Olivares appeared as a realistic critic of Spanish power. In 1629 he even spoke of two "unexpected and almost miraculous events," the assassination of Henry IV and the victory on the White Mountain. Those events, he affirmed, had saved Spain from disaster which the country would hardly have been able to avoid if left to its own resources. There, perhaps, in the inability to follow the voice of his own reason, lay Olivares' guilt. The impoverishment of Spain proceeded under his rule at an ever quickening pace. Another forced conversion of loans was decreed in 1627, and still another was to come in 1647. Monetary machinations were the order of the day. The importation of bullion from America in the years 1641-45 declined to one-third of what had been imported in 1591-95. It was no wonder that foreigners, revisiting the Pyrenean peninsula, were taken aback by the outward signs of decadence. "This city," said one of them, writing from Lisbon in 1629, "has now lost all its ancient splendor since I was here seventeen years ago. It is now completely ruined. All the merchants are bankrupt, and all their commodities are gone except their diamonds, Brazil tobacco, and coarse sugar, all of which are dearer here than in Holland. There is a great discontent with Castilian rule, and especially with some new laws whose object is to bring the Portuguese more absolutely under the King."

But as far as foreign affairs were concerned and, above all, in matters of dynastic policy, Olivares was a true heir to the Spanish statesmen of the preceding generations. He had to witness the frustration of the scheme to ally Spain with England by a marriage between Charles, son of James I, and the Infanta Maria, sister of Philip IV, because he could not give way in matters of religious principle which required a Catholic husband for the Princess. Even the good offices of Peter Paul Rubens, the painter, could not help him to succeed in an affair in which his own axioms prohibited him from making any concession. And the same axioms proved his greatest disadvantage in his main struggle, the struggle against France, the country led by Cardinal Richelieu.

4

Seen from the point of view of a historian of nationalist policies, the whole story of Spanish preponderance in Europe seems like a prolonged fight between Spain and France, in which France, for almost a hundred years, was losing battles. To interpret history in such a way would mean, of course, a dangerous oversimplification. But perhaps it is not without significance that France succeeded in matching its forces with Spain only at a time when sheer and almost automatic nationalism prevailed in Spanish political thought.

The close collaboration between Spain and the Holy Roman Empire had alway been an object of French suspicion. And the Valtelline, the Alpine valley which had proved so useful to Oñate in 1619-20, was regarded by the French as a strategic artery of the Spanish-imperial alliance. In 1621 France decided to step into the international turmoil and restrict Spanish influence in the Valtelline by an agreement with Spain, which, for its part, certainly needed French friendship. The counselors of the dying Philip III were ready to negotiate. Baltasar Zúñiga himself suggested, as a halfway solution of the trouble, that the Valtelline should be ceded to the Pope. After prolonged discussions a treaty was signed in Madrid, in April, 1621, according to which the Valtelline was to be placed under the joint protection of France and the Swiss confederation. But the inhabitants of the valley did not want to come again under the power of the Protestant Grisons. Nor was the Duke of Feria, governor of Milan, ready to comply with the terms of the treaty. When the Grisons attempted to restore their authority in the valley, they were defeated by the combined forces of the Duke of Feria and of the Emperor's younger brother, Leopold.

The ascendancy of France, however, interrupted by the assassination of Henry IV in 1610, was fully revived at the close of 1622, after the peril of an internal revolution had been reduced by the agreement between the King and the Huguenots reached at Montpellier. In February, 1623, France joined Venice and Savoy in a solemn pledge to oust the Spaniards from the Valtelline. Pope Gregory XV then decided to prevent a conflict by occupying the valley with his own troops. But even this solution proved of only temporary value.

In the meantime, Oñate's idea of a new principality on the Rhine pushed France directly into the net of Mansfeld's diplomatic plans. In April, 1624, Richelieu again became the leading minister of Louis XIII and revived fully his policy of opposing Spanish power everywhere. The papal troops in the Valtelline were attacked, at the end of 1624, by the combined French and Swiss forces, commanded by the Marquis of Cœuvres; this was Richelieu's first major action in the field of foreign policy. But during the year 1625 Huguenot resistance in France revived, and Richelieu had to conclude the treaty of Monzon, which left the fortified places in the Valtelline in the hands of the Pope and did not expressly forbid the passage of Spanish troops through the valley. To cover his temporary impotence, nevertheless, the French statesman let loose the Danish attack upon the imperial forces in Germany. Courmenin, his diplomatic agent, encouraged Christian IV of Denmark and promised him French help. The result was an offensive, assumed by Lutherans as well as by Calvinists in the spring of 1626 and led by King Christian and by Mansfeld. Richelieu, the instigator, stayed, of course, in the background, but he had achieved his purpose: the conflict which had started in 1618 was rekindled again.

5

In its Danish period, the years 1626-29, the Thirty Years' War was rapidly assuming a character which differed widely from that of its first phase. The religious cause was becoming a mere pretext for the belligerents. Albrecht Valdštýn, the Czech nobleman whom we have mentioned in connection with the Prague rebellion and who had recently acquired immense wealth in the lands which had been confiscated from the rebels, had now become the imperial commander-in-chief. He was no better in his moral outlook than Mansfeld. And, above all, few people were still able to believe that any religious values could be restored by his murderous, rapacious troops. Pope Urban VIII now clearly disapproved of the continuation of the war. But Spanish policy, directed by Olivares, was not to be influenced by any admonishing. On the contrary, when the Duke of Mantua, Vincent Gonzaga, died in December, 1627, and the French Duke of Nevers, Charles Gonzague, appeared as his only male heir, Olivares started another conflict, the so-called "War of the Mantuan Succession," which for several years, until the spring of 1631, ravaged the entirely Catholic provinces of northwestern Italy.

It is interesting to observe how, in the oscillating course of events which shaped the story of the Thirty Years' War, imperialist strategies disrupted what had formerly been unified by a common ideology. In the autumn of 1627, for instance, Valdštýn came forward with the plan to attack the heartland of Denmark; the Spanish as well as the Hanseatic vessels were expected to participate. But his suggestion was not even considered seriously in Madrid. The Mantuan affair absorbed all the Spanish energies. On the other hand, the presence of Spanish troops in Germany was more and more resented even by the German Catholic princes. And so was Valdštýn's influence upon the execution of the Edict of Restitution, which marked off the imperial victory in the Danish war.

Religious enthusiasm was also completely absent from the events which took place in 1629 in Italy. Richelieu was able to step in again after the fall of the Huguenot fortress of La Rochelle. The main French attack against the Spanish forces in Italy almost coincided with the peace between the Emperor and the King of Denmark, concluded in May, 1629. Not only Spanish but also imperial troops had to be transferred from Germany into Italy, and Ambrosio Spinola, as well as Valdštýn's lieutenant Collalto, were directed there to take charge of the operations around Casale and Mantua.

The war of the Mantuan Succession showed the weakness and exhaustion of Spain. When it finally ended, in April, 1631, by the treaty of Cherasco, Olivares had to give the Duchy of Mantua to the Duke of Nevers. But the conflict had dragged on long enough to bridge the gap between the Danish and the subsequent, Swedish, stage of the Thirty Years' War. It fulfilled almost the same role as did the Netherlands campaign of Spinola between the Bohemian and the Danish war. It brought the Spaniards new enemies.

6

The Swedish war, resulting from the attack of King Gustavus Adolphus—the "Restitutor Germaniae"—on the Empire, witnessed the last stage of the traditional collaboration between Spain and the Empire. In February, 1632, Ferdinand II signed a treaty of mutual help, and Olivares, disillusioned and melancholy as never before, exerted himself to effectuate it. In 1633 and 1634, two armies, one commanded by the Duke of Feria and the other by the Cardinal Infante Ferdinand, younger brother of Philip IV, crossed the Alpine passes to the north. Even Oñate, the first architect of the war, came again to Vienna, in October, 1633, as envoy extraordinary.

A crisis followed, resulting not only from the victories of Gustavus Adolphus but also from the rapidly growing enmity between the Spaniards and Valdštýn, who was jealous of the authority of the Spanish generals and critical of their imperialism. It was only after the decreed assassination of Valdštýn, in February, 1634, that the culminating point of the Swedish war was reached by the smashing victory of the Cardinal Infante Ferdinand and the imperial general Gallas over the Swedes at Nördlingen, in September, 1634.

The victory of Nördlingen, however, turned against the Spanish interests in so far as it influenced Richelieu's decision to enter the stage once more—this time with the full military might of the strengthened Kingdom of France. The French-Spanish war, presaged as early as 1631 by French military actions in the bishopric of Trèves, was actually declared in May, 1635. The French victory with which it finally ended was by no means an easy one. The initial successes of the Duke of Rohan in the Valtelline valley ended in the settlement of 1639, which authorized the Spaniards to pass through the valley. In 1637 the offensive directed by the Cardinal Infante Ferdinand from the Low Countries had almost reached Paris. The loss of Portugal in 1640 and the insurrection in Catalonia were not able to destroy the Spanish power to resist. Nor did the fall into disgrace of Olivares, which took place in the spring of 1642, prove decisive; on the contrary, it was welcomed by the Emperor, Ferdinand III, who did not like the minister's intransigent imperialism, and it brought relief to the hidalgos themselves who had learned to hate the "Herod of Spain."

Nevertheless, after the defeat which they had suffered at Rocroi in 1643, the Spaniards had to give up in the Empire and to restrict themselves to the defense of their own territory. Four and half years afterward, the Emperor's representatives concluded the peace treaty of Westphalia. The Holy Roman Empire emerged from the Thirty Years' War changed into an absolutist, centralized state, but restricted to the area of the upper Danubian valley and with less influence in Germany or Italy than ever before. It was to be called, from now onward, the "Austrian Empire." The ascent of Leopold I to the imperial throne in 1657 completely reversed the relation between the two branches of the Hapsburg family; the Austrian branch was now to play the leading role not only because Spain had exhausted its material forces and impoverished itself but also because the political ideology of the Spaniards was dead.

Spain, in spite of all that, remained on the battlefields, fighting desperately against the troops of young Louis XIV, whose policies were now directed by a former subject of the King of Spain, Cardinal Mazarin. Even Count Oñate, who had died in 1644, would hardly have recognized the war of whose beginnings he had been the main witness. It was the last stand of men who had survived their own times. The same Condé, who had defeated the Spaniards at Rocroi, fled to them in September, 1652, when he had become involved in the conspiracy of the French noblemen against Mazarin. He was given a high post of command in the Spanish army but was not able to achieve anything with its antiquated equipment. The defeat inflicted on the Spaniards by Turenne on the dunes near Dunkirk in June, 1658, the last major battle of the war, thus became, ironically enough, a French victory over the Spanish army commanded by a French officer.

The peace treaty of the Pyrenees between France and Spain was concluded in 1659. It meant not only the confirmation of France's possession of Roussillon and Artois, together with some towns on her eastern frontier but also, and above all, the recognition by Spain of French leadership in Europe. The days were gone in which the fabulous wealth and military might of the Spanish kings had served as background to idealist plans.

And the results of those plans? Let us not judge them by the material devastation left in their wake. The dramatic power of a tale is in the tale itself, not in the silence which follows it.

NOTES

PREFACE

The following is a list of the archives from which I have been able—in most cases directly, in some indirectly, with the help of copyists—to draw my material. Each name is preceded by an abbreviation which is used in the subsequent notes.

BBP	Besançon, Bibliothèque publique
BZA	Brno, Zemský Archiv
EBM	Escorial, Biblioteca del Monasterio
HSA	Hannover, Staatsarchiv
KAA	Kroměříž, Arcibiskupský Archiv
MAHN	Madrid, Archivo Histórico Nacional
MAP	Madrid, Archivo de Palacio Nacional
MARAH	Madrid, Archivo de Real Academia de Historia
MAV	Madrid, Archivo de los Duques de Villahermosa
MBN	Madrid, Biblioteca Nacional
MBP	Madrid, Biblioteca del Palacio Nacional
MDA	Mikulov, Dietrichsteinský Archiv
MIVJ	Madrid, Instituto de Valencia de Don Juan
NAF	Naples, Archivio dello Stato, Archivio Farnese
NGN	Nuremberg, Germanisches Nationalmuseum
PAČ	Prague, Archiv země České
PAMV	Prague, Archiv ministerstva vnitra
PAN	Paris, Archives nationales
PMÉ	Paris, Archive du Ministère des affaires étrangères
RAAE	Rome, Archivio della Ambasciata Espagnola presso la S. Sede
RASV	Rome, Archivio Segreto Vaticano
RLA	Roudnice, Lobkowiczský Archiv
RLK	Roudnice, Lobkowiczská Knihovna
SAG	Simancas, Archivo General de España
WNB	Vienna, Nationalbibliothek, Manuscripta
WRKA	Vienna, Reichskammerarchiv
WSA	Vienna, Staatsarchiv

Some of the above-listed archives have been made more easily accessible by the publication of detailed indexes to their abundant material. I am specially indebted to three publications of this kind: M. Acocer, *Consultas del Consejo de Estado* (Valladolid, 1930); Julian Paz, "Archivo general de Simancas" (Vienna, 1913), in *Archiv für oesterreichische Geschichte;* and, by the same author, *Secretaria de Estado: Documentos de las negociaciones de Flandes, Holanda y Bruselas* (2d ed.; Madrid, 1946). Also of aid to me were: B. Sánchez Alonso, *Fuentes de la historia española;* and R. Ballester y Castell, *Las Fuentes narrativas de la historia de España*, both published in Madrid in 1927.

There are also published collections of documents, of which the following have been used for the present work: the large *Colección de documentos inéditos* (abbrev. "CDI") and its continuation, the *Nueva CDI;* the English collection, *Calendar of Letters*, the Spanish volumes of which have been edited by M. A. S. Hume; the *Briefe und Akten zur Geschichte des 30jährigen Krieges;* the Czech collection, *Sněmy české;* the *Relazioni degli ambasciatori veneti*, published by Albéri; similar collections of Venetian diplomatic reports, edited by Gachard and Fiedler; reports of the papal nonces published by German historians *(Nuntiaturberichte aus Deutschland)*, as well as by their Czech *(Epistulae nuntiorum)* and Spanish colleagues (Hinojosa, *Los Despachos de la diplomatia pontifitia*, and Serrano, *Correspondencia diplomatica entre España y la Santa Sede).*

It goes without saying that even extended investigations of archives would hardly be sufficient if they were not supported by a study of literature. Among the basic works dealing with subjects related more or less closely to the theme of this book, I would like to note, in the first place, the second, third, and fourth volumes of the *Cambridge Modern History;* H. Hauser's *La Prépondérance espagnole* (Paris, 1934); and Roger B. Merriman's *The Spanish Empire* (New York, 1912-34). A thorough survey of Spanish history, as well as a detailed bibliography, may be found in *The Golden Century of Spain* by R. Trevor Davies (London, 1937), in *Historia de España y su influencia en la historia universal* by Antonio Ballesteros y Beretta (Barcelona, 1920-26), and in the old, but still useful, *Geschichte Spaniens unter den Habsburgen* by K. Haebler (Gotha, 1907).

I cannot conceal that, as far as the appreciation of Spanish political ideals is concerned, the essays of A. Cánovas del Castillo *(Casa de Austria en España* [Madrid, 1869]; "De las ideas políticas," *Revista de España*, [1868], and *Revista contemporánea* [1889] seem to me, in spite of their age, more fair and more brilliant than the more modern works on the same theme—with the exception perhaps of José Antonio Maravall's *Teoría española del estado en el siglo XVII* (Madrid, 1944) and F. Javier de Ayala's *Ideas políticas de Juan de Solórzano* (Seville, 1946). As to the religious and economic aspects of the story, I have tried to reach the truth by carefully reading even such works as seemed to me too distant from what I had been able to find in the documents. Thus not only Pastor's *History of the Popes* but also Gothein's *Reformation und Gegenreformation* (Munich, 1924) and other works disapproving of the Catholic point of view have helped me. Among the basic works discussing the economic character of the epoch I would like to mention K. Haebler's *Die wirtschaftliche Blüte Spaniens im 16ten Jahrhundert* (Berlin, 1888), Artiñana's *Historia del comercio con las Indias* (Barcelona, 1907), R. H. Tawney's *Religion and the Rise of Capitalism* (London, 1916), R. Ehrenberg's *Capital and Finance in the Age of the Renaissance* (English trans. of *Das Zeitalter der Fugger* [London, 1928]), Earl J. Hamilton's *American Treasure and the Price Revolution in Spain* ("Harvard Economic Studies" [1934]), and Jaime Carrera Pujal's *Historia de la economía española* (Madrid, 1943).

THE ENIGMA OF AN AGE

The quotation from Herbert Butterfield is from his book *Christianity and History* (New York, 1950), p. 42. The author acknowledges the kindness of Charles Scribner's Sons, New York, in granting him permission to include this quotation in his text.

Edward Armstrong published his book *The Emperor Charles V* in 1910, Ramón Menéndez Pidal his study, *Idea imperial de Carlos V,* in 1941. Cf. p. 9 of Menéndez Pidal's work, where he speaks of Charles as of "esta figura tan española"; and F. Cereceda's article, "Origen español de la idea imperial en Carlos," in *Razón y fé,* 1942, pp. 239 ff.

AN IMPERIAL PROGRAM

Among the older books concerning Charles V, those by Gossart *(Charles-Quint et Philippe II: Étude sur les origines de la prépondérance politique de l'Espagne en Europe* [Brussels, 1896] and *Charles-Quint et Philippe II dans l'ancien drame historique espagnol* [Brussels, 1923]) are still well worth reading. Ludwig Pfandl *(Johanna die Wahnsinnige* [Freiburg, 1930]) studies Charles's family, as well as the general characteristics of his age. Two modern biographies of the Emperor are outstanding: Karl Brandi's *The Emperor Charles V* (New York, 1939) and D. B. Wyndham Lewis' *Charles of Europe* (New York, 1931). Some researchers have studied the so-called "Testament of Charles V" (E. W. Mayer in *Historische Zeitschrift,* Vol. CXX; Bruno Stuebel in *Mitteilungen des Instituts für oesterreichische Geschichtsforschung,* Vol. XXIII; J. K. Mayr in *Historische Blätter des Staatsarchivs* [1921]). Charles's ideas about the duties of the imperial office have been analyzed by Peter Rassow *(Die Kaiser-Idee Karls V* [Berlin, 1932]; also "Der Kaiser und sein Kanzler" in *Nachrichten der Gesellschaft der Wissenschaften zu Göttingen* [1933]); but some of his more important conclusions have been modified by Ramón Menéndez Pidal in his *Idea imperial de Carlos V* (Buenos Aires, 1941), in which full use has also been made of C. Bornate's conclusive study, *Memorias de Gattinara* ("Miscellanea di storia italiana," Vol. XVII [Turin, 1915]). A substantial part of Charles's correspondence has been dealt with by O. A. Looz-Corswarem *(Die Korrespondenz Karls V* [Göttingen, 1936]).

Charles's declaration before the Cortes at La Coruña has been published in *Cortes de León y Castilla,* II, 293.

At the beginning of Charles's career as emperor, a certain Georg Sauermann (Sauromano), a German whose identity I have not been able to establish, published a treatise, *Hispaniae consolatio,* in which he tried to show to the Spaniards the advantages of Charles's new office for their own kingdom. It does not seem likely, however, that his arguments had any influence on Spanish opinion.

The part played by Charles in the religious disputes of the time has certainly been misunderstood by historians, who treated him as if he had participated in the post-Tridentine sharp division between the Catholics and the Protestants. There is hardly any better book to initiate us into the spiritual atmosphere of the century and, at the same time, introduce us to the vast literature of the subject than the first volume of Hubert Jedin's *History of the Council of Trent,* of which I have been able to peruse the Italian version, *Storia del Concilio di Trento* (Brescia, 1950). The large *Historia de los heterodoxos Españoles* by M. Menéndez y Pelayo (Madrid, 1881) is still the most penetrating study of the Spanish quest for religious purity. But I would also like to draw the reader's attention to three more specialized but highly important works: *Influencia que tuvieron en el derecho público los filósofos y teólogos españoles* by Eduardo Hinojosa (Madrid, 1890); *Pedro de Soto y las controversias político-teológicas en el siglo XVI* by V. D. Carro (Salamanca, 1931); and *L'Élément historique dans la controverse religieuse du XVIe siècle* by Pontien Polman (Gembloux, 1932).

The quotation containing Luther's decision of 1520 is from Enders, *Luthers Briefwechsel*, II, 432.

The quotation on enthusiasm is from S. T. Coleridge's address delivered at Bristol in 1795. Pedro de Medina's words are from his *Libro de grandezas y cosas memorables en España* (Alcalá de Henares, 1548), p. xxx. The re-establishment of the Inquisition in Spain has been related in detail by W. T. Walsh in his essay on Torquemada (*Characters of the Inquisition* [New York, 1940]).

Some of the characteristic utterances of Martin Luther concerning the relation between faith and reason ("the greatest prostitute of all," as he called it) may be found in his *Sämtliche Werke* (published in Erlangen), XVI, 142-48; in his *Tischreden (Werke,* published in Weimar), III, 62, No. 2904*a;* and in his *Briefwechsel,* ed. Enders, VIII, 160-61. It is interesting to note the close connection between Luther's divorcing of faith from reason, on the one hand, and his principle, "Pecca fortiter, crede firmius," on the other hand. In fact, Luther did not preach merely the insignificance of human sin in comparison with the merits of Jesus Christ; he preached active and wilful sinning as the best method of fighting the devil. See, for example, *Tischreden* (ed. Weimar), III, 258, and *Opera exeg. Lat.* (Weimar), XLII, 8-10: "O, that I may find some true sin to be able to hoax the devil and to prove that I do not recognize any sin and that my conscience is in peace because it does not know of any; we, who are constantly attacked and tortured by the devil, have the greatest need to get rid of the Decalogue altogether and not to think of it any more."

Quevedo's scene with Luther, Mohammed, and Judas may be found in his *El Sueño de las Calaveras* ("Clásicos castellanos," Vol. XXXI [Madrid, 1931]), p. 50.

EUROPE—THE DYNAMIC CONTINENT

Guicciardini's opinion concerning the relations between the Papacy and the Empire is taken from his *Proposta di alleanza di Carlo V a Clemente VII.*

The Lutheran point of view, as defended at the Diet of Augsburg in 1530, is particularly well explained by Melanchthon himself in a letter to Johannes Brenz, dated May, 1531, and published in Enders' edition of Luther's letters (*Luthers Briefwechsel,* IX, 18–21). See also Luther's treatise *Zwei kaiserliche meinige und widerwertige Gebote.*

Juan de la Vega's advice to the Emperor ("quittar aquella cirimonia de elección de manera que viniesse hereditario el imperio como los otros estados") has been discussed by Buschbell ("Die Sendung des Pedro Marquina," *Spanische Forschungen der Görresgesellschaft,* I, No. 10, 316).

Fray Alfonso à Castro's preaching in England is discussed by D. B. Wyndham Lewis *(Charles of Europe* [New York, 1931], p. 298). Marcel Bataillon, who in his *Erasme et l'Espagne* stresses the "illuminated" character of the religious ideas of Cazalla and the other Spanish "Lutherans," forgets that there was no basic difference between the irrationalism of the *illuminados*—an old Gnostic sect which also did not recognize any value in practical morality—and that of the Lutheran doctrine of justification; in this case, the Spaniards were certainly entitled to speak of Lutheranism.

ON THE LAND, ON THE SEA

Since Leopold Ranke published his book on the *Ottoman and Spanish Empires in the 16th and 17th Centuries* (an English translation with this title appeared in London in 1843), many historians have been interested in the conflict between the Turkish Empire and the empire of the Spaniards, founded by Charles V. Very few of them, however, have stressed the fact that not the Protestants but the Turks had been the main concern of Spanish foreign policy up to the 1580's. Among those who did, Fernand Braudel, author of the large and minutious study, *La Mediterranée et le monde méditerranéen à l'époque de Philippe II* (Paris, 1949), has to be mentioned in the first place. The bibliography which he gives is exhaustive.

The quotation from the *Tercera Canción* by Garcilaso de la Vega is from his *Obras* (Buenos Aires, 1946), pp. 131 ff.

The legends commemorating St. Orosia have been studied by Ramón Menéndez Pidal in his *Floresta de leyendas heroicas españolas* (Madrid, 1926).

The participation of Spanish troops in the campaigns in Austria and Hungary was recorded by several Central European chroniclers of the sixteenth and early seventeenth centuries, particularly by Slavata in his Czech "Story of the Kingdom of Hungary." See also A. Lefaivre, *Les Magyars pendant la domination ottomane en Hongrie* (Paris, 1902).

Gabriel Salamanca's activities in Austria have been discussed by J. V. Goehlert (*Archiv für oesterreichische Geschichte* [1869]) and Alfred Stern (*Historische Zeitschrift*, Vol. CXXXI).

I, THE KING

The mutual relations between Charles, Ferdinand, Philip, and Maximilian are reflected in the reports of two Spanish diplomats, Martin de Salinas and Gamiz, WSA, Span. Dipl. Korr. 2. Also WSA, Span. Dipl. Korr. 3, contains reports of Pedro Lasso concerning the young men around Maximilan. Charles's "Documentos y avisos," addressed to Philip and dated in Augsburg, January 18, 1548, are kept in WSA, Span. Hofkorr. 1. In WSA, Span. Hofkorr. 1, a fascicle can also be found containing the letters which the Emperor sent to Maximilian during the years 1549–52. The atmosphere of the family conference in Augsburg is depicted in a report sent to Rome and preserved in SAG, Libros de Berzosa 5, fol. 124. The draft of an agreement between Ferdinand and Philip, dated March 9, 1551, is in SAG, Estado 649. The attempts of the Emperor to win Austria for Philip again are discussed by Luis Cabrera de Córdoba in his *Filipe Secundo,* Book I, chap. vii. The letters of Vanegas are kept in SAG, Patr. Real 57, MS 125 and Estado 649. See also MBN, MS 10988, "Correspondencia entre D. Fernando, rey de Romanos, y su sobrino Felipe Segundo, 1555–1563."

Some documents concerning the life and political activities of Maximilian have been published by Maurenbrecher, Koch, and Perger. There is a good book on Maximilian's formative years by Holtzmann, *Maximilian II bis zu seiner Thronbesteigung* (Berlin, 1903). The book which Victor Bibl has written on the same subject, *Maximilian II* (Hellerau bei Dresden), is not to be trusted because of its complete lack of knowledge of documents.

For the rebellion of the Moriscos in southern Spain see P. Boronat Barrachina, *Los Moriscos españoles* (Valencia, 1901). Philip's instruction to Bishop Aguila is in CDI, XCVIII, 6–10. A short bibliography concerning Miques-Mandes-Nasi, Duke of Naxos, may be found in Braudel's *La Méditerranée à l'epoque de Philippe II* (Paris, 1949), p. 537; see also W. T. Walsh, *Philip II* (New York, 1937), *passim.*

The negotiations between Philip and Maximilian concerning the defense of Hungary as well as Spanish interests in Eastern Europe during the first twenty years of the reign of Philip II may be studied in the following sources: RAAE, leg. 17; SAG, Estado 654, 668, 670, 675, 688, 693, 694, 697, 700, 701, 702, 703, 704, 705, 706, 927, 956, 2450, and 2864; CDI, 98, 101, 110, and 111; PMÉ, Mém. et cons., Espagne 236; WSA, Span. Dipl. Korr. 6–10, 12, and 13; WSA, Span. Varia 1*b* and 2, Kriegsakten 24, Span. Hofkorr. 3 and 4; MDA, HA 11, 156, and 167; NGNM, Khev. Kpb. I–III and V; HSA, III, Y17; RLK, Genealogia; KAA, Kop. (letters of Bishop Pavlovský to St. Clemente), and "Volná korespondence." See also F. C. Khevenhueller, *Annales;* J. Macůrek, *Zápas Polska a Habsburků* (Prague, 1931); Janko, *Lazarus Schwendi* (Vienna, 1871); Eiermann, *Lazarus von Schwendi* (Freiburg, 1904).

Among the books dealing with the reign of Philip II, that of the well-informed and critical Luis Cabrera de Córdoba (*Filipe Secundo,* a new edition of which was published in Madrid in 1876) is still of great importance. The nineteenth-century historians, such as Hume, Maurenbrecher, Justi, and Philippson, whose minds were full of prejudices, and also some of their more modern followers—among others Merriman (Vol. IV of his *Rise of the Spanish Empire*)—were hardly able to grasp the ideological basis of Philip's policy. The detailed studies of Ricardo de Hinojosa (*Felipe II y el conclave de 1559* [Madrid, 1889]) and of J. Fernández Montaña brought new light into some of the more problematic chapters of the story of Philip's reign. The tide was reversed completely by the small but profound book of the Danish historian, Karl Bratli, of which a French version, *Philippe II,* was published in Paris in 1912. Bratli's conclusions have been confirmed by a number of studies of more special interest, among which perhaps the most important are those of Angela Valente (Filippo II e l'Italia [*"Nuova rivista storica,"* 1926]) and Julián Zarco Cuevas ("Ideas y normas de gobierno de Felipe II," *Boletín de la Academia de Historia* [Madrid, 1927]). Among the most recent biographies of Philip, we may quote those by L. M. E. Bertrand (*Philippe II* [Paris, 1929]), Rheinhold Schneider (*Philipp II* [Leipzig, 1931]), W. T. Walsh (*Philip II* [New York, 1937]), and Mariano Tomás (*Felipe II* [Madrid, 1939]).

Philip's administration has been discussed by M. J. Gounon-Loubens in his *Essai sur l'administration de la Castille au XVI⁰ siècle* (1861). See also Agustín Alvarez de Toledo, "El Gobierno de España" (MBN, Manuscritos, E 31, MS 904). The idea of "dissimulation" was analyzed by Pedro de Ribadaneyra (*Tratado de la religión y virtudes que debe tener el príncipe christiano* [Madrid, 1595]) and by Juan de Santa Maria (*Tratado de la república y policía christiana* [Valencia, 1619]).

THE PRINCES AND THE BISHOPS

The dissenting views of the Hapsburgs in matters of religious policy in the 1550's may be studied in: MBN, MSS 9390 and 10988; MBP, T 2289; MDA, HA 11 and 157; SAG, Estado 649, 893, and 2688; PMÉ, Mém. et doc. 232/58; WSA, Span. Hofkorr. 1, Saxonica 2*b*, Span. Dipl. Korr. 1, 5, and 6, Röm. Korr. 11, HA Saml. 1 and Röm. Ber. 15; CDI 98 and 101. Bromato's *Storia di Paolo IV* is, in spite of its age, an indispensable background to this story.

Ferdinand's negotiations with the papal Curia concerning an authorization for the Czech laity to communicate under both species are recorded in RASV, Germania 10, fols. 182 ff.

Dietrichstein's mission is commented upon in a very peculiar way by Professor Steinherz in the volume of *Nuntiaturberichte aus Deutschland* which he edited. Steinherz found that, on the same day on which Charles Borromeo received the visit of the Spanish ambassador and gave him his negative reply, he also wrote a private letter in which there was mention that Dietrichstein had already succeeded in obtaining from the Pope the privilege "which he had come to request in the name of Piuscosque." Not knowing what the word "Piuscosque" could mean, Steinherz reached a conclusion which was as quick as it was far-reaching. "Piuscosque," he affirmed, cannot be anything else than Maximilian's pseudonym used to conceal the real name of the petitioner; subsequently—and this was the conclusion Professor Steinherz was especially proud of—Cardinal Charles Borromeo, who had assured the Spanish ambassador that he knew of no mission on behalf of Maximilian but mentioned it in a private letter of his written on the same day, was a liar. Had Steinherz taken the trouble to investigate the Dietrichstein archive in Mikulov, he would have found there letters addressed to Adam Dietrichstein by Jiří Proskovský, a Czech nobleman, member of the Order of St. John. As a Johannite knight, Proskovský, although not a priest, was not allowed to marry; but, as his older brother had recently died, he wished to marry to preserve the name of his family for future generations. A papal dispensation was necessary. Having heard about Dietrichstein's forthcoming journey to Rome, he asked him to take his petition with him. Dietrichstein willingly accepted this secondary mission, and, once in Rome, he obtained the dispensation for Proskovský through ordinary channels, so that several officials of the papal court knew about it, and even Cardinal Borromeo mentioned it in one of his letters—spelling Proskovský's name in a rather distorted way. Maximilian had nothing in common with "Piuscosque," and Cardinal Borromeo did not know of a petition on behalf of Maximilian which Dietrichstein had brought to the Pope in all secrecy. See also PAMV, RG 77, p. 38.

The following sources have been used in reconstructing the story of the Hapsburg policy concerning the third stage of the Council of Trent: SAG, Libros de Berzosa 4, Patr. Real 21, Estado 141, 143, 641, 650–53, 674, 886, 890, 895, and 896; WSA, Span. Hofkorr. 2, Span. Dipl. Korr. 6, Religionsakten 8–12; MBN, MS 10988; CDI, 9, 98, and 101; RASV, Germ. 4 and 10, Spagna 39; EBM, O II 24, "Petri Martinez Muro Commentaria"; MDA, HA 11. Many documents have been published by Šusta (*Die römische Kurie und das Konzil von Trient unter Pius IV* [Vienna, 1909]); Eder (*Concilii Tridentini Diaria* [Freiburg i. Br.]); Grisar (*Jacobi Lainez disputationes Tridentinae* [Innsbruck, 1886]); and Manuel Ferrandis Torres ("Algunos documentos inéditos sobre el concilio de Trento," *Annales de la Universidad de Valladolid*, Vol. V, and *Archivo Histórico Español*, Vol. I [Valladolid, 1928]). As to the literature on the subject which has appeared since the publication of Sforza Pallavicini's *Istoria di Concilio di Trento* (Faenza, 1795) and to which many industrious researchers like Sickel, Astrain, and Reimann have contributed, it may be expected that all of it, including Richard's *Concil de Trente* (Paris, 1931), will be superseded by the third volume of Hubert Jedin's monumental work when it is published. Among the recently published shorter studies, that by Constant (*Concession à l'Allemagne de la communion sous les deux espèces* [Paris, 1932]) is one of the most interesting.

The trends of religious policy during the last years of the reign of Ferdinand I and especially the new authorization of Communion under both species in the Kingdom of Bohemia may be reconstructed from the following sources: SAG, Estado 893, Patr. Real 21; WBN, MS 6621; CDI, 98 and 101; WSA, Span. Hofkorr. 2, Span. Dipl. Korr. 6, Saxonica 2*b*, Röm. Dipl. Korr. 22 and Röm. Hofkorr. 5; HSA, Erskeinsche Sammlung I, Reichssachen N 32; RASV, Germania 4.

THE REBELS

The number of recently published books devoted to the study of Spanish philosophy of law is not small. Two of them deal with the subject in a general way: Ernest Nys, *Le Droit des gens et les anciens jurisconsultes espagnols* (La Haye, 1914), and James Brown Scott, *The Spanish Origin of International Law* (Washington, 1928). Francisco de Vitoria's most important treatise is *De Indis relectio prior* (see *Francisci de Victoria Relectiones morales,"* ed. James Brown Scott and Ernest Nys [Washington, 1917] and Alonso Getino's *Francisco de Vitoria* [Madrid, 1930]). Among Vitoria's followers, Domingo Soto, whose *De iustitia et iure* was published in 1553, is discussed by V. D. Carro in *Domingo Soto y el derecho de gentes* (Madrid, 1930); the much younger Francisco Suárez, whose *De legibus et Deo legislatore* was published in 1612, is studied by Joaquin Carreras Artau in *Doctrinas de F. Suárez acerca del derecho de gentes* (Madrid, 1925). As an illustration of the wide interest aroused by the writings of the Spanish jurisprudents see the Italian manuscript in WSA, B 16: "Discorso delle ragioni che ha il rè catolico sopra il novo hemispero." Among Sepúlveda's disciples, the most prominent were Juan de Solorzano Pereira, later active as judge in Lima (*Disputatio de Indiarum iure*) and Martin de Azpilcueta (*Consilia*). Many works of a more practical nature have spread the ideas of the Spanish theoreticians of law; *De iusta hereticorum punitione* and *De potestate legis poenalis* by Alfonso de Castro, as well as Ayala's *De iure et officiis bellicis* (1581) are well known; there is, however, also that queer book by Luis al Alcazar, *Vestigatio arcani sensus in Apocalypsi* (Antwerp, 1614), which seems to have been one of the main sources of Hugo Grotius.

Cabrera de Córdoba's words on the danger coming from France are taken from his *Filipe Secundo*, V, 10.

The development of diplomatic relations between the Hapsburg courts: NGN, Khev. Kpb. I; MDA, HA, 157; WSA, Span. Dipl. Korr. 5 and 6; WRKA, Reichsakten 177; SAG, Estado 641, 653, 658, 664, 675, 689, and 893. The activities of Johann Khevenhueller are described in the *Annales Ferdinandei,* published in the first half of the seventeenth century by his nephew, Franz Christopher Khevenhueller, and founded on a manuscript, written probably by Georg Mosshammer, secretary of the younger Khevenhueller, and preserved in RLK, VI, Fc 10, and in MBN, MS 2751. It is rather an interesting fact that Adam Dietrichstein, after having returned home from his mission, started sending regular reports to Madrid about the developments at the imperial court (see SAG, Estado 669, 670, and 672).

The case of Vratislav and Maria Pernštýn: MDA, HA 157; CDI, 37, 38, 101, 110, and 111; RLA, B 127 and 129; KAA, Breve, A I C, 27*b;* WSA, HA, Sammelbände 1, Priv. Korr. Maxm. II, Span. Varia 1*b,* Grosse Korr. Alph. Nachtrag, Span. Dipl. Korr. 6 and 8; RLK, Genealogia; SAG, Estado 650, 651, and 2688; RASV, Arm. 44, T 14; MBP, T 2289; MARAH, MS 9/60; PMÉ, Mém. et doc. 232/58; also *Lettere familiare del com. Annibal Caro* (published in 1572). The group with which Isabella de Bresegno was in contact has been frequently studied by Italian historians; see, among others: Benedetto Croce, *Vite di avventure di fede;* Rodocanachi, *La Réforme en Italie* (Paris, 1921); B. Nicolini, *B. Ochino e la riforma in Italia* (Naples, 1935); D. Cantimori, *Eretici italiani del cinquecento* (Florence, 1939); and F. Lemmi, *La Riforma in Italia* (Milan, 1939); also F. C. Church, *The Italian Reformers* (New York, 1931); R. H. Bainton, *Bernardino Ochino* (Florence, 1941); and Edmondo Cione, *Juan de Valdés* (Bari, 1938).

The beginnings of the uprising in the Netherlands: WSA, Span. Hofkorr. 2, Röm. Hofkorr. 5, Span. Dipl. Korr. 6, 7, and 8, Belgien P/C 71 and 88, Belg. Korr. 2 and 3, Röm. Korr. 28, Reichssachen in gen. 50 and 80; MDA, HA 11, 156, and 157; SAG, Estado 654, 658, 902, 903; RLA, B 129; RLK, Genealogia de los Khevenhilleros; CDI, 98 and 101. An excellent introduction to the developments in the Low Countries is P. Geyl's *The Revolt of the Netherlands* (London, 1932). See also the correspondence of the Spanish statesmen in the Netherlands published by Gachard, Weiss, and Bakhuizen-Theissen, and the following three monographs: B. de Meester, *Le Saint-Siège et les troubles des Pays-Bas* (Louvain, 1934); Léon van der Essen, *Alexandre Farnèse* (Brussels, 1933); and G. Slocombe, *Don John of Austria* (London, 1935).

The mission of the Archduke Charles: SAG, Estado 658–62, 906, 910, and 911, Patr. Real 57; MDA, HA 11, 156, and 157; WSA, Span. Dipl. Korr. 8, Belg. Korr. 3, Röm. Dipl. Korr. 31 and 31*b,* Span. Varia 1*b,* Span. Hofkorr. 2, and Reichssachen in gen. 53; CDI 37, 38, 101, and 103. It is necessary to compare these documents with Serrano's *Correspondencia diplomática entre España y la Santa Sede.* Three researchers have so far dealt with the mission in special studies, but none of them on the ground of sufficient documentary material: Frettensattel (*Mitteilungen des Instituts für oesterreichische Geschichtsforschung,* Vol. XXIV); Bibl (*Mit-*

teilungen des Instituts für oesterreichische Geschichtsforschung, Vol. XXXVIII); and Loserth (*Mitteilungen des Historischen Vereines für Steiermark* [1896]). Compare the present author's study in *Mitteilungen des Instituts für oesterreichische Geschichtsforschung* (1934).

The rebellion in the Netherlands during the last years of the reign of Maximilian II and Philip's attempts to win over the German princes: SAG, Estado 545, 661, 663, 664, 667, 668, 674, 910, and 920; CDI 37, 38, 98, 101, 103, 110, 111; RLK, Genealogia de los Khevenhilleros; WSA, Belg. Korr. 3, 4, and 7; WSA, Span. Dipl. Korr. 6–9, Span. Hofkorr. 3; MDA, HA 11, 156, and 157; NGNM, Khev. Kpb. I; KAA, Volná korespondence; PMÉ, Espagne, Mém. et cons. 236.

The Empire, Spain, and Italy: CDI 98, 103, and 110; SAG, Estado 649, 653, 913, and 916; NGNM, Khev. Kpb. I; WSA, Span. Dipl. Korr. 5–10; WSA, Span. Varia 1*b*, Span. Hofkorr. 1–3, Miscellanea Gratialia 40 and HA Sam. 1; WRKA, Reichsakten 170; RLK, Genealogia de los Khevenhilleros; MDA, HA 11, 12, 156, and 157; MBN, MS 10988; NAF, fasc. 258.

PREACHERS, DIPLOMATS, AND ASTROLOGERS

Family relations of the Hapsburgs during the reign of Maximilian II: WSA, Span. Dipl. Korr. 5–9; Span. Hofkorr. 1 and 2; Belg. Korr. 2; CDI, 98, 101–3, 110, 111; MDA, HA 156 and 157; SAG, Estado 141, 651–55, Hazienda 37/55; MIVJ, Emvio 38/109; HSA, Cod. Y, 17*a*, 407; NGNM, Khev. Kpb. I.

Maximilian II's last years: KAA, Volná korespondence; MDA, HA 157; RLA, B 175; RASV, Spagna 7, 8, and 72; CDI, 37, 98, 101, 103, 110, 111; WSA, Span. Dipl. Korr. 7, Span. Varia 1*b*, Span. Hofkorr. 2 and 3; SAG, Estado 652, 653, 659, 660, 662–76, 898, 899, 906, 907, 925; see also Cyprianus, *Tabularium* (Frankfort, 1743).

Philip's letters to his daughters have been published by Gachard, *Lettres de Philippe II à ses filles* (Paris, 1884).

Among the books and shorter studies published during the last twenty-five years and concerned with Philip's attempts to save the coherence of the western European bloc, three are of outstanding importance: L. van der Essen's *Alexandre Farnèse* (Brussels, 1935); P. O. de Törne's "Philippe II et Henri de Guise," *Revue historique* (Paris, 1931); and J. B. Black's "Queen Elizabeth, the Sea Beggars, and the Capture of Brill," *English Historical Review* (1931).

The personal relations between Philip and Rudolf and the family problems of the Hapsburgs in the years 1576–98: WSA, Span. Dipl. Korr. 10 and 11; HSA, Y 17, Vol. III; SAG, Patr. Real 57, MS 150, Estado 614, 677, 683, 687, 689, 704, 927, 928, 969, and 2323; NGNM, Khev. Kpb. III, IV, and V; see also Mayer-Loewenschwerdt, *Der Aufenhalt der Erzherzöge Rudolf und Ernst in Spanien* (Vienna, 1927).

Italy and the Netherlands in the last twenty years of Philip II's reign: Italy: WSA, Span. Dipl. Korr. 10 and 14, Span. Varia 2, Span. Hofkorr. 3 and 4; SAG, Estado 680, 683, 707, 708, 935, and 2449; CDI 98; HSA, III Y 17; NGNM, Khev. Kpb. V. The Netherlands: WSA, Belg. Korr. 5, Span. Hofkorr. 3 and 4, Span. Varia 2, Span. Dipl. Korr. 10, 11, 13, and 14; WSA, Belg. P/C 67; SAG, Estado 570–72, 578, 604, 607, 609, 617, 679, 680, 683–88, 691, 692, 696, 699, 701, 702, 707, 708, 930, 932, 933, 943, 953, 2449, 2492, 2844, 2845; RASV, Spagna 2 and 45; NGNM, Khev. Kpb. I–VI; MDA, HA 156; HSA, III Y 17. See also Mathorez, "Les Espagnols et la crise nationale française," *Bulletin hispanique* (Bordeaux, 1916).

Spanish interest in eastern Europe at the close of the sixteenth century: RAAE, leg. 17; SAG, Estado 654, 668, 670, 675, 688, 693, 694, 697, 700, 701–6, 927, 956, 2450, and 2864; CDI 98, 101, 110, 111; PMÉ, Mém. et cons., Espagne 236; WSA, Span. Dipl. Korr. 6–13, Span. Varia 1*b*, 2, Kriegsakten 24, Span. Hofkorr. 3 and 4; MDA, HA 11, 156, 167; NGNM, Khev. Kpb. I–III; HSA, III Y 17; KAA Kop. (correspondence between St. Clemente and Bishop Pavlovský) and Volná korespondence. See also F. C. Khevenhueller, *Annales Ferdinandei;* J. Macůrek, *Zápas Polska a Habsburků* (Prague, 1931); Janko, *Lazarus Schwendi* (Vienna, 1871); Eiermann, *Lazarus von Schwendi* (Freiburg, 1904).

Economic contacts between Spain and the Empire under Philip II: General characteristics: SAG, Estado 217 and 273; NGNM, Khev. Kpb. V; RLK, Genealogia de los Khevenhilleros, III, 1243 ff.; RASV, Spagna 10, fols. 80 ff.; WRKA, Reichsakten 151; MDA, HA 157; WSA, Span. Dipl. Korr. 7–10, Belg. Korr. 2; MIVJ, Emvio 44/6. See also "Disputatio de usura variisque negotiis mercatorum" in *Iacobi Lainez disputationes Tridentinae;* Eduard van Roey, "Le Contractus Germanicus," *Revue d'histoire ecclésiastique* (Louvain, 1902); and H. Sée, *Les Origines du capitalisme moderne* (Paris, 1930). The economic co-operation of the Hapsburgs and their diplomats: WSA, Span. Dipl. Korr. 5, 11, 13; RLK, Genealogia de los Khevenhilleros, III, p. 1242; NGNM, Khev. Kpb. II, IV, and VI; see also *Annales Ferdinandei*, Vol. II, col. 345; and Fynes

Moryson, *Itinerary*, Part IV. Salt: WSA, Span. Dipl. Korr. 5; MBN, MS 10988; NGNM, Khev. Kpb. IV. Corn: NGNM, Khev. Kpb. II, IV, and V; HSA, III Y 17, fols. 696 ff.; MIVJ, Emvio 44/5; SAG, Estado 691, 692, 697, 704, 2449, 2450; RASV, Spagna 40. Copper: SAG, Estado 672; WSA, Span. Dipl. Korr. 10; NGNM, Khev. Kpb. I and II. Quicksilver: WRKA, Hoffinanz, Exped. 1561, 34, Exped. 1562, 14, and Protocoll, Reg. 1562, 10; WSA, Span. Dipl. Korr. 6 and 7; CDI 98; SAG, Estado 663 and 665.

ANOTHER EMPIRE?

The general situation of Spain in the two decades preceding the Thirty Years' War: SAG, Estado 617, 624, 705–8, 2323, 2492, and 2496; WSA, Span. Dipl. Korr. 14 and Span. Hofkorr. 4; RASV, Fondo Borghese III, 102*ab;* NGNM, Khev. Kpb. V and VI; RLK, Genealogia de los Khevenhilleros; WRKA, Reichsakten 156; PMÉ, Mém. et doc. 265/905; CDI 55, Memoria sobre las causas de la decadencia de España escrita al parecer de orden de conde duque Olivares. See also A. Danvila y Burguero, *Diplomáticos españoles* (Madrid, 1900), and Jerónimo de Sepúlveda, *Sucesos del reinado de Felipe III* (published by "Ciudad de Dios").

The political career of Zdeněk Vojtěch Lobkovic: RLA, B 228 and 232; SAG, Estado 709, 2494, 2495, and 2496; MBN, MS 18196, fols. 97 ff.; WNB, Cod. 12011, Synopsis historica collegii pragensis. See also: *Zápisky Viléma Slavaty z let 1601–1603* (published by Rezek); Pavel Skála, *Historie Česká* (published by Tieftrunk); František Stloukal, *Papežská politika a císařský dvůr* (Prague, 1925) and *Česká kancelář dvorská* (Prague, 1931); Josef Borovička, "Pád Zelinského," *Český časopis historický* (Prague, 1928), and "Počátky kancléřování Zdeňka z Lobkovic," *Friedrichův sborník* (Prague, 1931).

The last years of St. Clemente's mission in Prague: WSA, Span. Hofkorr. 4; SAG, Estado 617, 706, 708, 972, 980, 988, 2323, 2326, 2451, 2452, 2492, 2493, 2494; NGNM, Khev. Kpb. VI; MDA, HA 156. See also Atakar Odložilík, *Karel z Žerotína* (Prague, 1936).

Cardinal Dietrichstein's participation in political developments up to 1608: SAG, Estado 706, 707, 970, 971, 980, 984, 1858, 1861, 1870, 2495; RASV, Fondo Borghese III, 70*bef,* 87*ab,* 102*ab,* 125*fk;* KAA, Volná korespondence; NGNM, Khev. Kpb. VI; WSA, MS W 290/1, Span. Varia 3, Span. Dipl. Korr. 14; MIVJ, Emvio 82, 456. See also Jan Tenora, *Dietrichsteinovo mládí* (Brno, 1906) and *Dietrichstein za boje mezi Matyášem a Rudolfem* (Brno, 1917).

THE BARTERED KINGDOM

Zúñiga's share in the dispute between Matthias and Rudolf in the years 1608–9: SAG, Estado 708, 709, 988, 991, 992–95, 1860–62, 2323, 2324, 2452, 2494–98, 2862, 2865, 2868; WSA, Span. Hofkorr. 4, Span. Dipl. Korr. 14 and 15, Belgien DD/B 242, Belg. Korr. 8, MS W 290; WRKA, Reichsakten 178; RASV, Germania 114 C, 114 D, 443, Barberini 6911, Fondo Borghese III 59*a*, 102*ab*, 127*ef*, IV 44, Nunz. div. 8, 233; MAHN, Estado 712*d* Alemania, 730*d* Santa Sede; RAAE, leg. 55; MBN, MS 687; KAA, Volná korespondence; NGNM, Khev. Kpb. 17 and 19; J. Glück-lich, *Korespondence Václava Budovce* (Prague); K. Stloukal, *Karel z Liechtensteina* (Prague, 1912); *Paměti Viléma Slavaty,* ed. Jireček (Prague, 1866).

The invasion of Archduke Leopold's troops into Bohemia has been investigated by O. Opočenský, "Zajetí F. Tengnagla," in *Věstník král. čes. spol. nauk* (Prague, 1910), and V. Líva, "Spiknutí Vchynských," in *Věstník král. čes. spol. nauk* (Prague, 1928).

The problem of the Bohemian succession in the years 1612–16: SAG, Estado 710, 711, 999, 2324–26, 2426, 2454, 2498–2502, 2865, 2868; KAA, Volná korespondence and Kop. Dietrichstein; RASV, Spagna 337 and 338, Germania 114 G, Nunz. div. 8, Fondo Borghese III 60*fg;* WSA, Span. Dipl. Korr. 15 and 16, Span. Hofkorr. 4, MS W 290/13, Span. Varia 3; BZA, Dep. Collalto; RLA, B 19; MAHN, Estado 712*d* Ale-mania; MBP T 2152 Avisos de Roma, T 2168 Cartas de Gondomar. Of particular value is the fascicle MS 18435 in MBN, entitled "Minutas de cartas que el Conde de Oñate escrivió a SM desde que salió de Madrid a la primer embajada de Alemania." The memoirs of Vilém Slavata are preserved in the department of MSS of the library of Charles University in Prague.

THE "WHITE MOUNTAIN"

The following documents have been used to reconstruct the story of the Prague insurrection:

SAG, Estado 633, 634, 711, 712, 1867, 1868, 1882, 1883, 1922–24, 1930, 1934, 1935, 2032, 2034, 2138, 2232, 2305–9, 2327, 2402, 2454, 2503–6, 2515, 2572, 2573, 2599–2601, 2850, 2994, 3918; RASV, Spagna 341, Fondo Bor-ghese II, 63, 488, Fondo Borghese III, 12*a*, Francia 296–99, Miscell. Arm.

XV/69, 70, 71, Napoli 20 F, Nunz. div. 42–44; NGNM, Khev. Kpb. 1618 and 1619; the Khev. Kpb. 1620 may be found in WSA, Span. Varia 3; WSA, Belg. P/C 25–28, 54–56, Span. Varia 3–4, Span. Hofkorr. 4–5, Span. Dipl. Korr. 16–17, Belg. Dipl. Korr. 10–12, 35–36, Protocoll 1619 and 1620; PME, Mém. et doc. 274/148, Espagne 265; MBN, MS 9408 and 18435; MBP, T 2108, 2116, 2134, 2160, 2185, and 2221; CDI, 41 and 46; KAA, Div. corr.; RAAE, leg. 57; PAN, K 1431, 1455, 1468, 1474–77, 1593; EBM, G IV, 2; RLA, B 228 and 230; BZA, Dep. Collalto; WRKA, Reichsakten 177.

I also had the opportunity to study the copies of a number of documents preserved in the National Archives in Brussels (Secrétariat d'État et de Guerre) and in the Archives of the Ministry of Foreign Affairs in Madrid; the copies are now in the archives of the Kingdom of Bohemia in Prague.

Among books and shorter studies the following have been used to prepare this chapter:

A. Gindely, *History of the Thirty Years' War* (1884); S. R. Gardiner, *The Thirty Years' War* (1874); F. Sánchez Cantón, *Don Diego de Sarmiento de Acuña conde de Gondomar* (Madrid, 1935); C. Pérez Bustamente, *El Conde de Gondomar y su intervención en el proceso de Sir Walter Raleigh* (Santiago, 1928); F. Hrubý, *Ladislav Velen z Žerotína* (Prague); S. R. Gardiner, *Letters and Other Documents Illustrating the Relations between England and Germany at the Commencement of the Thirty Years' War* (ed. Camden Society, London); Z. Kalista, "Buquoyův itinerář," *Vojensko-historický sborník*, Vol. V; Weigel, *Franken, Kurpfalz und der böhmische Aufstand* (Erlangen, 1932); Rossi, "La Politica di Carlo Emanuele I," *Nuova rivista storica* (1937); R. Stanka, *Die böhmischen Conföderationsakte von 1619* (Berlin, 1932).

Of the contemporary books and leaflets, I have used especially: Quido Bentivoglio, *Memorie* (Venetia, 1668); *La famosa victoria junto a la villa de Praga* (Malaga: Juan Regné, 1620); *The Manifest or Declaration of His Sacred Imperial Majesty* (translated from Latin [1620]); "Informatio fundamentalis" and "An Answere to the Question: Whether the Emperour that now is can be Judge in the Bohemian Controversie or not?" The last three can all be found in WSA, Belg. P/C, 55–56.

ON THE WAY TO ROCROI

The persistence of inherited ideas in Spanish foreign policy during the epoch of the Thirty Years' War is well characterized in Jaime Carrera Pujal's *Historia de la economía española* (Barcelona, 1943), I, 512 ff. A detailed story of the diplomatic relations between Vienna and Madrid during the Thirty Years' War may be found in Anton Gindely's *Geschichte des Dreissigjährigen Krieges* and in Jaroslav Goll's *Poměry evropské po Bílé hoře* ("Časopis českého musea" [Prague, 1875]). Among the hitherto unused sources of documents, I would like to stress the following: RLA, B 230; WSA, Span. Hofkorr. 5, Belg. Korr. 12; KAA, Volná korespondence; SAG, Estado 2510; WNB, MS 12479. See also *Moravské korespondence a akta z let 1620–1636,* ed. F. Hrubý (Brno, 1934).

The complicated personality, as well as the policy, of the Count Duke of Olivares has been studied by Gregorio Marañón (*El Conde-Duque de Olivares* [Madrid, 1936]), who also gives an ample biography. It is interesting to note that not only the expulsion of the *validos* of Philip III from the court of his son but also the revival of hostilities in the Low Countries in 1621 were attributed exclusively to Baltasar Zúñiga by the pamphlet *El Nicandro,* in which the Count Duke was defended after his career had come to an abrupt end in 1642: "Respecto de la prisión de Duque de Uceda y del de Osuna, dice que quando se hicieron estas prisiones el que mandaba era Don Baltasar de Zúñiga. Otro cargo es el haber roto las treguas con Holanda; responde a él que el que las rompió fué Don Baltasar de Zúñiga" (Marañón, *op. cit.*). The memorandum dated November 28, 1621, called "Documento del gobierno del Conde de Olivares al Rey," is printed by Marañón, *op. cit.,* pp. 422 ff. The remark of an English visitor in 1629 is quoted by M. Hume, *The Court of Philip IV* (new ed.; n.d.), p. 227.

GENEALOGICAL TABLES

THE HAPSBURG FAMILY IN THE FIRST HALF OF THE SIXTEENTH CENTURY

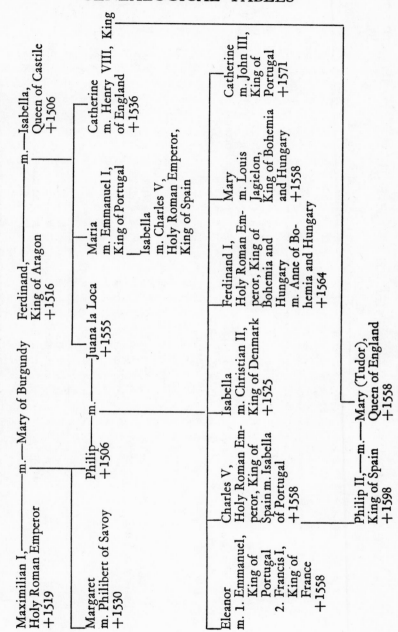

THE SPANISH HAPSBURGS IN THE SIXTEENTH AND SEVENTEENTH CENTURIES

Charles V, Holy Roman Emperor, King of Spain +1558 — m. — Isabella of Portugal +1539

Margaret m. 1. Alessandro de Medici 2. Ottavio Farnese of Parma +1586

Philip II, King of Spain m. 1. Maria of Portugal 2. Mary Tudor 3. Elizabeth of France 4. Anne of Austria +1598

Maria m. Maximilian II, Holy Roman Emperor +1603

Juana m. John, son of John III of Portugal +1578

Juan of Austria +1578

Alessandro Farnese of Parma +1592

(1) Carlos +1568

(3) Isabella Clara Eugenia m. Albert, Archduke of Austria +1633

(3) Catherine m. Charles Emmanuel of Savoy +1597

(4) Philip III, King of Spain m. Margaret of Styria +1621

Philip IV, King of Spain +1665

Carlos +1632

Ferdinand, Cardinal-Infante +1640

Maria m. Ferdinand III, Holy Roman Emperor

Anne m. Louis XIII, King of France

Baltasar Carlos

Charles II, King of Spain +1700

Margaret Theresa m. Leopold I, Holy Roman Emperor

Maria Theresa — m. — Louis XIV, King of France

THE AUSTRIAN HAPSBURGS IN THE SIXTEENTH AND SEVENTEENTH CENTURIES

Ferdinand I, Holy Roman Emperor, King of Bohemia and Hungary +1564 — m. — Anne, Sister of Louis Jagielon, King of Bohemia and Hungary

- Maximilian II, Holy Roman Emperor, King of Bohemia and Hungary m. Maria, sister of Philip II of Spain +1576
  - Anne m. Philip II of Spain
  - Rudolf II Holy Roman Emperor, King of Bohemia and Hungary +1612
  - Ernest +1595
  - Elizabeth m. Charles IX, King of France
  - Matthias Holy Roman Emperor, King of Bohemia and Hungary +1619
  - Maximilian of Tyrol +1620
  - Albert m. Isabella Clara Eugenia, daughter of Philip II of Spain +1621
  - Wenceslas +1578
- Anne m. Albert of Bavaria
- Ferdinand of Tyrol
- Maria m. William of Cleves
- Elizabeth m. Sigismund II of Poland
- Joanna m. Francesco Medici
- Charles of Styria m. Mary of Bavaria
  - Margaret m. Philip III, King of Spain
  - Maximilian Ernest
  - Leopold of Passau
  - Ferdinand II, Holy Roman Emperor, King of Bohemia and Hungary +1637 → Ferdinand III, Holy Roman Emperor, King of Bohemia and Hungary +1657 → Leopold I, Holy Roman Emperor, King of Bohemia and Hungary +1705

INDEX

Aachen, 164
Abbas, Shah, 166
Abbasids, the, 60
Abbot, George, 236
Aben Humeya, 87
Abyssinia, 166, 181
Acuña, Hernando de, 52
Acuña, Martín de, 92
Adda, 242
Adige, 51, 225
Adrian VI, Pope, 21, 22, 24, 45, 46
Adriatic Sea, 59, 60, 69, 92, 145, 172, 173
Aegean Sea, 69
Africa, 57, 66, 67, 68, 87, 88, 167, 171, 176
Aguila, Bishop, 88
Aigues Mortes, 44
Alba, Fernando Alvarez, Duke of, 52, 65, 69, 80, 85, 86, 93, 98, 137, 138, 139, 140, 142, 143, 144, 150, 153, 154
Albania, 59
Albergati, Fabio, 186
Albert II, Holy Roman Emperor, 15
Albert Hapsburg, Archduke, 126, 155, 161, 165, 175, 183, 184, 191, 194, 201, 210, 217, 219, 220, 223, 233, 235, 251, 254
Albrecht of Bavaria, 83, 105
Albret, 35
Albuquerque, Duke of, 146
Alcalá de Ebro, 159
Alcalá de Henares, 28
Alcantara, Orden of, 73
Alcantara, Pedro de, 47
Aldobrandini, Giovanni Francesco, 171
Aldobrandini, Hippolito; see Clement VIII
Alfonso el Sabio, King of Castile, 18, 58, 129
Algiers, 66, 67, 68, 87, 176
Aliaga, Luis, 223
Almagro, Diego de, 3, 77
Almazan, Marquis of; see Monteagudo, Count of

Almeria, 57
Alps, 35, 42, 73, 78, 231
Alsatia, 35, 208, 212, 217, 223, 225, 242, 252
Altaemps, Cardinal, 115
Althan, Adolf, 228
Amberger, 12
Amboise, 130
America, 3, 78, 99, 100, 127, 172, 188, 254
Amsterdam, 3
Andalusia, 1
Angoulême, Duke of, 233, 240
Anhalt, Christian, 198, 212, 246, 247, 252
Anjou, family of, 2
Anne, daughter Maximilian II, Holy Roman Emperor, 147, 149, 158, 190, 191
Anne, daughter of Philip III of Spain, 205
Anne, sister of Louis Jagielon, 62, 79
Anne Boleyn, 85
Antwerp, 135, 175, 186, 244
Apertola, 210
Arabs, 1, 14, 60
Aragon, 1, 2, 12, 14, 36, 41, 57, 97, 156, 157, 182
Aragón, Almirante de; see Mendoza, Francisco
Aragón, Carlos de; see Terranova, Duke of
Aragón, Fernando de; see Villahermosa, Duke of
Areyzaga, Philip, 247
Argos, 72
Arians, the, 119
Aristotle, 31
Armstrong, Edward, 8
Arnoux, 232
Arras, 154
Arslan Pasha, 91
Artois, 35, 261
Ashkenazi, Salomon, 166
Asia, 58, 63
Astrakhan, 59, 89, 93

285